For David Wasserstein

with warmest regards

from

Dina and Edward.

Oxford   7th Aug. 1989

The Two Zions

The Two Zions
Reminiscences of Jerusalem and Ethiopia

EDWARD ULLENDORFF

Oxford New York
OXFORD UNIVERSITY PRESS
1988

Oxford University Press, Walton Street, Oxford OX2 6DP
Oxford New York Toronto
Delhi Bombay Calcutta Madras Karachi
Petaling Jaya Singapore Hong Kong Tokyo
Nairobi Dar es Salaam Cape Town
Melbourne Auckland
and associated companies in
Berlin Ibadan

Oxford is a trade mark of Oxford University Press

First published 1988

British Library Cataloguing in Publication Data
Ullendorff, Edward
The two Zions: reminiscences of
Jerusalem and Ethiopia.
1. Israel. Jerusalem. Social conditions, 1930-1948
2. Ethiopia. Social conditions, 1930-1987
I. Title
956.94´404
ISBN 0-19-212275-4

Library of Congress Cataloging in Publication Data
Ullendorff, Edward.
The two Zions/Edward Ullendorff.
p. cm. Includes index.
1. Jews—Jerusalem—Biography. 2. Jerusalem—Biography.
3. Eritrea (Ethiopia)—Politics and government—1941-1952.
4. Ethiopia—Description and travel—1945-1980. 5. Ullendorff,
Edward. I. Title. DS109.85.U45 1988 956.94´4004924—dc19 88-3211
ISBN 0-19-212275-4

Set by Downdell Ltd.
Printed in Great Britain
at the University Press, Oxford
by David Stanford
Printer to the University

To Dina

Preface

This book sets out some of my reminiscences of Jerusalem, half a century ago, and of my war service in Eritrea and Ethiopia, as well as a few impressions of many return visits to Ethiopia. It is called *The Two Zions* because Ethiopians have traditionally referred to their country as 'the Second Zion' and to themselves as the heirs of Jerusalem and ancient Israel.

The idea of writing such a book is that of Yoram Bronowski of the *Ha'arets* newspaper; and when I recently lectured on Jerusalem and the Hebrew University to the Oxford Centre for Postgraduate Hebrew Studies, at the invitation of its President, Dr David Patterson, several of my listeners were rash and kind enough to urge me to embody those recollections in a book. Wilfred Thesiger did the same as far as the Ethiopian part is concerned and also spoke to Mr Michael Shaw of Curtis Brown. And when the latter encouraged me to go ahead, I decided to make the attempt.

I should explain, perhaps, that this is not by way of being an autobiography. In these reminiscences, the prerogative of the aged, I am the link, not the centre.

I owe a debt to Miss Christine Nuttall, OBE, and to Miss Carolyn Beckingham; and my indebtedness to, and affection for, Jerusalem and Ethiopia will, I trust, be transparent on every one of the following pages.

E. U.
January 1987

N.B. The spelling 'mandatary' is correct.

Contents

PART ONE
THE FIRST ZION

I

Jerusalem

Introduction

Half a century ago, the view over Jerusalem, the Old and the New City, from the loftiness of Mount Scopus was truly sublime. Mount Scopus is the continuation of the Mount of Olives, the great ridge to the north-east of the city, and (as its name implies—Greek *skopos* is a translation of Hebrew *hatsofim*, 'watchers, looking out or over') it affords matchless vistas over the Holy City to the west, with the great and noble edifice of the Dome of the Rock its ever demanding focal point; and to the east over the wilderness of Judea, the mountains of Moab, and the Dead Sea, the bottom of the world, the deepest depression on the surface of the earth.

The Roman legions of Titus had been encamped here in AD 70 poised to destroy City and Temple; the Crusaders were positioned here towards the end of the eleventh century; and the British Forces halted here after they had entered Jerusalem in 1917. The starkly beautiful British War-cemetery, just north of the crest of the hill, is a constant reminder of those battles of the First World War.

The Hebrew University has occupied this great ridge on Mount Scopus ever since the site was purchased from the estate of Sir John Gray-Hill. The foundation stones (twelve in number, to symbolize the twelve tribes of Israel) were laid in 1918 by Dr Weizmann, and the university was formally inaugurated in 1925 by Lord Balfour in the amphitheatre overlooking the stark and mighty scenery of the mountains to the east.

Jerusalem was still empty in the 1930s; there were no buildings between Mount Scopus and the walls of the Old City. In the summer, the early morning air had a peculiar haze and a fragrant smell; in the winter, under the skies of the rainy season, the views were wonderfully clear; and in the 'fifty' days of the *khamsin* (hence the name), the hot desert wind, all was blurred and leaden, and man and beast were heavy and depressed. But the sudden lifting of the dense curtain brought back the beauty of Jerusalem, its majestic hills and deep valleys, as well as its aura of tranquillity and serenity, which even the sounds of bombs and battle could not efface.

Coming to Jerusalem and to the university on Mount Scopus in the 1930s was a profoundly moving experience. Not only was the city still small and beautiful (at that time Jerusalem had 55,000 Jewish inhabitants, 58,000 Muslims, and 20,000 Christians, according to the Report of the Palestine Royal Commission (Cmd. 5479, 1937, p. 304, the 'Peel Report') but the Mounts of Olives and Scopus were still real mountains rather than built-up slopes. Nearly every morning, before attending lectures, I would walk to the eastern and western edges of the hill to be uplifted by those views of true grandeur. I had just read Sir Ronald Storrs' *Orientations* (he had been the first governor of Jerusalem under the British Mandate and the founder of the 'Pro-Jerusalem' Preservation Society) and was constantly reminded of his words: 'For me Jerusalem stood and stands alone among the cities of the world. There are many positions of greater authority and renown . . . but in a sense that I cannot explain there is no promotion after Jerusalem' (*Orientations*, 1937; p. 440 of the 1943 edition).

Even twenty years after he had left Jerusalem, when I met Storrs at Asmara, Eritrea, towards the end of the war in 1945, he still asked me to introduce him as 'Governor of Jerusalem', although he had subsequently held more senior offices as Governor of Cyprus and of Northern Rhodesia. Storrs looked the quintessential proconsul, though by inclination he was a scholar, artist, musician—a highly cultivated polymath who preferred literature, conversation, and good food to the drudgery of administration. He was a fine linguist, fluent in Arabic and Italian, and a splendid lecturer on Dante, Shakespeare, the Bible —and especially on his friend T. E. Lawrence. During his visit to Eritrea, when I had the pleasure of showing him around the country and Northern Ethiopia, he gave me a copy of his Penguin book *Lawrence of Arabia—Zionism and Palestine*, generously inscribed. Eric Kennington's famous drawing in *Seven Pillars of Wisdom* splendidly catches the hauteur, the slight vanity, as well as his fine head and good looks.

The people who lived in that most historic of cities, at that time, were divided into watertight compartments, with virtually no intercourse between them. The Arabs were, in the inter-war years, still the largest community in Palestine. Outside the urban areas, their lives had not changed very greatly over the centuries. But the Mandatary Government had brought education and other modern services to them, and in most respects the British administration was primarily concerned with the Arab inhabitants. The Jews led an entirely autonomous cultural life, and neither the Arabs nor the British impinged on that life in any important or meaningful way. The language barrier was well-nigh total. Fifty years ago, there were hardly any Jews in Palestine who could speak English, and fewer still who were able to sustain a conversation in Arabic. It is now almost unimaginable that, when the High Commissioner visited the Hebrew University at that time, the President of the university had the greatest difficulty in finding three or four professors and half a dozen students who could talk to their distinguished visitor.

The British, outside office-hours, had a social life in which the indigenous or immigrant communities had no part. I do not think there was any resentment on that score: the Arabs had begun to withdraw and to become resentful, indeed violent, as they witnessed the influx of large numbers of immigrants (instead of the earlier trickle) with the advent of Hitler and all he stood for. The Jews were content to be left alone; virtually the only demand they made of the government was to obtain an accelerated flow of immigration in response to the increasingly serious situation in central Europe.

The Arab disturbances, which began in earnest in 1936 and did not cease until the outbreak of war in 1939 (which, paradoxically, turned out to be the most peaceful era in Mandatary Palestine), brought about two important developments: (*a*) the appointment of the Palestine Royal Commission under Lord Peel; and (*b*) the resolve by the *Yishuv* (the collective designation of the Jewish community settled in Palestine) to observe a policy of self-restraint, self-discipline (called *havlaga* in Hebrew), forswearing any violent reaction, other than in self-defence, to whatever provocation might be offered. This policy, I am glad to say, was approved and adhered to by the great majority of the Yishuv. Of course, there were anxious debates whether such a

stance might not be misunderstood and lead to serious consequences in the future—and, indeed, whether the moral gain
was not outweighed by grave political and military disadvantages.
The White Paper of 1939, which virtually closed the door to
further immigration and, at any rate on the surface, appeared to
reward the campaign of violence, was seen by many Jews as the
pay-off for their long and patient restraint. This view, though
understandable in 1939 in what was probably the most fateful
time in Jewish history, took insufficient account of global
realities and of the imminence of a war in which it was
imperative to keep the Near East as calm as possible.

The 1936 Royal Commission, which had been appointed to
look into the Palestine problem and whose report was published
in 1937, was led by Earl Peel, grandson of the nineteenth-
century Prime Minister and a man renowned for his services in
Indian affairs. His Vice-Chairman was Sir Horace Rumbold, a
diplomat with a long career in the foreign service culminating in
his ambassadorship to Berlin from 1928 to 1933. He was thus the
first British envoy with direct experience of the Nazi regime and
its propensities. The most influential member of the Commission
was no doubt Professor Sir Reginald Coupland, Beit Professor of
Colonial History in the University of Oxford. The Peel Report is
probably the most accurate, dispassionate, and beautifully
crafted document ever composed on the Palestine problem. And
although it was never implemented, it has remained the authoritative handbook on all questions bearing on the British administration of Palestine between the two world wars and on the Arab
and Jewish communities at that time. In 1948, when I was interviewed for an appointment at the Oxford University Institute of
Colonial Studies, Coupland was a prominent member of the
interviewing committee. We had a most interesting conversation
on the Peel Report, and Coupland did own—though with proper
reticence and decorum—to 'a hand in the final drafting of "Peel"'.

Of course, there was a Palestine outside Jerusalem. There was
the beautiful city of Haifa built along the slopes of Mount
Carmel, with wonderful views over its harbour and the Mediterranean coast; on clear days one could see Mount Hermon and
southern Lebanon. The hinterland of Haifa was the area of the
early Jewish colonists who established their collective farms,
Kibbutzim, in these regions; with the movement spreading over

all parts of the country, the Kibbutz became the moral and physical pivot, the great pioneering achievement, of the Jewish renaissance in Palestine. If in the modern State of Israel the Kibbutz has lost something of its central position, this is due partly to sheer weight of numbers, which mass immigration has inevitably entailed, and partly to a certain loss of the idealistic and missionary zeal of the pioneers, who no longer constitute the backbone of developed and organized contemporary Israeli society.

And there was Tel-Aviv, at first only the northern outskirts of the ancient port of Jaffa, but gradually an independent town and the first all-Jewish city for close on two millennia. This thriving and bustling metropolis had none of Jerusalem's austere beauty, but it possessed fine Mediterranean beaches, wide avenues, theatres and concert halls, and a shrill liveliness all its own.

But it is to Jerusalem that I must return, for, while Haifa, Tel-Aviv, the Kibbutz, or a settlement like Ramoth Hashavim (where I taught Hebrew during the long summer vacation in order to eke out a meagre study allowance) were agreeable holiday breaks, Jerusalem was the place I knew best and where my university studies were concentrated.

Life at Jerusalem

Life in Palestine was hard in those days. Study during the day was intense, without any of the high jinks usually associated with student activities. Most undergraduates (and graduates for that matter) had to earn money to support their studies. There were no state grants, and the majority did not have parents in Palestine to come to their aid. And during the night we had to be on guard duty, for during the 1936-9 disturbances many of us were sworn in as special constables (*ghafir*), armed with antiquated rifles after a perfunctory course of training, in order to protect and preserve the nocturnal peace in the neighbourhood to which we had been assigned. *Shemirah* (guard duty) from 9 p.m. to midnight was not too bad, but midnight to 3 a.m. or 3 to 6 a.m. was pretty grim. Yet living in Jerusalem and studying at its university seemed ample compensation and provided a spiritual and psychological uplift, coupled with a sense of history and achievement, which it is hard to imagine now, let alone to describe. I think all of us were profoundly conscious of being among the

first to receive a university education entirely in the Hebrew
language.

Not only were we, the students, poor, but it has to be recalled
that there were no rich Jews in Palestine in those days. The
highest paid Jewish official in the country was said to be the
chairman of the *Keren Hayessod* ('Foundation Fund'), who
earned £720 per annum. Full university professors had an annual
salary of £480. To receive a bona fide students' certificate of
entry into Palestine, the Government stipulated the transfer
from abroad of £120 to be deposited with the university. The
university deducted £24 from this sum as tuition fees for two
years, and the remaining £96 was deemed to be sufficient for two
years' study, that is, £4 per month. Since the minimum period of
study up to the first degree (MA) was four years, it was assumed
that one was able to find a job to finance the second half of one's
undergraduate career.

In those days Palestine was a country with a remarkably low
cost of living. It is now barely believable that the total annual
budget of Jerusalem University in the mid-1930s was £87,000—
for all academic and administrative purposes. It rose to £100,000
by the outbreak of the Second World War and is now, I understand, in excess of eighty million dollars!

When I first came to Jerusalem I visited a distant relative who
had married a gentleman who was said to be well-to-do. The
husband asked me how I would finance my studies, and I told
him of the £4 per month that had been deposited with the university (incidentally, £ Pal. = £ sterling—divided into 100 piastres or
1,000 mils). He seemed somewhat sceptical that I could manage
on that sum but suggested that I should visit them again once I
had had some experience of living in Jerusalem. A month or two
later I returned and announced that I could manage—just—on
my monthly allowance. He evinced an avid interest in my
budgetary arrangements and asked me to give him a detailed
breakdown of the figures, a request with which I readily
complied:

Rent	£1.50
Food	1.80*
Fares to university	0.20
Laundry	0.15

* That is, 6 piastres a day: 1½ for breakfast, 3 for lunch, 1½ for supper

Miscellaneous	0.15
Entertainment	0.20
	£4.00

He seemed impressed with this analysis, asked a few further questions, and then suggested that I might perhaps accept an invitation to dinner at their home. When I turned up on the appointed evening, I found a large concourse of people, perhaps thirty altogether. We were seated in the entrance hall, the dining-room, and the adjoining spacious balcony. Somewhat to my surprise, I was bidden to sit next to my host at the lengthways centre of the dining-room table, from where I could see the guests both in the hall and on the balcony. At the conclusion of the meal our host rose and, without prior warning, invited me to tell the assembled company how one could manage on £4 per month. I felt I had no choice and explained, with some hesitation but also with a measure of pride, how I had contrived to stretch this exiguous allowance to last for the whole month. At the end of my brief exposé only our host applauded and, to my intense embarrassment, announced that all the ladies and gentlemen at dinner were his hangers-on and were in receipt of an allowance from him of £6 per month which, in the light of my detailed budgetary analysis, would forthwith be reduced to £4. I took my leave as soon as possible and was thankful that no physical harm befell me in consequence of this wholly unexpected denouement.

By a curious coincidence (in view of the fact that twenty-five years later I was elected to the first, and only, Chair of Ethiopian Studies anywhere—tenable at the School of Oriental and African Studies, London University) my first lodgings in Jerusalem were in Abyssinian Street, in a fine Arab house close to the beautiful Ethiopian Church called Dabra Gannat (= 'Hill of Paradise'). As I was studying Semitic languages (among which the major Ethiopian tongues have an important place), this turned out to be a very fortunate fluke. I met there some of the priests and monks, as well as Ethiopian scholars such as Jacques Faitlovitch (of Falasha fame—about whom I shall say more later on) and A. Z. Aescoly. While the former was a missionary, intent on converting the Falashas of Ethiopia to normative Judaism, and also possessed a good practical knowledge of Ethiopia as well as a fine library, the latter was primarily a student of Falasha lore who contributed some valuable studies to this subject.

The Ethiopians, living in a number of huts within the church compound, had a life-style which differed very little from that of their compatriots in Ethiopia, as I came to find out a few years later when war service took me to that country. Although some of them spent most of their lives in Jerusalem, they kept very much to themselves, usually spoke no language other than their native Amharic or Tigrinya, the two principal modern Semitic Ethiopian tongues, and seemed to be content with their ghetto-like existence.

A few hundred yards to the east was another, though very different, ghetto-like quarter, that of Me'ah She'arim ('a hundred gates' or 'a hundredfold', Genesis 26:12, derived from Isaac sowing the land and reaping in the same year 'a hundredfold'). When, about the middle of the nineteenth century, the Old walled City of Jerusalem could accommodate no further inhabitants within its Jewish, Muslim, and Christian quarters, the three major communities began to expand beyond the walls and to establish the foundations of the New City which, within a fairly short period, began to outgrow the Old City by a large margin. On the whole, the various religious groups settled in carefully segregated communities (usually along the pattern of the Old City) also in their new habitat: the Christians founded the Greek, German, etc., colonies in the south of the new parts (other Christian settlements included the important Russian Compound, in the centre of the New City, and the American colony in the north of Jerusalem), the Muslims went to live in the north, and the Jews in the west, at first mainly along the Jaffa Road, the principal approach to Jerusalem. Moreover, the Jews, in their new settlements, reflected very largely their country of origin, that is, the 'Houses of Warsaw' or of Hungary, the Bukharian quarter, etc.

But the most important quarter, built in the 1870s, was the ultra-orthodox Me'ah She'arim whose inhabitants lived almost exclusively for study and prayer. They recognized the government of those days as reluctantly as they do now in relation to the State of Israel and shunned all possible contact with secular authority. Most of their two-storeyed houses have balconies with iron grilles, a kind of stockade or enclosure of upright stakes, which overhang the cloistered lanes and alleys. This mode of building was transplanted from their *shtetls* in Eastern Europe whence their forebears had come. They spoke and speak Yiddish and regard Hebrew, the holy tongue, as unsuitable for secular purposes.

Their side-curls (*pe'ot*) grow long over their ears and hang down their pale cheeks—untouched by the sun, for their faces are almost continually buried in the Talmudic texts whose elucidation is the prime aim of their lives. They wear long black garbs, a form of frock-coat, black stockings, and black fur-hats called *shtreimels*. Their schools (*cheder* or, at a higher level, *yeshivah*) emit the constant and monotonous sound of the recitations of the pupils who are usually grouped around their rabbinical masters. It would be foolhardy to drive a vehicle through their streets on the sabbath or for women to wear dresses that do not offer full and ample cover.

From my house in Abyssinian Street it was less than five minutes' walk down the hill to Me'ah She'arim, where there were many small shops from which I would buy my groceries for breakfast and supper. For a shilling one could buy a loaf of bread, some butter, and half a dozen very small eggs. For five mils (=one two-hundredth of a pound) one could get an armful of oranges. And as I walked back slowly up the hill, I would stop at the Ethiopian Church, chat with the monks, and ask them for the Ethiopian, that is, Amharic, names of my purchases. I am still surprised at my ignorance when I enquired after their word for marmalade, which is obviously unknown in their diet and, to this day, is simply rendered as *marmälata*, that is, the Italian *marmellata* (from Greek *meli-melon* 'honey-apple').

My Arab-style room was spacious and reasonably well furnished, but it lacked a wardrobe. So my first major investment at Jerusalem was in the purchase of a wardrobe. I found an adequate one at a small Jewish shop of second-hand goods, most of whose wares were exhibited on the pavement outside the shop. The agreed price for the wardrobe was four shillings, which included transport (about half a mile) in the salesman's cart. Unfortunately, the Arab house in Abyssinian Street was sold three or four months later and I had to move; the new room which I rented had a perfectly serviceable wardrobe and there

was no space for a second one. So I returned to the same shop
and enquired whether they would take their wardrobe back. The
owner readily agreed, collected it on his little cart, and gave me
five shillings. And when I reminded him that I had paid him only
four shillings a few months ago, his rejoinder was: 'Do you run
my business or I!' My girlfriend (and future wife), on hearing of
this transaction, opined that perhaps I was not cut out for a
career in business!?

The idea of having to move rooms upset me greatly, for any
interruption to one's studies and ordered mode of life was disturbing; and shifting even a small library of about a thousand
books was both expensive and a nuisance. I sought, therefore, a
new home where I could be reasonably certain of spending the
remaining three-and-a-half years of my undergraduate studies.
A friend of mine told me of a small new settlement of only eight
houses, built and owned by officials of both mandatary and
Jewish authorities. The place, called North Talpioth, was
situated between Abu Tor and the High Commissioner's Palace
at the outskirts of Jerusalem; it was directly adjoining the massive
walls of St Claire's Convent and possessed superb panoramic
views of the Old City, the Hinnom Valley (that is, Gehenna, at
whose edge it was built), and the road down to Jericho. The eight
houses of whitewashed concrete were comfortable inside but were
no architectural gems and assorted ill with the grandeur of their
natural setting. Since then many more houses have been added,
and the conifers, which fifty years ago were mere saplings, have by
now produced an improved landscape.

The owners of the original eight houses were architects,
engineers, Jewish Agency functionaries, a Director of the Zionist
Archives, and a doctor in charge of Jewish medical services. It
was a highly congenial cultural as well as physical milieu for a
university student and proved to offer almost ideal conditions for
both serious study and leisure. The only disadvantage was the
distance from the town centre, where I had previously lived, and
especially from the university. It also added fares, from North
Talpioth to central Jerusalem, to my tightly arranged budget; but
fortunately my kindly landlady offered to deduct the additional
twenty-five piastres for fares from my monthly rent.

North Talpioth was a mere five to ten minutes' leisurely walk,
along Allenby Barracks and the Jerusalem golf course, from the

beautifully wooded suburb of Talpioth which had been established as long ago as 1922. As far as I know, this was the only golf
course in Palestine at that time. The Allenby Barracks were a
small township of army huts, and a considerable number of the
large garrison then stationed in Palestine were quartered there.
The troops were predominantly Scottish regiments, and I shall
never forget the sound of bagpipes which were a constant accom-
paniment—at first unaccustomed, later almost indispensable—to
my studies: Cuneiform texts or Arabic syntax without the haunting tunes of bagpipes became quite unthinkable. Many of these
tunes remain firmly lodged in my memory. The two High Commissioners during my student days were Scotsmen, Sir Arthur
Wauchope and Sir Harold MacMichael; their hearts must have
rejoiced at the sound of this music which carried well across the
half-mile or so from the barracks to Government House. These
bagpipes were the first element in my great love for Scotland; the
second was the wonderfully happy period of close on ten years
my wife and I spent at St Andrews University in Scotland during
the 1950s; and the third is the Scottish landscape, a scenery of
such beauty and seclusion as I have otherwise only encountered
in Ethiopia—alas, since 1974, virtually closed to civilized man.

The half-mile or so from North Talpioth to Government
House, the High Commissioner's fine residence, was virtually
empty ground, traversed only by the road leading to his 'palace'
(that at any rate was the Hebrew designation, *armon*, for Government House). My room at that time did not, unfortunately, look
out towards the east, the Old City, the Hinnom valley, and the
mountains of Transjordan (as it then was). But it did, in its west-
ward exposure, have fine views upwards towards the fields and
the road. In the evening in particular it was a picturesque sight to
watch Arab men and women (the latter with their baskets
skilfully poised upon their heads), as well as their camels and
donkeys, returning to their villages, their outlines beautifully
silhouetted against the setting sun. By day I often watched the
High Commissioner's splendid Rolls Royce (the only one in the
country), preceded by outriders and followed by an armoured
vehicle, issuing forth from Government House and later returning. It was an impressive and, at any rate at first, unaccustomed
spectacle for me.

I vividly recall an occasion when I saw the High Commissioner's

young daughter, a beautiful blonde girl of about 17, being thrown
by her donkey, on which she used to ride along the fields between Government House and North Talpioth. She was un-
injured, and I managed to capture the donkey. She thanked
me and invited me to tea for the next afternoon. The following
morning, however, an equerry appeared at the French windows
of my room and politely cancelled the invitation. It seemed that
on security grounds (always an important consideration in
Palestine) it was not thought prudent to extend such an invitation to a complete stranger. There was an amusing sequel to this
—some thirty-three years later. When Emperor Haile Sellassie
was on a visit to Britain in 1972, the Prime Minister gave a
dinner party at 10 Downing Street to which my wife and I were
invited. After dinner small groups formed in the drawing-room
and I came to sit next to the Emperor's daughter, Princess
Tenagne Worq, whom I had known in Ethiopia for many years.
A lady next to us asked me where I had learnt the 'Ethiopian
language'. When I told her that I had studied it at Jerusalem
before the war, it emerged that she had been there at the same
time; in fact, she turned out to be the young lady whose donkey I
had caught. So our afternoon tea had become after-dinner coffee
—postponed by a third of a century.

Arabic is, of course, one of the principal Semitic languages,
and the opportunities in Jerusalem for hearing and speaking it
were most helpful—quite apart from excellent study facilities at
the university, with the fine library of the late Professor I.
Goldziher, the great Hungarian Islamic scholar, as the
centrepiece of the oriental collections. All of us (alas, in fact, very
few) who were privileged to study Near Eastern languages at
Jerusalem were in an extremely fortunate position, for, beyond
the usual means existing for the pursuit of the classical tongues,
Jerusalem offered a fertile field—indeed unparalleled opportunities—for research on the *living* Semitic languages. Obviously,
there were Hebrew and Arabic, first and foremost, with their
ample reservoir of indigenous speakers; but also modern
Aramaic languages, still spoken by a handful of people, could be
heard in Jerusalem by those who took the trouble to search out
for these comparatively rare chances. It was much easier to find
speakers of modern Ethiopian languages, Amharic, Tigrinya,
Gurage (in this order), which were used by members of the

Ethiopian Christian communities for so long resident in Jerusalem. They were concentrated in and around the Ethiopian Church in Abyssinian Street (initiated during the reign of Emperor Yohannes IV, 1872-89, and completed during that of Emperor Menelik II, 1889-1913), in the fine Ethiopian house and consulate in the Street of the Prophets, and in the Ethiopian Orthodox Patriarchate in the Old City, between the New Gate and the Damascus Gate.

The first to exploit these singular opportunities was my teacher, Professor H. J. Polotsky, about whom I shall have more to say later on. At the present time no one is more assiduous in search of speakers of modern Aramaic dialects than my erstwhile pupil, Professor Simon Hopkins. After an exceptionally distinguished undergraduate and postgraduate career at the School of Oriental and African Studies, London University, he held a research post at the Genizah Unit of the Cambridge University Library before being appointed, at the early age of 27, to the Chair of Hebrew in the University of Cape Town. Since January 1984 he has been teaching Arabic at the Hebrew University of Jerusalem and has also been working on the great dictionary of the Hebrew Language Academy, the first non-Jew to hold such central positions. His main research interest now is the pursuit (quite literally) of Aramaic-speaking remnants, a search in which he has been marvellously successful. Of course, there is one technical aid available now which was not at our disposal fifty years ago—the tape-recorder.

Apart from conversations—alas, no systematic research—with some Ethiopians whom I encountered in the 1930s, I endeavoured to engage Arabs in some pretty elementary exchanges of words and sentences. When working in my room in North Talpioth I would look out for some of their little caravans passing along the road outside my window. At first it was mainly a question of exchanging greetings and enquiries after their health and that of their animals. With time and increasing acquaintance with classical Arabic—a most challenging language of great subtlety—my command of the colloquial tongue improved, but it never became fluent or easy. I was too much constrained by the classical language which in the case of Arabic is pretty far removed from the contemporary colloquials, in themselves fairly distinct, of Palestine or Egypt, Iraq, Arabia, the

Sudan, or the Maghreb, etc. The problem of diglossia in Arabic
is acute—that is the co-existence in the same region of a
colloquial idiom side by side with a more learned and literary
language. The gulf between the two can be very profound
indeed. The language of the Qur'an, of Arabic literature, and of
newspapers, indeed of most means of literate expression, is
supra-national and is generally understood wherever Arabic is
read, while the ordinary mode of daily conversation is a patois
which differs in all aspects of linguistic realization.

My attempts, however, were on a fairly mundane level and,
certainly at first, caused a good deal of hilarity to my casual inter-
locutors. I was quite content if they understood what I wanted to
say and if I comprehended their fluent utterances. One factor
that complicated mutual comprehension was naturally connected
with the very distinct range of interest and vocabulary which
divided me from those I tried to engage in conversation. Eliciting
information, in practical linguistics as well as in matters of substance, is a skill which requires a great deal of practice. This is
especially the case when the chasm of culture, experience, and
mode of life is as wide and yawning as it inevitably was (and
generally still is) between Europeans and, say, Arabs along the
Bethlehem Road or Ethiopians in remote villages in the
inaccessible mountains of Northern Ethiopia.

My greenness as regards their mode of life was such that, when
I first saw an Arab woman give birth to a baby by the side of the
road leading to Government House—with her husband standing
by her side, idly and seemingly unconcerned—I ran for medical
help. The doctor just smiled at me, and when I returned to the
spot ten or fifteen minutes later, she had gone, no doubt carrying
a healthy baby in her arms—and without the aid of obstetrics.

My immediate neighbour was the vast complex of the Convent
of St Claire. I never saw any of the sisters, the Clarisses who
were devoted to a life of poverty and total seclusion. This last
element seemed to me immensely attractive at that time, for it
would permit uninterrupted study without disturbance and
without having to worry over board and lodging. The only sign
of life emanating from the Convent was the regular chime of
monotonous but strangely haunting bells which called the sisters
to prayer. The walls were so high that it was totally impossible to
look into the large compound; and it was not until shortly after

the war, when a ninth house was built at North Talpioth, much closer to the wall, that it was possible to see from its roof that the terrain inside was beautifully green, with lovely gardens, trees, and fine buildings. By that time I no longer sought such total seclusion, but the mystery of that hidden world is not forgotten.

The settlement and its inhabitants at the edge of Gehenna

I must now say a little more about some of the inhabitants of the original eight houses (*skekhunah*, as it was termed, that is, 'neighbourhood, quarter') of North Talpioth at the edge of Gē Hinnom (=Gehenna). The owner of the small villa in which I lodged was the head of the Zionist Archives at Jerusalem and had held similar posts abroad before immigrating into Palestine. By training he was a historian, but by inclination he was more of an annalist, lexicographer, and chronicler of events. He was upright, worthy, and conventional in his views and habits—what would be called *bieder* in his native Silesia. His principal published work was invested in the co-editorship of the *Jüdisches Lexikon* which, in five volumes, managed to give an excellent outline of available knowledge in the area of Jewish studies and related fields. He had served for many years as Secretary of the Presidium of Zionist Congresses, a fact of which he was—not unreasonably—very proud. In that capacity he had met many of the prominent Zionist leaders, including Weizmann, Sokolow, Ussishkin, Ben-Gurion, and many others.

His wife was an excellent home-maker and created an atmosphere of harmony and well-being. They had two daughters, the elder of whom rose to senior positions, including an ambassadorship, in the Israeli Foreign Service. And although my wife and I see her, and correspond with her, at infrequent intervals only, we have remained friends all these many years. The sixth inhabitant (in addition to parents, daughters, and lodger) was an elderly aunt who usually lived at the house. In retrospect, though not at the time, I find it remarkable how six people managed to co-exist in close proximity in a small bungalow of five rooms without any friction or disturbance, particularly in the climate of Jerusalem with extreme heat on *khamsin* days and occasionally freezing weather, at times even snow, in the winter—and with fairly rudimentary means of heating. When I reflect that I have always found it difficult to do any scholarly work except in conditions of almost total seclusion (and have shunned, whenever possible, even the reading rooms of university libraries) and, moreover, that I have throughout my life unsociably recoiled from accommodating overnight guests at my home (to my wife's chagrin), then I marvel at the congenial conditions and atmosphere I was fortunate enough to enjoy at that 'temporary' home for three-and-a-half years.

The only meals which I had with the whole family were Friday dinners and Saturday lunches, when the university refectory and the restaurants in town were closed. After dinner on Fridays my landlord and his wife were 'at home' to members of our small community. More often than not we first listened to the Sabbath Eve recorded concert of classical music on the Palestine Broadcasting Service and then had discussions on a remarkable variety of subjects. Palestine politics was inevitably of prime interest, but I still remember vividly conversations on music, Hebrew grammar and diction, the physical defence of our settlement—or the wives of Henry VIII, a most heated debate. I often wonder why there were such stimulating arguments on matters which could quite easily have been settled by recourse to the ample library resources available in most of the houses. Every Friday evening more or less the same company, with only minor variations, assembled and partook of light refreshments. As the inhabitants of North Talpioth had such different careers and occupations, different backgrounds and accomplishments, these occasions were never dull or repetitive. One was 'expected' to turn up; if someone failed to do so, a gentle enquiry might, at the next meeting, be directed at those who had played truant.

Of course, there were also the 'village bores', such as the erudite insurance executive and art expert, the frequent and hapless butt of endless teasing. He had discovered a minor factual error in Arnold Toynbee's *Study of History* which he would parade at every conceivable opportunity. To him it was, of course, a major flaw which invalidated the entire work—until, many months later, he received an answer from Toynbee to his no doubt gentle rebuke. At that point the capital mistake shrank to a trivial oversight: 'After all, we are all prone to error', he now said, and 'Have I shown you the text of his careful rejoinder to my letter?' Everyone cautiously refrained from demanding to inspect the great Toynbee's declaration of submission for fear of prolonging the discussion or of encouraging our neighbour to search for other mistakes. But a few weeks later a newcomer to our circle evinced an interest in the matter and wanted to see Professor Toynbee's dissertation on the subject of that crucial error. To our surprise, our learned neighbour showed himself curiously and uncharacteristically reluctant to produce the actual missive, but when challenged he had no choice and went to fetch the letter from his home. It read: 'Dear Dr X, you may well be right in your supposition. Yours sincerely, Arnold Toynbee.' Poor wretch! And he was such a genuinely learned man.

The house next to 'mine', some thirty or forty yards away, was that of my future father-in-law, his wife, and their three daughters. He was a doctor but had for most of his life been a senior medical administrator. In some ways he was perhaps—like whisky—an acquired taste, but he was a man of astonishingly wide reading and knowledge, both in the sciences and in the humanities. By inclination he was a teacher and liked to challenge and instruct his family and friends. Though given to soliloquy, his disquisitions were never dull and were always enlivened by humour and informed by genuine learning. He was a university professor *manqué*, and this fact was probably the cause of a certain tetchiness towards professional academics. In the course of his official duties he had reached the conclusion that the stable-fly, *stomoxys calcitrans*, was the real cause of typhoid rather than the bacillus *salmonella typhosa* ingested with food, milk, or water. He was deeply wedded to this theory and believed that academic medicine prevented his hypothesis from being properly tested. I was to understand later that the theory was unlikely to be well-founded and that his concern in regard to medical professors was probably the result of frustration.

He presided over a wonderfully harmonious family who looked up to him with respect and deep affection. The atmosphere at his home was at all times intellectually stimulating, and I came to admire the impressive width of his learning which he liked to share with others. He would invite friends, particularly among the young acquaintances of his daughters, and read with them Dante or Goethe and discourse knowledgeably on background, literary parallels, etc. At some stage he felt he ought to learn Arabic, and I volunteered to give him lessons—a small token in return for all the hospitality I had enjoyed at his home. He was not naturally gifted for languages (unlike his eldest daughter), but he showed an intelligent interest in the *modus operandi* of Arabic. The only mutually convenient time we could find was early in the morning when he was having breakfast. While I was matutinal in my habits, his metabolism was decidedly nocturnal, and the early hour was not the best time for his cerebral functions. His example encouraged at least one of his neighbours, an engineer, to follow in his footsteps and take Arabic lessons from me. This proved to be a hard slog for me (and no doubt for him), and as the remuneration for these strenuous efforts was exiguous in the extreme, we decided, by mutual agreement, to leave him in a state of ignorance in matters Arabic. Dr N., my prospective in-law, on the other hand, was made of sterner stuff, intellectually and otherwise; he persevered until the approach of my final examinations forced me to concentrate on my studies.

When war broke out I was engaged on writing my MA thesis. Its subject, the definite article in the Semitic languages, caused much mirth to Dr N. who was anxious to know what contribution to the war effort the definite article was likely to make. To my obvious rejoinder he would respond that his solution to the typhoid scourge would have a salutary effect on the course of the war. His banter became more muted when I was despatched to Eritrea and Ethiopia to utilize my knowledge of Ethiopian languages. He seemed almost impressed.

His wife was the ideal helpmeet to him, in a long marriage of unimpaired happiness, and a wonderful mother to their three daughters. As a young student, between the ages of 18 and 21, I found in her a substitute-mother who was always tactful as well as helpful. And although it was generally thought that all three daughters were nice-looking, everyone considered their mother the most handsome. Each of the daughters possessed aptitudes and qualities quite distinct from the other two; these characteristics developed further in later life and account for the very different paths and roles they pursued subsequently. I met the eldest, my future wife, at a New Year's Eve party within a week or ten days of my coming to live at North Talpioth, and developed a penchant for her at this very first meeting. The friendship matured slowly in its initial stages but was firmly established within fifteen months. Her parents seemed pleased in the early phases but became a little concerned when they realized that I considered myself far too young to think of marriage or of a binding commitment—quite apart from the fact that, as a student, I had neither an income nor a job, not even any immediate prospect of finding one. This last element was changed by the war and its vicissitudes, but that belongs to a different section of this book. There was one curious—almost superstitious—factor which affected us all: one day we discovered that my parents and hers were married on the same day in the same year, and in the same place (without, of course, knowing each other).

Opposite the house of my future parents-in-law was the home of a very impressive man and his family. When my wife and I returned to Jerusalem from Ethiopia shortly after the end of the war, we lived for a year in a small flat at the top of their house. The flat had a large terrace which commanded incomparable views over the Old City of Jerusalem, the Mount of Olives, and the wilderness of Judea. My desk was under a window looking out on this unique scene, which made it hard for me to concentrate on my work.

Dr Markus Reiner, the owner of the house, had come to Palestine in 1922. After working briefly as an agricultural labourer, he joined the Public Works Department of the Government. He rose to senior positions and remained there until the surrender of the Mandate in 1948. He had been engaged in major public works projects as well as in the restoration of historical sites. He was also a physicist and mechanical engineer of note, the founder of a new branch of physics called rheology, which is concerned, I understand, with the flow and change of the shape of matter, particularly the viscosity of liquids. He used to visit Dr Scott Blair of the National Institute of Dairying, Reading University, and told me that the flow of milk had important lessons for asphalting and road-building. In 1948, at the age of 62, he became Professor of Mechanics at the Technion, the Israel Institute of Technology at Haifa, and eventually was appointed one of the founder-members of the Israel Academy of Sciences.

When I knew him in the 1930s and 1940s he seemed to me a remarkable man, although I could understand nothing of his professional work. He was a curious amalgam of jolliness and aloofness—normally, one would think, mutually exclusive attributes. Our views on Palestine politics converged closely, and he was

one of the founders of the movement for Arab-Jewish understanding (*Brith Shalom*, 'covenant of peace', later *Ichud*, 'unity').
I cherish his memory.

An even earlier and wholly devoted advocate of Arab-Jewish
understanding was, alas, only an occasional resident of North
Talpioth, the distinguished father of one of our neighbours,
Hermona Simon, who was among the very early *sabras* (natives
of Palestine/Israel, literally 'prickly pears', allegedly thus called
because of their prickly exteriors and tender hearts). Haim
(Margolis-)Kalvaryski (1868-1947) was one of the great pioneers
of Jewish settlement in Palestine. Born in Russia where his
parents were landowners, he studied agriculture at Montpellier
and went to Palestine in 1895. He taught there at agricultural
schools and subsequently worked on behalf of Baron Edmond de
Rothschild, the great philanthropist, in the settlements established by the Baron's munificence. In 1900 he became the
principal administrator of the settlements that ICA (the Jewish
Colonization Association) had founded in Galilee, again largely
financed by Edmond de Rothschild.

Apart from this great pioneering enterprise of establishing
these early settlements in Palestine, Kalvaryski was a wholehearted advocate of Arab-Jewish accord, an aim which he
pursued with singleminded dedication. Already in 1913 he and
Sokolow, the Zionist leader, had met Arab representatives in
Damascus in order to reach an understanding between them and
the Zionist Organization. He was one of the few Jewish leaders
who had close contacts with his Arab neighbours and moderate
Arab groups. He could speak their language, and they were
convinced of the genuine sympathy he had for their anxieties. On
the Jewish side the movement for close accord with the Arabs
was largely, though by no means exclusively, supported by an
intellectual élite, connected in part with J. L. Magnes of the
Hebrew University and some of his colleagues. But Kalvaryski
was the principal personality in the *Yishuv* who had genuine
rapport at the grassroots and was able to evoke a response from
the other side. By and large it is unhappily true to say that those
Arabs who saw some prospect of a *rapprochement* were severely
intimidated, often by violent means, by their compatriots. It
required courage of a high order to have contacts on the other
side of an ever taller fence. In the course of time extremism grew

in both camps—to a point when even today I would hesitate to name Arab friends and colleagues with whom one was in touch forty-five to fifty years ago.

Kalvaryski saw Palestine as a homeland common to both Arabs and Jews. In his earlier years he had served as a member of the Palestine Government Advisory Council as well as head of the Bureau for Arab Affairs of the Jewish Agency and the *Va'ad Le'umi* (the Jewish National Council) but towards the end of his life he was increasingly out of sympathy with official Zionist policy. I knew him only in the course of his last ten years, mostly during his visits to his daughter in North Talpioth. He would tell me fascinating stories of the early settlements in the 1890s and the period before the First World War—and of *hanadiv hayadu'a* ('the well-known benefactor', as he used to be described), the great Baron Edmond de Rothschild, his friend. His store of knowledge of early Palestine was immense, if not unique.

He would ask me about my Arabic studies and the attitudes of my fellow-students in Arabic. Did their work in the language, literature, and history of the Arabs influence their political orientation? I was not sure of the answer then—nor am I now. Both he and I deplored the intransigence, as we saw it, of the Arab and Jewish leaderships. Kalvaryski was, above all, a gentleman with an old-world courtesy, an amalgam of Russian and French elements. It is a great privilege to have known him, even on so superficial a level as I did.

The little road bisecting North Talpioth, with four houses on either side, was the hub of our small settlement and one used to meet one's neighbours there very regularly. One daily excitement was the arrival of the postman, a charming young Arab who served in that area throughout the three-and-a-half years I lived at North Talpioth. His knowledge of English, Hebrew, and his native Arabic must have been sufficient at least to decipher the handwritten addresses in those languages—no mean undertaking. I used to address him in Arabic and quite often he would respond in his serviceable Hebrew. I learned a good deal from him, but I rather doubt that he will ever see this acknowledgement of my debt.

In the course of time the owners of two of the houses moved back into the centre of Jerusalem and let their houses. In those

days, fifty years ago, nobody I knew owned a car, and the nearest
bus stop was either at Talpioth or in the Arab suburbs of Abu
Tor or Bak'a, a good ten minutes' walk. In the heat of the
summer this could be quite an effort, but it was far worse in the
winter during the rainy season when torrential downpours
turned the rough roads on the outskirts of Jerusalem into mud
flats and the severe western gales gave one a hefty buffeting.
Moreover, the security situation caused some anxiety, and it was
therefore not surprising that a few abandoned the seclusion of
North Talpioth to go back to the inner city. A third house, the
largest in our tiny hamlet, was suitable for sub-letting. The
owner and his family moved into a small wing of the house and
let the remainder of the two-storey building to two English
tenants.

One was a family with two charming little twin daughters,
aged 3 or 4. They would play on our small road and chatter in
English with great fluency. It had apparently not occurred to any
of us that in England little boys and girls could speak English
without having to study it laboriously as we had to do. In fact, of
course, it was much more curious that in Palestine little boys and
girls could speak the language—or at any rate a reasonable
semblance of it—once uttered by King Solomon and by at least
some of his wives. The twins' father was Registrar of Co-
operative Societies in the Palestine Government. I remember an
occasion when a Scots Major, in kilt and full uniform, visited this
English family. His unaccustomed attire in a 'skirt' caused great
hilarity to all the children playing on the road. The Major
appeared displeased by this reception which seemed to him very
ill-mannered. He demanded a formal apology which was in due
course delivered to the neighbouring Allenby Barracks.

The other tenant was a most charming man, a Mr Ralph
Poston, who had been Private Secretary to Sir Arthur
Wauchope, the former High Commissioner, and now held a
senior position in the Palestine Broadcasting Service. Pro-
grammes on the PBS were broadcast in the three official
languages of the country: English, Arabic, and Hebrew; and on
rare occasions, when there were announcements or news
bulletins of particular importance, Mr Poston himself would
read these in English—rather like his counterparts on the BBC,
Messrs Stuart Hibberd and John Snagge. We were very pleased

to have such a prominent and delightful person as our neighbour. Mr Poston had one other inestimable advantage which made him even more popular: he possessed, unlike anyone else, a motor car—and a smart sports model into the bargain. He was invariably generous with lifts, and a ride with him across Jerusalem was always enjoyable as well as instructive. Even my future mother-in-law, who was shy and very reticent, would gratefully accept a lift from Mr Poston. She would tell him that she felt quite embarrassed by the tiny and extremely noisy and unreliable scooter (or rather the forerunner of such a machine) on which her husband drove himself to his office, wearing the most remarkable and unbecoming outfit for this hazardous journey. But Mr Poston consoled her and assured her that it was merely a crazed sewing-machine and not a motorbike.

The two houses which had been vacated by their owners were eventually let to the Youth Aliyah, the organization initiated in 1932 by Mrs Recha Freier (the mother of a schoolfriend of mine) to rescue children from the Nazis and settle them in Palestine, first for education and training in residential schools and subsequently in a kibbutz. Such a residential school was now set up in those two houses at North Talpioth. I think the children were aged between 13 and 16, and there were some thirty of them. Apart from formal instruction during school hours, they had quite a number of extra-curricular activities such as music, gardening, amateur theatricals, etc. Their instructor was a close friend of mine, Dr Edgar Freund, some twelve years my senior, a highly gifted mathematician, physicist, and philosopher. My own involvement with this group of youngsters was marginal and was mainly on account of my friendship with Edgar. I would occasionally tutor some of them in Hebrew language and literature, especially those considered good enough to go to university at a later stage.

Edgar Freund's wide-ranging aptitudes included, *inter alia*, music and agriculture. He conducted concerts given by these children, and I recall with pleasure a spirited public performance of Beethoven's Choral Fantasia. He was immensely hard-working and totally devoted to whatever task he undertook. He got permission to use the half-acre of land between two houses for agricultural training and managed to transform the unpromising soil into a vegetable garden of real quality. He would invite me to read Kant under his guidance, and occasionally we would be extravagant—despite our meagre financial resources—and go out for a meal together. There was a vegetarian restaurant in the centre of Jaffa Road whose speciality was a fruit risotto of ample quantity and good quality; this was one of the few opportunities when we could afford to eat our fill.

Edgar also had a wife who was (and is) a lady of great beauty, blonde, blue-eyed, and possessed of remarkable cheekbones. She was a doctor and later specialized in paediatrics. In those far-off days she was not fond of cooking (nor were the facilities at her disposal adequate), and Edgar and I would at times cruelly abandon her and go out to eat. When my future wife joined us and we became a foursome, our manners gradually improved under her influence and we would all go out together. The most expensive as well as the most *recherché* restaurant in Jerusalem was called Hesse; it was mostly frequented by members of the British administration. I think we could afford (no—we could not really) to go there only twice or at most three times throughout those years. The three-course menu was priced 16 piastres (= 16 pence) and was quite splendid; alas, wine was far beyond our means.

Edgar's later career was spent as Director of a technical and handicraft school. But his intellectual potential was never turned to full account; he was always unfulfilled. In many ways he was too gifted and too versatile to accept the narrow discipline of a university career, though he would have liked to do so; but he was much too self-effacing and upright ever to think of applying or pulling strings or making himself agreeable to those in a position of influence. He was and remained a man of exemplary probity and integrity. After his retirement he read, studied, and visited university libraries, but the books he could and should have written never materialized. While his personal life with his wife was happy and unclouded, his mind was ever searching for something that would offer him real stimulus and give him intellectual satisfaction. He died suddenly in 1986. His family and his few close friends are very conscious of their great loss. He was, perhaps, a typical representative of a generation caught between Hitler and a life away from their indigenous ambience. Once uprooted, the new roots were too tenuous to sustain so demanding a mind.

Talpioth

Nearby Talpioth was an old-established and fairly exclusive residential suburb of Jerusalem, beautifully wooded and with fine houses. There was a small school, a tiny synagogue in a wooden hut, an attractive café-restaurant, a corner-shop, and a lovely copse. Among the residents were some of the ornaments of the Hebrew University's professorial cadre and of the country's intellectual and literary élite. To a young student it was a wonderful experience to meet some of these men and women whose names were living concepts throughout the country and beyond, wherever Hebrew and Semitic studies were pursued.

One of the oldest residents was Joseph Klausner (1874-1958), Professor of Hebrew Literature, who was also internationally known as a historian, publicist, and Zionist leader, as well as for his important book *Jesus of Nazareth* (Hebrew edition 1922; English translation 1925) which described the background of Jesus' life, sayings, and general activities. His knowledge of Rabbinic sources enabled him to see Jesus as he was regarded by his contemporaries—and without any doctrinal preconceptions. Klausner possessed a ready fluency in contemporary Hebrew speech and had a natural command of the language, which at that time was still very unusual among university professors, who had mostly come to Palestine fairly recently. Klausner had settled in Jerusalem in 1919, having left Russia shortly after the Bolshevik revolution.

He had strong views on the type of Hebrew that ought to be spoken and written. He insisted that linguistic development demanded the abandonment of biblical forms in favour of mishnaic usage. Here, as in his political views, he was given to extreme positions. By and large, his opinions on the biblical genre have not carried the day, for in general present-day Hebrew is an amalgam of many styles; yet the contemporary linguistic forms and developments of Hebrew show considerable autonomy and a fairly rapid distancing from traditional modes.

Klausner was as renowned outside the university as he was within it. His political involvements, as a follower of Jabotinsky and of a strongly nationalistic line, mattered to him greatly. His lectures on modern Hebrew literature and other subjects were informed by a spirit of profound Jewish nationalism. While he mourned, I believe genuinely, any acts of terrorism or murder, he would not condemn them and thought that 'history has at times to be written in blood'. I deplored his views, but I could see that they were held with much fervour and sincerity. In 1949 he stood as a right-wing nationalist candidate for the Presidency of Israel in opposition to Weizmann.

His personal life seemed to me to contrast sharply with some of those extreme views. He was courteous, humane, and kind in his demeanour, was easily close to tears, and was uxorious to the point of absurdity: when his wife had a cold or a similarly trivial affliction he would cancel his lectures and announce, when eventually he reappeared: 'We were ill.' In his scholarship he was essentially a man of wide sweeps rather than pedantic minutiae. His practical knowledge of languages was extensive rather than profound. When I left for Eritrea and Ethiopia on war service, he asked me to find him a copy of the Books of the Prophets in classical Ethiopic. He possessed the other parts of the Bible in that language but claimed that the Catholic Mission at Asmara had deliberately withheld the prophets from him, a notion of which I failed to disabuse him. Despite our divergent political views and the discrepancy in our respective positions at opposite ends of the hierarchical scale, he was invariably considerate and hospitable to me. He deplored that I did not possess a Hebrew name, and as a guest in his home I was too timid to point out that his surname at any rate did not have a markedly Semitic appearance. Forty-five years later I am still glad to have known him.

The only other among my teachers who could compare with Klausner in the fluency of his Hebrew delivery—indeed outstripped him—was Mr Gedalya Allon (1901–50). He was at the lowest rung of the academic ladder, a mere instructor, but was quite obviously a man of vast erudition with a genuine spark of genius. He was invariably referred to as an *illuy* ('prodigy'). By the mid-1930s he had as yet published very little—and that was still largely true when he died, tragically early, in 1950. But a considerable number of truly important works by him appeared posthumously, and even now the stream of such writings has not run quite dry. His main interest lay in the text of the Talmud and in the history of the Jews in the period of the Mishnah and the Talmud. To me, as a listener to his lectures, the most remarkable thing about him was the speed of his Hebrew utterance, the beauty of his style, and the extraordinary range of his vocabulary. Even a brief moment's inattention to his words, fired at machine-gun velocity, caused one to lose the thread of his argument. I recall one particular occasion when, without changing either the rhythm or the voice level of his delivery and without any caesura at either end, he contrived to intercalate into his learned discourse the following remark (whose flavour is, unfortunately, lost in translation): 'I observe and point out that a boy and a girl in the last row are engaged in what can only be described as acts of indecency.' By the time it had dawned on us what he had just said, without the slightest alteration in his facial or vocal expression, he had long been back to the explication of his Talmudic passage. And by the time we had turned round to observe the happenings in the last row of the lecture hall, the offending events had—to our chagrin—long ceased.

At the farthest end of Talpioth, at Arnona, in a house that was dangerously exposed in times of trouble, lived one of my principal teachers, M. H. Segal (1876–1968), Professor of Bible. Segal was born in Lithuania, obtained his BA degree at Oxford, and for some years served as Tutor in Old Testament and Semitic Languages at Oxford. He worked under the great S. R. Driver, Regius Professor of Hebrew in the University of Oxford and one of the most renowned English Hebraists, whose abiding influence on his scholarly development he always gratefully acknowledged. He joined the recently founded Hebrew University of Jerusalem in 1926 as head of its Bible Department.

Segal developed the academic study of the Hebrew Bible with exquisite tact and scholarly integrity, and thus established as a recognized university discipline a subject for whose academic safety many had expressed forebodings, especially in the atmosphere of Jerusalem, charged with deeply felt religious emotions. During his long tenure of the Chair Segal demonstrated how orthodox beliefs can co-exist with the concepts of modern critical biblical scholarship. Of particular significance among his writings were a pioneering study of Hebrew phonetics, a comprehensive grammar of Mishnaic Hebrew (still the standard work in this field), and an edition of Ecclesiasticus (Ben

Sira). Like S. R. Driver before him, he frequently returned to the text and composition of the books of Samuel; he was a nonagenarian when his last work on this subject was published. He was a sensitive teacher and cared for his students' welfare. His English university experience was probably partly responsible for the generosity and kindness with which he welcomed undergraduates to his home, particularly on Saturday afternoons. I think he was the only one of my teachers who evinced enough interest in how I lived and worked, and what books I possessed, to come and visit me at my room at North Talpioth. His charming wife (*née* Frumkin, a family of early pioneer settlers in Palestine) had first come to the Holy Land in 1884 at the age of 9. She later composed her memoirs in Hebrew, about which her son, J. B. Segal, wrote a delightful article (*Jewish Chronicle Literary Supplement*, 25 Dec. 1981). The Segals would invite me on Passover Eve for the *Seder* ceremony, and I greatly enjoyed both the homely atmosphere (in the presence of their daughter on a visit from England) and the instruction I derived from Professor Segal's reading and commentary of the text of the *Haggadah*, the tale of the exodus from Egypt.

I also met, at about that time, their younger son Ben, who was then serving in the Sudan Government and later won an MC on active service in the Middle East. I doubt whether either of us would then have thought that we would both become Professors of Semitic Languages and enjoy a long professional and personal friendship. I did not meet his elder brother Sam, later Lord Segal of Wytham, until the 1950s, when I accosted a gentleman in the street in Bloomsbury and informed him with a high measure of confidence that he must be a son of Professor Segal of Jerusalem, my erstwhile teacher. He could not gainsay that piece of intelligence, even though proffered by a total stranger. The resemblance was striking, in both appearance and movement. He later told me how much that recognition had pleased him, for he was greatly attached to his father.

The success of their children was naturally a source of pride and deep satisfaction to my late teacher and his wife.

Another prominent resident of Talpioth was the widow of Eliezer Ben-Yehuda (1858-1922), the man who is generally regarded as the father of modern Hebrew. I shall briefly refer elsewhere in this volume to the question whether this epithet can be applied to Ben-Yehuda *simpliciter* or whether he was, perhaps, just a factor, albeit an important one, in the revival of spoken Hebrew. The latter position has of late been advocated in some revisionist writings on the subject (there usually is a swing of the pendulum in scholarship, as elsewhere, at times as a result of fresh or refined information, but often merely for the sake of novelty or, perhaps, to dethrone the gods who are thought to have outlived their time).

Ben-Yehuda's wife had died in 1891, and about six months later her sister Hemdah went from Lithuania to Jerusalem to marry Ben-Yehuda. Mrs Hemdah Ben-Yehuda (1873–1951) was a considerable personality in her own right. She helped her husband in his literary work and shared his singleminded devotion to the cause of Hebrew as a spoken language, the natural tongue of the Jews in Palestine. After his death in 1922, she applied her energies first and foremost to the continued publication of his orphaned multi-volume dictionary of Hebrew, the *Thesaurus totius Hebraitatis*, a work of immense labour and erudition. She also wrote a biography of Ben-Yehuda and his work and a similar book on her stepson (and nephew) Ithamar Ben-Avi, Ben-Yehuda's son, believed to have been the first modern Jewish child whose mother tongue was Hebrew.

Ben-Yehuda died at his house in Abyssinian Street (where, incidentally, several other prominent citizens had lived at one time or another—including Professor A. Feigenbaum, the first and foremost ophthalmologist in Palestine, G. Scholem, and my teacher H. J. Polotsky—about whom more anon). I do not know when Mrs Ben-Yehuda moved from Abyssinian Street to Talpioth (this suburb was founded, as mentioned earlier on, only in 1922), but I believe it was not very long after her husband's death. To me it was an exciting moment just to see the great Ben-Yehuda's widow—as I did very frequently—at the bus-stop at Talpioth, usually accompanied by her youngest and strikingly beautiful daughter (who is happily still with us and who lectured, not long ago, at Oxford on the work of her famous father). Jerusalem—and indeed Jewish Palestine as a whole at that time—was so small, even perhaps provincial, that it was not unusual to encounter those who carried well-known or famous names. In the somewhat austere atmosphere of mandatary Palestine fame seemed an incongruous attribute; yet it was an elevating and poignant experience to meet in the flesh those who had played (or were still playing) a prominent role in Hebrew letters (such as Agnon) or in recent history (such as Weizmann or Ben-Zvi).

I never knew Hemdah Ben-Yehuda at all well. Apart from brief bus-stop encounters, my meetings with her were generally connected with the proofs of her late husband's posthumously appearing dictionary. My teacher, Professor N. H. Torczyner (later Tur-Sinai), was the principal editor of the volumes left unfinished at the time of Ben-Yehuda's death. Torczyner knew that I lived close to Talpioth and occasionally used me as a not unwilling messenger to hand proof-sheets to Mrs Ben-Yehuda and later collect them from her with any marginal glosses she might have penned. I formed the impression that the lexicographer's widow did not invariably see eye to eye with the way the editor discharged his task; and I believe that the latter, in his turn, did not always offer hospitality to all those marginalia in the published version. I confess that I cared little about these minor manifestations of the *odium scholasticum* (no doubt much too strong an expression), but was pleased at the opportunity of being admitted, however briefly and superficially, into the presence of someone who had been so intimately associated with the early phases of the revival of Hebrew as the everyday medium of spoken communication.

Talpioth is now a large district of outer (perhaps no longer even that) Jerusalem. When my wife and I wanted to visit old haunts there, in 1980, we failed to find the famous bus-stop. It may have been moved, or the bus route may have been altered— or, quite possibly, we may have lost our bearings; but the lovely little copse we had known so well in our youth was still there— except that it was by now more of a forest.

The most self-effacing citizen of Talpioth and, probably even then, the internationally most renowned was the great Hebrew writer S. Y. Agnon (1888-1970), later the first Nobel laureate for Hebrew literature. When I knew him he was barely 50 and at the height of his powers. He had already published a great deal, but most of his important work was yet to come. Indeed, in the course of his Nobel address (in Hebrew) in 1966, he disclosed that the majority of his writings were still in manuscript. Since his death, a stream of highly significant books by him has been published posthumously, thanks to the considerable endeavours of his daughter, Mrs Emunah Yaron.

I had long been familiar with his writings, mainly short (and not so short) stories which were avidly read wherever Hebrew was known, perhaps as much for their beguiling and highly characteristic style, imbued with deep knowledge of, and feeling for, the Rabbinical genre and flavour, as for their contents and depiction of atmosphere. But when I came to know the man who had created this singular opus, it was revealing to find someone shy, self-effacing, almost withdrawn, and quite unspoilt by his reputation. I did not see him in his later years (except at a reception in London on his way back from receiving the Nobel Prize in Stockholm), but I have no reason to think that his attitude or demeanour changed.

It is odd that, half a century ago, we never met (as far as I can now remember) at that well-known bus-stop at Talpioth, but I frequently saw him in bus No. 7, both into Jerusalem and back to Talpioth, almost invariably seated in the same corner of the vehicle. I often wondered where he had boarded the bus and how he had managed to get his accustomed seat. He would invite me on many occasions to sit next to him and tell him about my studies and my teachers. He seemed most interested in Talmud classes I had attended and in the methodology by which such an essentially 'traditional' subject would be taught at a university. He was an excellent listener, and his own contributions to the conversation sounded very much like those sayings, parables, allegories, and adages which made the narrative of his works so appealing. A good example of that particular style can be found in his posthumously published *Me'atsmi el atsmi* ('from myself to myself'), a collection of miscellaneous addresses, short speeches, obituaries, *éloges*, and occasional writings of that nature. In later years, when I recalled the picture of Agnon inconspicuously huddled in his seat on the bus, I was often reminded of a remark on the radio by the late Gilbert Harding: on one occasion, when travelling on the London Underground, he was asked for his autograph by some of his fellow-travellers. And then he observed the solitary figure of T. S. Eliot, seated in a corner, away from the throng and unnoticed by autograph hunters. Harding felt deeply embarrassed.

On a few occasions in the 1930s I was invited to Agnon's home where I met his equally shy and diffident wife Esther. I had already heard a good deal about her charming ways from my future wife, who had been Mrs Agnon's pupil in elementary Arabic at the local Talpioth school. In 1983 Agnon's daughter published a volume of most interesting letters which her parents had exchanged between 1924 and 1931. This collection adds appreciably to our knowledge of Agnon's life, character, and mode of work. Thus we learn more of the terrible fire which largely destroyed the house the Agnons had occupied in 1924, at Bad Homburg in Germany, and in which many of the valuable manuscripts and rare books he had collected perished, together with large numbers of his own still unpublished writings. A similar disaster befell Agnon at his first residence at Talpioth where his home was plundered during the 1929 riots and many of his books and manuscripts were once more destroyed. Undaunted, he now built his own house at Talpioth, into which he and his family moved in 1931. The volume of letters to which I have referred also contains a pictorial record of the destruction in Homburg and at Talpioth as well as photographs of the new Talpioth home and of Agnon's study. I was quite shattered when he first told me of the terrible loss of two libraries and of two separate collections of his as yet unpublished writings. I greatly admired his courage and persistence in the face of such adversity. By the time I saw his library, in the second half of the 1930s, it seemed to me a splendid assemblage of rare and important works.

The last book which Agnon wrote, and on which he was still working at the time of his death, was a novel entitled *Shirah* (published by his daughter, together with a postscript, in 1971). In my view, none of his works is of greater weight and conceived on a grander scale than this last creation, which may well be considered his most remarkable single composition. It differs in subject-matter, atmosphere, style, and ambience from most of his other writings.

The story of *Shirah* is very briefly as follows. The central character is a Lecturer in Byzantine History at the Hebrew University of Jerusalem, and the academic community in and around that small university in the mid-1930s constitutes the backcloth of the novel. Academic rivalries, pressure for promotion, the need to publish, absorption in narrow scholarly pursuits, are all described with consummate skill and subtle irony. And behind these daily preoccupations unfold the cataclysmic events of that period, the rise of Hitler, the large-scale migration from Germany and central Europe, Arab reactions, violence in Palestine, and the looming menace of the Second World War. But the central theme is the personality of the Byzantinist torn between his affection for and loyalty to his devoted wife and family and his infatuation with a nurse, the eponymous Shirah. It is a powerful physical attraction which he fights by immersing himself in his work and his long-delayed *magnum opus* (failure to publish it had prevented his promotion to a professorship) and by added devotion to his family. The contrast between the weak and vacillating character of the Byzantinist scholar and the abrasive personality of the nurse is described with infinite care and remarkable psychological insight.

The blurb states that the delicate subject of the book made Agnon hesitate to publish it during his lifetime. I am not quite certain what precise inferences are to be drawn from that statement. Is it the theme of extra-marital love, and physical love in particular, that caused Agnon's hesitation? Or is it the realistic depiction of actual events that form the background to the novel which has at times been described as a *roman à clef*? Although I was reasonably familiar with the personalities of the Hebrew University at the operative period, I find it difficult to disentangle a real character from the complex skein presented to us. No doubt the Byzantinist is a conflated figure and probably sufficiently well disguised to put the reader off the scent—yet apparently not enough to assuage Agnon's anxieties about publication during his lifetime. Professor H. J. Polotsky, probably the principal professorial survivor of the period in which the novel is set, is in broad agreement with this assessment.

A few years ago I had arranged with Agnon's daughter and with publishers to prepare an annotated translation of the *Shirah* novel. I had done some preliminary work on this and had been very much looking forward to this undertaking, both *per se* and on sentimental grounds. I was particularly interested in the attempt to render the complexities and the flavour of Agnon's style into a register of English that might not be considered unacceptably *outré*. I was equally attracted by the challenge of annotating the language as well as the background of this remarkable novel, which covers a period in the life of the Hebrew University and of Jerusalem with which I had been reasonably familiar. Alas, a severe illness put paid to any thought of carrying through an enterprise of such difficulty and duration. I hope that someone will soon be found to make this work accessible to those who do not read Hebrew.

I should like to conclude this brief sketch of my acquaintance with Agnon and our meetings at Talpioth, in those now very distant days of my undergraduate studies at Jerusalem, with another, to me very poignant, recollection. When I served as Professor of Semitic Languages and Literatures in the University of Manchester, I received (as no doubt most professors of literature do) from the Nobel authorities the annual proposal form on which one is expected to make a reasoned submission for the award of the literature prize. I had no doubt who was the most worthy candidate in the field in which I was expected to have some professional competence. I made my submission on two or three successive occasions, and I was greatly moved when in due course, no doubt supported by names weightier than mine, Agnon became the first Hebrew writer to receive the Nobel Prize in Literature. Those who proposed him and those who made the final decision at Stockholm could not have known that much of his most significant work was yet to be published.

In 1938 I would not have thought that in my lifetime a Hebrew writer would be awarded that most prestigious and coveted of prizes; nor could I have imagined, for all my admiration and respect for him, that the diffident man on the Talpioth bus would be the recipient of that signal honour; and least of all could I have dreamed that in the fullness of time I would have a minuscule part in that consummation.

The new city

The Old City of Jerusalem, where, within the confined space circumscribed by the massive wall, Jews and Arabs as well as the various Christian denominations had lived for centuries in an uneasy (and at times turbulent) symbiosis, impinged curiously little on the life of the new city during the 1930s. Of course, residents of the newer parts went there, security permitting, when they first arrived in Jerusalem and had to discharge the *de rigueur* pilgrimage to the Dome of the Rock, the Wailing Wall, and the Christian shrines. Later on, one would occasionally conduct visitors and tourists (in small numbers—unlike the American, German, and Japanese inundation of today) through the narrow alleys and navigate a cautious path through shop-keepers, vendors, and importunate hawkers and beggars. The Wailing Wall was still a place of private devotions rather than the giant spectacle for clicking cameras and flash-bulbs. The Dome of the Rock, that most beautiful of all buildings, was viewed and admired from a respectful distance, without upsetting the susceptibilities of those to whom these places were holy and exclusive.

But the real and vibrant life of Jerusalem lay outside the wall in the manifold quarters of the new and unwalled city. Of course, here, too, there were the older parts, those dating from Ottoman times up to the First World War, and the more recent ones built during the Mandate, especially the smarter districts of Rehavia and Talbiye, the latter with its fine Arab houses. It is difficult now to envisage that the great arterial avenues issuing from the central Jaffa Road, the Ben-Yehuda and King George V streets, were not built until the 1920s. The hub of all urban activity in my time was situated in Zion Square where the Jaffa and Ben-Yehuda streets met and the 'new' Zion Cinema had been built. Everything happened here: it was at Zion Square that one joined one's friends by appointment or encountered numerous acquaint-ances by chance (scarcely by accident, for it was so central that one was virtually bound to run into everybody at this point). It is only a slight exaggeration to say that in that central part of the city one recognized almost every face; somehow one had seen everyone at some time. Jerusalem was still small enough to have a village-community feel about it.

The houses in the centre, in contrast to the newer and smarter residential quarters, were small and old-fashioned, but made of stone and durable. There were no skyscrapers in those days; Sir Ronald Storrs' Preservation Society and its ordinances had seen to that. Of course, there were some fine buildings, old and new, such as the Citadel (or Tower of David) to the right of the Jaffa Gate as you walk towards the Old City, or the Monastery of the Cross (at that time in the wilderness beyond Rehavia), or the Russian Compound, just off the Jaffa Road, with the green-domed towers of the Cathedral of the Holy Trinity. Or the buildings of the Jewish Agency and the Keren Kayemeth (the National Fund established to acquire land for settlement), the Yeshurun Synagogue—or the Terra Sancta College, and the Augusta Victoria Hospital on Mount Scopus, the first residence of British High Commissioners. Among the (then) most modern and most impressive buildings were the YMCA, with its unjustly maligned 'phallic' tower, and the King David Hotel opposite it. The former could be inspected inside, with its fine indoor swimming-pool (the only one at Jerusalem at that time?), excellent concert hall, and regular organ recitals, while the latter seemed inordinately expensive and presented an atmosphere of opulence and (for Palestine) unaccustomed luxury.

In the commercial centre, off Zion Square, were shops and cafés and restaurants as well as some excellent bookshops. There were also, curiously enough, a very large number of barbers. My barber in Ben-Yehuda Street, although long-established, seemed very modern and hygienic; there was never any dearth of customers, and many of them, in addition to a haircut, would also have a shave (nowadays a vanished accomplishment, I think). The owner of the shop had some six or eight constantly busy assistants; he himself was a man of substance presiding over a flourishing business. His son, Yehuda Ha'ezrahi (in my day still called Brisker), was a fellow-student of mine and became a well-known novelist and playwright as well as a champion of the society to preserve the beauty of Jerusalem. He died, tragically young, in 1974 at the age of 54. His wife Pepita had predeceased him in 1963. She had become a philosopher and taught at Jerusalem and Cambridge. In our undergraduate days she had been a girl of unusual beauty and equally unusual comportment: she always wore, in hottest summer and coldest winter, a simple black dress, hat, and brown leather gloves. On one occasion, on a particularly hot day, I was fortunate enough to have her sit next to me in a lecture on Psalms. She had forgotten her copy of the Bible and asked me for permission to share mine. At the end of the class her leather glove stuck to the margin of my book and left a mark near Psalm 22, by the verse 'O my God, I cry in the day-time, but thou hearest not'. The mark has been carefully preserved; it is still clearly visible. Shortly before her death, when she was teaching philosophy at Cambridge, I heard from Professor Leon Roth that she had become an important figure in contemporary philosophy, particularly (and not surprisingly) in the field of aesthetics.

More than twenty years after those events, in 1961, my wife and I walked up Ben-Yehuda Street on a visit to Jerusalem. When we passed the barber's shop, Mr Brisker's senior assistant, who had since taken over as proprietor, recognized me (to my intense surprise) and insisted that I have a haircut, a service which he performed himself. In the constantly and rapidly changing kaleidoscope of Palestine-Israel, here was a tiny corner that was untouched by the march of events. Even more astonishing was an encounter in the same part of Jerusalem in 1977, when we went to book seats in a shared taxi (*sherut*) to Haifa. Outside the office we were stopped by a heavily bearded old man who asked me why I did not recognize him. 'I know who you are; forty years ago I had a *gazoz* stall [fizzy orangeade, thirst-quenching mainly by virtue of its sheer awfulness] up on Mount Scopus, outside the university, and you were such a good customer; you were very thirsty'. And then he produced a passable approximation of my name. We were flabbergasted and even curiously moved: forty years had passed; Israel and the world had been transformed; and I had turned from a callow and hirsute youth into an elderly and bald professor (*tempora mutantur, nos et mutamur in illis*)—yet that old man had retained a clear impression of his student-customer across that chasm of time.

One of the most remarkable experiences for a newcomer to Jerusalem was (and no doubt still is) the onset of the sabbath when, with dusk, city life came to a complete standstill, to return to normal twenty-four hours later. It was a strange sight, poignant even to the agnostic, to observe the cessation of all activity on Friday afternoons or evenings (depending on the season), when shops, restaurants, and places of entertainment closed suddenly; when buses and taxis vanished from the streets (not before people had hurried to catch the last ones); and when the street scene was one of virtually total emptiness and desolation. And then, on Saturday evenings, almost miraculously, the streets filled, cafés and cinemas reopened, and the urban bustle was greater than ever. Everyone made for the newly lit and clamorous focal points of the city, as if some great centripetal force had been unleashed. It was a scene from the slumber of the

Sleeping Beauty ('Dornröschen', the briar rose), where life had come to a halt suddenly and everyone and everything had stopped in their tracks—only to awaken twenty-four hours later and continue where they had left off.

In those days entertainment was virtually identical with cinema-going. There were four large picture-houses in Jerusalem into which everybody seemed to crowd on Saturday nights. They were invariably chock-a-block, almost irrespective of the films they showed. Of course, there was also the Hebrew theatre, but that required greater mental concentration as well as a good knowledge of Hebrew. The cinemas exhibited films in various European languages, though increasingly in English and decreasingly in German which, with the consolidation of the Nazi regime, became taboo. (The only kind of strong-arm tactics of which I seemed to approve at that time was, I think, the inter-dicting of the use of German in public places such as buses, cafés, shops, streets, etc.) As most of the populace knew little or no English or French, there were 'side-titles' in Hebrew and Arabic on either side of the screen, summarizing the dialogue rather than translating it. There was another picture-house in the predominantly Arab part of Jerusalem, where one could see either Arabic films (interesting mainly from a linguistic point of view) or the usual American entertainment showing also elsewhere.

The theatre was intermittently, and not regularly, available. There were original Hebrew plays as well as translations from other languages. I recall a very enjoyable performance at Haifa, to which I took my girlfriend, of Ibsen's *Pillars of Society* (*amude ha-hevra*) in a well-turned Hebrew rendering. Lehar's *Merry Widow*, sung in Hebrew, at the Edison Theatre in Jerusalem was, perhaps, less successful, both vocally and in its linguistic adaptation. In 1936 the violinist Bronislaw Hubermann founded the Palestine Symphony (later Israel Philharmonic) Orchestra which, with Toscanini conducting the inaugural concert, soon gained international recognition and standing. I remember with particular pleasure an open-air performance, in the exhibition grounds near the Yarkon river at Tel Aviv, of Schubert's *Unfinished Symphony* and Ravel's *Bolero*, a romantic setting for a fine rendering of these two great works.

Among the bookshops in Jerusalem, my favourite haunt was a deceptively small establishment, with plenty of back rooms full of shelving right up to the ceiling and crammed with books, thousands of them, in a remarkable state of disarray. Yet the two scholarly co-owners, Bamberger and Wahrmann, never failed to lay their hands at once on what was required. Theirs was an Aladdin's cave of orientalist and Judaistic treasures, immensely seductive to an impecunious, yet bibliophilically acquisitive, student. They seemed to part with their wares with regret, though they took an almost sadistic pleasure in placing some of the most recondite and desirable books in front of you and then watching your reaction with ill-concealed glee. However, they were true servants of scholarship: once they were assured that their treasures were going to a good and appreciative home, they were generous to a fault and would insist that you have the book. 'Pay when you can; do not worry; we trust you.' At times they had to wait for quite a while, yet they would never remind you.

The only other place of this kind I have come across was the Oxford treasure-house of J. Thornton & Son. The knowledge and helpfulness, the knack of finding out-of-the-way books, and the generosity towards young scholars shown by the late Mr Thornton and his son, 'young Mr Jack' (now himself in his 80s), must be almost unparalleled. During the Second World War they sent to me in Eritrea a precious copy of Dillmann's great Ethiopic Dictionary, but there was at that time a weight limit on parcels of that kind. So they carefully removed the original leather binding case and split the book into two, and then despatched it in three parts. All three arrived safely and were expertly re-assembled by an Italian book-binder at Asmara. No trace of that perilous operation can now be discerned. Thornton's have found hundreds, indeed thousands, of rare books for me, and, like my erstwhile Jerusalem booksellers, they were always willing to wait for payment in the case of scholars in the early stages of their careers. Such conduct earned deep loyalties from those thus favoured. *Habent sua fata libelli*—and so no doubt have booksellers and their customers. Quite a few of my books carry the names and marginal glosses of some of the great orientalists of the past. They are a treasured possession and an inspiration.

There were also some Arab booksellers who traded mainly in Arabic works published at Cairo, the principal place of Arabic publishing. I established friendly relations with one such trader, not far from the Jaffa Gate, who was helpful in obtaining both local and Egyptian-published books needed in connection with my studies. He had a reddish complexion and almost blond hair. When I first came to Jerusalem I was surprised that quite a number of Arabs, though wearing traditional dress of *thawb* (tunic), *'abaya* (cloak or mantle), and *kafiyya* (head scarf) with the familiar *'aqāl* (cord or rope, to fasten the *kafiyya*, worn by men only) and speaking 'normal' Arabic, were of distinctly non-Arab appearance. They had fair, often reddish hair, blue eyes, and a light complexion. I learnt later that they were supposed to be the descendants of crusaders who had intermarried with the indigenous population. The number of Franks thus assimilated must have been fairly sizeable, for there were certain towns, such as Jerusalem and Bethlehem (but also districts in the Lebanon), where the sight of such light-coloured men and women was not uncommon. Certain Christian Lebanese clans, such as the Faranjiyya ('Frankish') or Salibi ('Crusaders'), derive their names from those origins. The name of Baldwin, Crusader King of Jerusalem, was perpetuated in the topography of Palestine as Bardawil, and there was a Palestinian village, Sinjil, derived from Saint-Gilles.

I do not know whether the nineteenth- and twentieth-century German *Tempelgesellschaft* (modelled on the Templars) had any connection with this phenomenon of light-complexioned Arabs. These new Templars had established an agricultural settlement at Sarona (later the site of the Israeli Government Offices at Tel Aviv) in the 1870s, and by the turn of the century they had founded another one in the Lydda plain which they called Wilhelma after the Kaiser's much heralded visit to Palestine. Even earlier, about 1878, these Templars had occupied a residential quarter in the Emek Refaim district of Jerusalem which was generally called the 'German Colony'. Similar establishments existed in Haifa and Jaffa. By the mid-1930s there were more than 1,500 German settlers of allegedly Templar origin. In the Jerusalem German Colony they had shops, schools, a hospital, and a cinema, all of which were frequented by outsiders as well. With the outbreak of the Second World War they were interned and later deported. Their property was taken over by the Israel Government in 1948 and was subsequently taken into account as part of the Reparations Agreement entered into with the German Federal Republic. It has been my impression (but I am not certain) on visits to Jerusalem in recent years that those light-complexioned Arabs who had so fascinated me in my youth have disappeared from the street scene.

It may, perhaps, be thought surprising that on my meagre budget I could contemplate buying any books at all. I was naturally concerned to possess and to have ready access to the most important of the *instruments de travail* needed for the pursuit of my studies. I was equally concerned to make some provision for the remaining two years of my time at the university, for which no financial arrangements had been made. While I would have preferred to use the long summer vacations of the university for study and neglected reading, I felt I had to earn some money during those lengthy periods. When first I reached Palestine, I stayed for two or three weeks with friends at Ramoth Hashavim, a village famous for its poultry farms, situated in the (even then) densely settled plain of Sharon, along the road from Tel Aviv to Haifa. The only son of these friends had died suddenly of polio, and they thought they would be glad to have a friend of their deceased boy stay with them. On later occasions I would visit them and also renew acquaintances I had made among the poultry farmers of Ramoth Hashavim. At that time they were almost all professional men from central Europe, victims (or at any rate potential ones) of the Hitler regime, doctors, lawyers, architects, etc. They had established a co-operative settlement entirely given over to chickens and their products. The elected central administration of the co-operative looked after the marketing aspects of the business, while individuals were exclusively concerned with encouraging their hens to lay as many eggs as possible. I had always been (and still am) exceedingly fond of eggs, and for this reason, as well as others, invariably enjoyed my stays at Ramoth Hashavim.

At some stage the Mukhtar (Arabic for 'mayor') of this co-operative settlement suggested that I spend the long vacations at Ramoth Hashavim and teach Hebrew, and perhaps also some Arabic, to the residents. This proved to be a highly agreeable arrangement. Many of the poultry farmers and their wives took part in these classes. As their levels of attainment varied widely, it was necessary to hold quite a number of courses: beginners, whose spoken and written command of Hebrew was rudimentary, were a minority; most of my pupils fell into an intermediate category, where all the teaching took place in Hebrew, and fairly advanced literature or newspapers could be read; and then there was a small upper layer where the emphasis was on *explication de texte*. Some in that last category also took part in an Arabic class.

On each occasion I spent three consecutive months at Ramoth Hashavim and could afford to indulge my passion for eggs to the full. There was a small inn in the centre of the village, among orange groves and chicken pens, where one could put up an occasional visitor or drink a delicious grape-juice during the hot summer evenings. It was highly congenial teaching for one's first paid job and excellent training for more exacting tasks later. On my free day one of the poultry farmers would lend me his donkey and I would ride over to the next village to visit friends. I dare say I could have made the journey more quickly on foot, for the temperamental donkey would occasionally stop in his tracks, and no amount of persuasion, verbal or physical, would move him on until he was good and ready. But it was such unaccustomed fun to ride a donkey, and on arrival at my friends' farm I would tie up the animal at their gatepost and think of myself as an American cowboy.

During my second stay at Ramoth Hashavim the Italians entered the war, and a day or two later they sent planes over Tel Aviv and Haifa and some of the places along the coastal plain. As there were, of course, no air-raid shelters, we were ordered to take cover in the orange groves away from the houses. Despite the gravity of the international situation these were rather jolly occasions. I do not believe anyone in the rural areas was ever hit in those raids. In the larger cities there was some concern, and a few parents sent their children into the villages and settlements for greater protection. Near us two young girls with their mother were quartered in fairly cramped conditions. The younger one, aged 13, was very pretty and perhaps a little precocious. One day she told me that the smart young captain from the Antipodes, who had been billeted with her parents in Haifa, had seduced her.

While Ramoth Hashavim at first helped to eke out my limited funds, I soon reached the conclusion that whatever I might earn there could not be sufficient to finance the last two years of my studies or even the most modest book purchases. I then remembered that, before going to Jerusalem to study orientalia, I had been offered a scholarship to go to Cambridge. The money had been raised privately by a Dutch friend (and his associates) of the widow of my father's eldest brother. It occurred to me that if those funds were still available they might possibly be transferred to Jerusalem—or at any rate part of them. I mentioned this idea to a cousin of mine whom I had met for the first time on an early visit to Tel Aviv. (That meeting had, incidentally, happened by pure chance—simply because he answered to the same surname as myself.) He dissuaded me from writing to the Dutch donors, largely on the grounds that I could scarcely say that I was a conscientious and diligent student and deserved such support. Instead, he suggested that he should conduct the correspondence, especially as, being a *rentier*, he had nothing to occupy him, except for his daily swim in the Mediterranean. I agreed readily and gratefully.

A few weeks later he wrote to me and informed me that the Dutchman had transferred to him a sum of money which was now at my disposal. Whenever I happened to be in Tel Aviv, every few months or so, I would collect £25 from my cousin. By the end of my studies I had used £150 of that fund, both for living expenses and for book purchases. I felt very fortunate that these arrangements had been possible. When I returned from war service in Eritrea and Ethiopia, some years later, my wife and I saw my cousin in Tel Aviv on several occasions. In 1948 I visited my aunt, the widow of my father's brother, in London and told her of the generosity of her Dutch friend. She seemed somewhat puzzled and questioned me closely about dates. It then emerged that at the operative time the Dutchman had long been dead.

When I next met my cousin, on a visit by him to London, I tackled him on this point. He simply responded that he could not, at that time, be bothered to write a letter about so trivial a sum. He knew of the Dutchman's death but had never let on—until challenged now. My wife and I were deeply impressed by such sensitivity, delicacy, and generosity. Fortunately, I was then able to repay the monetary debt; the debt of gratitude is an abiding one and endures as devotion to his memory.

II

The University of Jerusalem

Peel Report

Early on in this book I briefly described the superb physical
setting of the University at Jerusalem. I would now like to say a
little more about its academic aspects and about some of the
people who worked in it—a few of them international celebrities
whose names are honoured all over the world, others humble
toilers without fame whose contribution to this historic venture
was yet of crucial importance, particularly in its initial stages.
I do not think I can do better than introduce these remarks by
quoting what the objective Peel Report of 1937 (p. 250) had to
say on the subject:

The apex of the Jewish educational system is the Hebrew University of
Jerusalem. The main purpose of its foundation was as a centre for postgraduate research in science and the humanities; but the demand for
university education among the Jews has been so great that there is now
a considerable body of undergraduates. The University has departments
of Jewish Studies, Oriental Studies, General Humanities, Mathematics,
Physics, Chemistry, Botany, and a number of allied sciences; also a
special department devoted to Cancer Research. There is a staff of
27 Professors, besides Lecturers and junior staff, and in 1935 there
were 391 students, about 30 per cent of whom had received their
secondary education in Palestine, the remainder coming from other
countries, notably Poland. The University is relatively well provided
with laboratories and class-rooms; its excellent library is constructed
and catalogued on modern lines; and on its magnificent site on Mount
Scopus it possesses ample room for further building when funds
permit.
   It is remarkable to find on the fringe of Asia a university which
maintains the highest standards of western scholarship. On its staff are
names well-known in Europe and America. Its research work can
compare with that of many older institutions. The scope of this research
is necessarily limited by the remoteness of Jerusalem from the centres of
modern civilization; and the University wisely concentrates, therefore,

in certain departments, on such an exhaustive study of Palestine and the neighbouring countries as cannot be made elsewhere. In so doing it has made a valuable contribution to our knowledge of the Near East and in particular of Arab life and culture. A notable instance of this is the recent publication by the University Press of the text of the Arab historian al-Baladhuri.

In its devotion to scholarship and good learning the Hebrew University sets an example to all Palestine. But it is not a Palestinian university. It is the crown of the Jewish educational system. All its teaching is in Hebrew. All its students are Jews. Its spirit, it is true, is not the spirit of Tel Aviv. It stands a little aloof from the popular life of the National Home.

There is only one minor, but perhaps not insignificant, rider I would wish to append to this fine statement: there were, in fact, a few (a very few) Arab students. I imagine that there were good reasons at the time not to publicize this fact in the Peel Report, for the lives of those few would probably have been endangered.

Student Life

In my time the total number of students was said to be about 600; it had risen to about 800 by the time I graduated. But many of these students were not full-time undergraduates or post-graduates, and their studies might extend over many years, as they had to earn their livelihood. Others again were not *bona fide* students, but had used the facility of students' certificates to gain entry into Palestine. The university authorities genuinely discouraged this practice for fear that abuse might cause discontinuance of this method of entry into the country.

There is, of course, no such thing as a typical day or week in the life of a student—just as there is no such fixed pattern in the life of anyone else—but perhaps the existence of a curriculum, the alternation of term-time, with lectures and seminars, and vacations, with the requirements of study and reading, prescribe a certain regularity which may be characteristic of student life. In many ways I was extremely fortunate that at any rate during term I could afford to be a full-time student. I often marvelled at the ability and attainments of some of my friends who had to work during much of the day and squeeze attendance at lectures and classes into a few hours snatched from their employment. All their evenings were devoted to study or to reading the lecture notes lent to them by some of their more fortunate colleagues. And, like many others, they also had to discharge guard duties, certainly during several nights in the course of the week. Some of these worker-students possessed impressive intellectual curiosity and ability as well as considerable physical stamina. In the face of such dedication to learning I was conscious not only of my own good fortune but also of all the obvious reasons for a measure of humility.

My day started early. In the spring and summer some of our professors liked to lecture at 8, and on Friday mornings there used to be an Assyriology class at 7 o'clock. This meant leaving North Talpioth well before 6 a.m., for one had to allow ten to fifteen minutes to walk to the nearest bus to central Jerusalem, another ten minutes in town to walk to the university bus; and the two bus rides were about fifteen minutes each. Early rising held no terrors for me, neither then nor now. I certainly liked those morning classes, as they allowed time for private study and reading afterwards. Of course, one might be unlucky and not have the next lecture until the afternoon. This meant the exercise of judgement whether that lecture was sufficiently vital to one's concerns to spend many hours in the reading room of the library rather than in the seclusion of one's own study at home.

In those days the university library, apart from such fields as Judaica and Orientalia, still had many sensitive lacunae. Some works could not easily be afforded on a tight university budget, while others were simply unavailable. The latter had probably long been out of print but might have considerable historical significance in the area of one's specialization. The reprint industry, so prevalent during the past quarter of a century, had not yet been invented, and ready photographic processes, such as xerox, were still unknown. My wife and I often look with astonishment at books we (that is, she, as a devoted and self-sacrificing girlfriend, and I) copied by hand. They are now treasured possessions of a vanished age of pre-xerography as well as tokens of a friendship and devotion that have endured into old age.

One's aim was to arrange classes in such a way that they could all be squeezed into three days a week. This saved not only fares but also a great deal of time travelling to and fro; and there is little doubt that preparation for language classes in particular and background reading in general could best be done in solitude. At Jerusalem in the 1930s there were virtually no corporate student life or activities. I cannot recall social meetings with one's colleagues outside the university precinct except on the rarest occasions. As far as I know, there were no such things as student societies devoted to extra-curricular activities. The social swing that is (or, perhaps, only seems to be) inseparable from an under-graduate's career in Britain was wholly absent at Jerusalem. I do not know what the position is now, nor can I assess how much we lost by this lack of an organized student life and the intellectual and social 'cross-fertilization' it is supposed to engender. While times were hard in the 1930s and the atmosphere in Europe doom-laden, the individual and collective zest in the Yishuv of inter-war Palestine was remarkable. It would, there-fore, be wrong if I gave the impression that the absence of a properly developed collegiate entity was an aspect of the austere times in which we lived. It was probably simply the want of a tradition which older universities and more affluent societies possessed.

There existed, incidentally, a student organization (*histadrut ha-studentim*), membership of which was, I believe, compulsory, but it was primarily concerned with student welfare and with representing the interests of those *in statu pupillari vis-à-vis* the university authorities in matters of fees and related aspects. The social life of students, like that of anyone else, was bound up with the society in which they lived; thus my own relaxation and entertainment were largely confined to North Talpioth and some personal friends elsewhere. In this context I remember quite a few parties held in the various houses in our little suburb, when we would dance through the night, fuelled by remarkably sparing alcoholic refreshments and frugal helpings of food—altogether very staid affairs in retrospect.

The university 'campus' (a term not actually current at Jerusalem in those days) was bisected by the road from the town to Mount Scopus and the Mount of Olives. On the eastern side of the road, the site of some of the original pre-university cottages, were the Einstein Building and other scientific institutes as well as the extremely austere administrative offices and, at the easternmost edge, the amphitheatre with its awe-inspiring panorama. On the western side was the University and

National Library with its reading room which also served, each
October/November, as a venue for the festive opening of the
academic year by the President of the university. His office was
above the library, under the little dome, with superb views over
Jerusalem. In this uniquely beautiful setting he received High
Commissioners and Jewish and Arab dignitaries (including, on
one occasion, the Amir (later King) Abdullah of Transjordan)
and not only conducted the affairs of the university but also
engaged in his wide-ranging work for Arab-Jewish understanding. No man in Palestine worked harder and more dedicatedly
for those profoundly important, yet seemingly ever elusive, aims.
Dr J. L. Magnes was (as we shall see later) the only Jewish leader
who was on easy and equal terms, by sheer dint of personality,
with the heads of the British Administration and such of the
Arab leaders as were willing to run the risks of espousing the
cause of accord and peace.

It was only in the course of my time on Mount Scopus that one
or two other buildings were added on the western side of the
road, in particular the so-called *Mo'adon*, with its spacious
lecture-hall and refectory, and the large Rosenbloom Building
for the humanities which was linked with the library by a beautiful colonnade. In those days these well-designed additions to the
Jerusalem skyline were still built in the fine mellow stone of the
region. Physically, then, ours was a small university with few
buildings and limited facilities—in all respects other than the
quality of its teaching body and its research capacity. And thus it
remained until the Arab-Israeli war of 1948 which cut off Mount
Scopus and the university and isolated it as a small enclave in the
Jordanian sector. This led to the construction of the Givat Ram
campus (now in the real sense of that American-style term), with
magnificent buildings and facilities—quite beyond the dreams of
my generation of students.

Of course, in the 1930s university professors and lecturers, at
Jerusalem or elsewhere (other than Oxbridge), did not expect to
have their own rooms in the university precinct (at any rate in
the humanities), but on arrival at the college they would go to the
communal teachers' room, leave their hats and coats there while
lecturing, and then return briefly to pick them up and go back
home to write their books, articles, and lectures. Contact with
students was generally fitful, but it remains, I would suppose, an

open question whether the loss this probably entails on both sides of the rostrum can justify the huge expense on vast building projects which are fully utilized only part of the year. Degrees in the full range of Semitic languages are very rarely available in universities anywhere. In this respect Jerusalem was in a uniquely privileged position. With Hebrew being both the language of the country and the exclusive language of instruction, a student working in this field set out with an inestimable advantage. Furthermore, Arabic was spoken and heard everywhere, and some other Semitic languages also survived here in their various modern forms. Thus it was fortunate that, when I came to Jerusalem, it was possible to take a degree in the full repertoire of Semitics—Arabic, Hebrew, Aramaic-Syriac, Akkadian (Babylonian-Assyrian), and Ethiopic, the latter with some of its modern tongues. Surprisingly, I was only the first or second student at Jerusalem to graduate in this subject; and the excellence of the course and of the available resources persuaded me in later years to institute similar degree courses at St. Andrews University, Scotland, at Manchester, and at SOAS, London University. It is, of course, a minority pursuit, but at Jerusalem there emerged some excellent candidates who later adorned the subject and about whom I shall say a little more presently. And at the other universities just mentioned half a dozen or so fine scholars came forward who have since been active and productive in teaching and research.

In Arabic we were fortunate to be able to benefit from the self-effacing erudition of D. H. Baneth, from lectures on indigenous Arab grammarians by G. Weil, and on Arabic syntax by H. J. Polotsky. I could have attended classes on Islamic art and archaeology given by L. A. Mayer, but I never did, though I came to know him reasonably well in later years. Hebrew was in the brilliant, though somewhat idiosyncratic, care of N. H. Torczyner (later Tur-Sinai), supported by M. H. Segal and later by Umberto Cassuto in the area of the Hebrew Bible (the latter also taught Ugaritic, the newly discovered (1929) Canaanite language of Ras Shamra in Syria), and by the aged David Yellin on medieval Hebrew grammarians. Biblical Aramaic was also taught by Torczyner, while J. N. Epstein lectured on Talmudic Aramaic and Polotsky on Syriac. Akkadian was once more the responsibility of Torczyner who discharged this task with characteristic verve, although some twenty years had passed since he had last contributed actively to the subject. Finally, H. J. Polotsky was in charge of things Ethiopian. Occasionally I would look in on the lectures given by such great masters as Gershom Scholem and Martin Buber—not because I wished to pursue these subjects seriously but because I was attracted by their personalities and by their fame. I shall say something about most of these great scholars later on.

These, then, were some of the classes I attended when I went up to Mount Scopus, occasionally just for the odd lecture or two, more often for four or five, punctuated by a frugal cold lunch at the refectory (I do not think that anything more elaborate was available then). When I was the only candidate in one of H. J. Polotsky's classes, we would sometimes meet at his home in the Rehavia quarter of Jerusalem, which saved the time and expense of the ascent to Mount Scopus.

My fellow-students mostly originated from Hungary (the cleverest of them), Poland, and Russia, with a sprinkling from Germany and Austria. At that time, half a century ago, sabras (native-born Palestinians) were still a tiny minority; and as far as I know there were no students then from English-speaking countries. The only sabra I can now think of was Yishaq Navon, a fine Arabic scholar and even then a man of character and distinctive personality; in the late 1970s and early 1980s he was a very popular President of Israel. His immediate predecessor as President, Ephraim Katzir (originally Katchalsky), was also a fellow-graduate of the Hebrew University (the first to attain such an exalted office), though of a slightly more senior vintage. He had become a distinguished natural scientist.

Among orientalists, I would mention, first and foremost, Joshua Blau and Samuel Stern, both of Hungarian origin. The former was an all-rounder as a Semitist and became Professor of Arabic at Jerusalem, a great specialist in Judaeo-Arabic; he is currently President of the Hebrew Language Academy, as well as being a Member of the Israel Academy of Sciences and a Corresponding Fellow of the British Academy. His prowess as an undergraduate presaged his success as a Semitist and tireless toiler in our field.

S. M. Stern, who died tragically young at the age of 49 (even then full of honour and singular achievements), was, I think by general consent, the most gifted among us. Already as a student he stood out in his singleminded devotion to his studies, constantly reading and working and never engaging in idle student chat. In an ambush on the university bus, or in a lesser shooting affray, when we were enjoined to lie on the floor of the bus, Stern would sit upright at the back of the vehicle reading pre-Islamic Arabic poetry, unperturbed by what was going on around him. At the age of 18 he was considered, by his teachers and colleagues alike, a mature scholar, possessed of remarkable knowledge as well as an uncanny sense of what mattered in his chosen field of Islamica. After the war he came to Oxford where we met up again; not long afterwards he was elected a Fellow of All Souls College and there he remained for the rest of his life, unseduced by offers of chairs and other preferments elsewhere. He lived at the home of Richard Walzer (the well-known student of Islamic and Greek philosophy) and his wife who created a congenial ambience for him. Being some twenty years Stern's seniors, they built a house for him opposite their own to provide for him after their death, though he continued to live at the Walzers' home. Alas, things turned out otherwise. In his will (which he and I discussed not many months before his wholly unexpected death, when I suggested to him that he leave his fine library to our *alma mater* at Jerusalem) he bequeathed both his house and his books to the Hebrew University. In 1970 I bought that house from the university, and my wife and I have lived there ever since. And although Stern himself had never occupied the house, I rejoice in its connection with both my deceased colleague and our university.

When Samuel Stern died so suddenly in mid-career and torn from a wonderful flow of creative ideas and productive work, there were quite remarkable manifestations of mourning and a sense of very genuine bereavement among his colleagues in the many disciplines which he bestrode as giant and genius, among students of Islam and Judaica, of Hispanic studies, and of medieval history. Personally I have one very particular regret: we had failed to elect him a Fellow of the British Academy while there was time to do so. It was a failure of initiative on our part rather than of insufficient attainments on his. He would have deserved it so much more than some of us who had had the good fortune to be elected. At one time I tried to console myself with the thought that being so withdrawn from mundane considerations he would not have cared—only to be told later by Richard Walzer that failure to be elected was the one thing that had rankled with him.

L. Kopf, mathematician and Arabist (an unusual combination) and subsequently in charge of the university library's oriental collections, also died sadly early. He had accomplished some excellent work on Arabic and Hebrew lexicography, but his considerable potential had been far from being fulfilled.

E. E. Kutscher was, as a fellow-undergraduate, some ten years older than most of us. He was, at the same time, working as a teacher and looking after his growing family. When finally he was able to devote himself full-time to academic work, he had significant achievements to his credit in Semitic languages in general and Aramaic dialectology in particular. He, too, was taken from us much too early, at the height of his career and creativity.

Yiga'el Yadin, the son of the Professor of Archaeology, E. L. Sukenik, made his considerable scholarly impact only much later. In our student days he was pre-eminent in the ranks of the Haganah, the semi-clandestine or semi-official defence organization, the nucleus of the future Israel defence forces. He became chief of staff of the army and a general; and it was only in his mid-30s that he returned to academic work, took his PhD, and rose meteorically on the hierarchical ladder of university promotion. His first forays into the scholarly field made use of his military experience, but later he was engaged in some dramatic and well-publicized excavations which made his name famous far beyond the academic world. Towards the end of his career he succumbed, probably unwisely, to the lure of politics. As Deputy Prime Minister in Begin's Government he had, for the first time, embarked on something he could not properly control. He died shortly afterwards—aware, I think, of the unwisdom of having ventured into fields which, for him, did not carry the well-nigh universal acclaim which archaeology and scholarship had earned him.

J. L. Magnes

Judah Leon Magnes (1877–1948) was the virtual founder of the Hebrew University of Jerusalem, its first Chancellor and President, and the principal purveyor of the wherewithal that made the creation of the university a reality. The pioneers of the idea of a Hebrew University at Jerusalem had been a number of Jewish thinkers in the nineteenth century, and the notion was embodied in an influential pamphlet, published in 1902 by Martin Buber, Chaim Weizmann, and Berthold Feiwel, which forcefully advocated the need to establish such an institution of higher learning at Jerusalem. But it was Magnes who transformed the idea into the tangible existence of a university in which Hebrew was to be the sole language of instruction and the vehicle by which knowledge and learning were to be acquired and disseminated; a university like other universities, but with that extra-dimension of being the principal institute of teaching and research in Judaica and Orientalia, allied with all other branches of learning, that was to extend benefits and advantages to the entire area in which it was situated.

While the establishment of the Hebrew University is no doubt Magnes' main achievement, the key to his importance and indeed fame has to be sought in his singular personality and in the quiet but unrivalled authority which he exercised almost in spite of himself. His entire life and work were devoted to the concerns of Jerusalem University and to the cause of Arab-Jewish accord. The latter aim he would pursue with great moral and physical courage, undeterred by the opprobrium he incurred at times in the Jewish community. His aristocratic, almost aloof, bearing, his fine stature and good looks, as well as his secure American background—all combined to give him that aura of authority and eminence which made him the natural and obvious confidant of successive High Commissioners and brought him into close contact with the apex of British, Arab, and Jewish society. Whether the leaders of the British Administration were always clearly aware that his views on the future of Palestine, while shared by some of the most distinguished scholars in the university, were (unhappily, to my mind) those of a small minority of the *Yishuv*, I am not competent to say. But I have little doubt that High Commissioners or Chief Secretaries would rather listen to Magnes than to Ben-Gurion, though the latter was at most times more representative of prevalent Jewish opinion and attitudes.

Magnes was born in San Francisco and became a reform rabbi. He subsequently (1900–3) studied at Heidelberg and Berlin, and during his sojourn in Germany made himself familiar with the plight of Jews in Eastern Europe as well as with their mode of life and the pervasive vitality of their culture. On his return to the United States he served as a rabbi to some of the most prominent communities in New York; he was also active in the Zionist movement in America. In 1917 he was deeply opposed to US entry into World War I—entirely on the basis of his general pacifist beliefs. Thus his career as one of the most prominent Jewish communal leaders ended at the age of 40, as American Jews were not only committed to US entry into the war but anxious not to be accused of unpatriotic sentiments.

Twenty-two years later, at the outbreak of the Second World War in 1939, Magnes stood before the professoriate and students of the Hebrew University, at the opening of the new academic session, and gave one of the most moving and memorable addresses I have ever listened to. It was a noble struggle and a truly agonizing reappraisal of everything he had stood for, when he gave public expression to his abandonment of that pacifist position which had made his communal work in New York untenable a generation ago. It may be said of that occasion in 1939, to paraphrase *Macbeth*, that nothing in his life became him like the [manner of his] leaving that long and profoundly held pacifist stance. The high drama of the moment was rendered the more poignant by his factual and unemotional rehearsal of the deep struggles and traumata that had forced upon him so fundamental a change of mind. He spoke of the uniqueness of the evil that had seized and deranged the Germany whose scholarship he had admired in the early years of the century. He called upon the student body to be prepared to help in removing the ghastly stain that had so grotesquely disfigured the face of humanity.

But I have been anticipating: the 1917 pacifist débâcle caused Magnes to take an even closer interest in the possibility of establishing a university at Jerusalem, particularly now after the British conquest of Palestine and the publication of the Balfour Declaration. In 1922 Magnes and his family moved to Jerusalem and settled there. From the inauguration of the Hebrew University in 1925 until his death in 1948 Magnes was, as Chancellor and later as President, titular head of the university. From his eyrie on top of the library building on Mount Scopus, with its views of unique grandeur, he observed what he had created and conducted the essential foreign affairs of the incipient and finance-starved university. Without Magnes and his worldwide influence the embryonic structure could never have survived. Curiously, despite the large measure of convergence in their pacifist and general orientation, Magnes and Einstein did not always see eye to eye as regards the former's stewardship of the university. Weizmann had tried to recruit Einstein to a university Chair at Jerusalem, and at a later stage Magnes had renewed these efforts; but it was clear that, despite Einstein's sympathy for the institution (on whose Board of Governors he served and one of whose buildings bore his name), the university at that time did not possess the facilities or the stature to encompass a man of his fame and calibre. This was apparently the case, although Einstein used to emphasize that all he required for his work was peace, pencil, and paper. It seems that neither Einstein nor Weizmann was entirely happy to see a 'theologian' at the head of a secular scholarly institution, and eventually a rector was elected by the Senate to serve as head of the academic affairs of the university.

Meanwhile Magnes continued with, and became increasingly absorbed in, his activities in the *Brith Shalom* ('Peace Covenant', later re-named *Ichud*, 'union') advocating the policy of establishing a binational state. He regarded accord with the Arabs in such a state not only as a political necessity but, perhaps above all, as of profound importance to the renaissance of the Jewish spirit and the Hebrew revival. At the opening of the academic year 1929/30, shortly after the 1929 disturbances, he made a speech which encapsulates his credo:

One of the greatest cultural duties of the Jewish people is the attempt to enter the promised land, not by means of conquest as Joshua did, but by peaceful and cultural means, through hard work, sacrifices, love, and with a decision not to do anything which cannot be justified before the world conscience.

Magnes adhered to these lofty ideals until the end, but the conscience of the world seemed a somewhat abstract entity once the full horror of the holocaust and the plight of its survivors had become apparent. Magnes and the group around him, though influential, were never numerically significant. When the total calamity that Hitler had wrought was finally realized, towards the end of the war and in its immediate aftermath, he became a tragic and heartbroken figure. For by now Jewish nationalism had been aroused, and men such as Begin and the heirs of Abraham Stern gained many adherents to the movement of terrorism or liberation (depending on one's viewpoint and judgement). When Magnes appeared before the Anglo-American Committee and later the United Nations Commission on Palestine he was, in truth, a lonely, isolated, yet heroic figure. The cruelty of events had overtaken and swept away the ethical ideals he represented and which now appeared attuned to a very different world. He died on a visit to New York in the autumn of 1948, a bitterly disappointed man; he was later re-interred at Jerusalem. His work of Arab–Jewish pacification had first come up against the intransigence of the Arab leadership under Hajj Amin el-Husseini, the Mufti of Jerusalem; later it fell victim, additionally, to the legacy of the Nazis and to the Jewish reaction it unleashed. No man can be blamed for having succumbed to odds of such magnitude.

However, Magnes's achievements in the sphere of the Hebrew University have lived on, and his name is not forgotten. No president after him has possessed the natural authority and charisma attached to the founding father of this foremost institution of Hebrew and general learning. The university press bears his name, and the road bisecting the post-war Givat Ram campus (which he himself did not live to see) is called after him, as is Magnes Square in West Jerusalem. In Oakland, California, a Judah L. Magnes Memorial Museum was set up in 1961, but I know little or nothing about its purpose or contents.

As a young undergraduate I naturally had only the most tenuous contact with the head of the university. I admired him from afar, and there were only three occasions during the 1930s when I actually spoke to him. The visits to the university by the High Commissioner, Sir Harold MacMichael, and—much more confidentially—by the Amir (later King) Abdullah were very formal occasions. The third time was a relatively relaxed conversation initiated and arranged by the administrator of the university, Dr D. W. Senator, who became a close friend of mine in later years—until his untimely death, at the age of 57, in 1953. Senator had been a prominent member of Magnes's peace group and also had the ear of the President. In 1938 or 1939 I had submitted a memorandum to Senator suggesting better training and absorption facilities for students who arrived from abroad with an inadequate knowledge of Hebrew and with little or no acquaintance with Palestine and its background. Senator passed my memorandum to Magnes who invited me to call on him at his office. He questioned me closely and then suggested a trial period for such an introductory course of orientation and language acquisition. In fact, he proposed that I might, perhaps, teach an hour or two per week within the framework of such a course. I did not, however, think that I possessed adequate qualifications for such a task. In the event, the trial period was cut short by the outbreak of the war, which interrupted the flow of students from abroad.

To be received by Magnes was an awesome experience. The impact of his remarkable personality I can only compare with that of Emperor Haile Sellassie, though the latter was, of course, surrounded by all the trappings of royalty. The trappings of Magnes's exalted office, both literally and metaphorically, were, however, sufficiently overwhelming to a young student unaccustomed to such company. When, during the war, I came to Jerusalem on short periods of leave from Eritrea-Ethiopia, Senator must have mentioned my presence to Magnes, for the latter invited me to visit him at his home, as he wished to meet (as he put it) a graduate who had 'made good'.

After the war, during my brief service in the Hebrew University and later in the Palestine Government, I saw much more of Magnes, not infrequently in the company of D. W. Senator, Leon Roth, or Norman Bentwich (about whom more anon). He had a somewhat exaggerated opinion of the importance of an Assistant or Acting Political Secretary of the British Military Administration in Eritrea, and I had to disabuse him of the notion that my experience in that office could have any conceivable bearing on judgements in the Palestine context. In Eritrea I possessed some professional knowledge of the Ethiopian background, languages, and general milieu. In Palestine I knew as much or as little as the next man—except that I judged (correctly, as it turned out) that the British Administration, and probably HMG as well, were growing increasingly tired of the thankless and costly burden of Palestine, particularly in the face of attack and abuse by both Arabs and Jews.

Magnes was a man of gravity and high seriousness. I can
remember only two occasions when I saw him laugh or show
genuine amusement (this may, of course, be due in part to my
limited acquaintance with him). The first time was when he read
me a letter he had received from an Austrian Jewish professor,
shortly after Hitler's *Anschluss* of Austria in March 1938. In it
the professor explained that he had never been a Zionist and had
not taken any great interest in the Jewish National Home in
Palestine. He could not, therefore, expect to receive a professorship at Jerusalem University, but did Dr Magnes think there
might be an opening for him 'at one of the provincial universities
of Palestine?' To the present generation of Israelis, with half a
dozen or so universities in Israel, there is nothing amusing about
this enquiry; but in 1938, with Jerusalem University only just
established and with its existence frequently queried by those
who thought that it was an expensive luxury and that the educational system should be built from the bottom upwards rather
than from the apex downwards, nobody imagined that there
would *ever* be another university in the country. So the nature
and wording of this letter were exquisitely funny in the writer's
total ignorance of conditions in Palestine.

The second time I saw Magnes really amused was when, on
my return to Jerusalem from war service, I told him about the
occasion when the Military Governor of Eritrea had sent me to
Kassala province in the Sudan to be present at a peace-making
ceremony between two tribes straddling the Eritrea-Sudan
frontier. On arrival at Kassala I duly presented my letter of introduction to the Provincial Commissioner. The letter must have
contained a reference to the fact that I possessed an MA degree.
The Commissioner looked up from the Governor's letter and
murmured: 'Oxford?' I had to reply in the negative at that time
and retorted, not without some pride, 'Jerusalem!', to which his
rejoinder was the most contemptuous grunt I had ever heard.
But he recovered his composure and his good manners at once
and added with a faint smile that was presumably intended to be
apologetic: 'No doubt a very ancient university!'

If it were possible to imagine that a man like Magnes was
capable of guffawing, then this is what he did—or, at any rate,
something closely resembling it. I later heard that he frequently
dined out on this story.

Magnes needs neither streets nor squares, neither presses nor volumes named after him: a visit to the campuses of the Hebrew University of Jerusalem will suffice: *si monumentum requiris, circumspice!*

Leon Roth

Leon Roth was the first Professor of Philosophy in the Hebrew University of Jerusalem. He was an ornament to that seat of learning in its early and heroic days. He served as Dean of the Faculty of Humanities and as Rector, the academic head of the university, in the crucial period of 1940 to 1943. He was for twenty-five years, virtually his entire active career, one of the three or four most influential men in the shaping of the academic structure and ethos of the university. With J. L. Magnes, the President of the university, Martin Buber, and Gershom Scholem (who are discussed elsewhere in this book) he stood for an Arab–Jewish partnership, for forbearance, disavowal of violence, and for genuinely civilized values. He was, to the best of my knowledge, the only scholar to be elected a Fellow of the British Academy whose working life had been spent abroad. He was an inspiring teacher, a true friend, and a man of uncompromising honesty. He did not suffer fools gladly. He could be impatient with those in positions of power, but he was uniformly kind and considerate to those who sought or needed his help or advice. He possessed wisdom, wit, and charm in equal measure. He was self-effacing (anything else would have appeared vulgar to him) but was endowed with an entirely natural and unselfconscious authority of a quite unusual order. He had exceptional courage, both physical and moral: in the worst days of the Palestine troubles he would insist on seeing me home, late at night, to a remote district of Jerusalem—pretending that his constitutional took him there in any event.

Roth was born in London, in 1896, to an observant Jewish family. His younger brother, Cecil, was an historian and Reader in Jewish Studies at Oxford. Leon was sent to the City of London School with its fine classical tradition which eventually took him to Exeter College, Oxford, with a scholarship in classics. His father had engaged, at an early stage, a private teacher for his tuition in Hebrew. During the First World War, which interrupted his Oxford studies, he saw active service in

France. On his return to the university he won two of the most prestigious scholarships in very disparate disciplines, the John Locke in Mental Philosophy and the James Mew in Hebrew. These scholarships laid the foundation of his work on Spinoza, Descartes, and Maimonides. In 1923 the philosopher Samuel Alexander called him to Manchester to join his department as lecturer in philosophy.

Many years afterwards, in the late 1950s and early 1960s, I would occasionally invite Leon Roth to lecture at Manchester University when I was serving there as Professor of Semitic Languages. He would then take me to the large entrance hall of the Faculty of Arts building to stand for a few moments in reverence before the bust of the great Samuel Alexander.

Between these two events, his first appointment to an academic post at Manchester in 1923, and his homage to Samuel Alexander thirty-six years later, lies a career of quite exceptional significance. A visit by him to Jerusalem in 1925 to represent Manchester University at the opening of the Hebrew University on Mount Scopus quickened his interest in the idea of such a university, which expressed the Hebrew renaissance in Palestine. In 1927 the renowned Hebrew essayist and philosopher Ahad Ha'am died in Tel Aviv, and the university at Jerusalem resolved to establish a Chair of Philosophy bearing his name. I do not know what the field of candidates was in 1927–8, but in retrospect the choice of Leon Roth as the first occupant of that Chair seems so obvious and natural that it is quite impossible now to envisage any other person in the foundation Chair of Philosophy at Jerusalem.

Thus in 1928, at the age of 32, Leon Roth came to Jerusalem to initiate the teaching of philosophy and to supervise research in it. He turned out to be the most mythopoeic of men. His mannerisms, conscious or unconscious, were numerous. They ranged from such trivia as the handkerchief, carefully lodged in his left jacket-sleeve and occasionally withdrawn during his lectures and then meticulously returned to that (to us unfamiliar) habitat, to his exceptionally beautiful, yet simple, Hebrew that was produced and modulated in an English voice and accent which, at any rate at first, were quite startling. There was, of course, no reason to suppose that, say, Isaiah or Jeremiah would have considered the usual Russian or Polish accent of Hebrew more authentic than Roth's English pronunciation, but in those days the Anglo-Saxon lilt was virtually unknown, and most certainly in conjunction with Hebrew. It was, in fact, confined to the Englishman Leon Roth and, to a much lesser extent, to the American Magnes. It must again be emphasized that, curiously enough, English in Palestine was an incidental result of the Second World War and came in when the British Administration went out.

Roth was philosopher, teacher, and educator *par excellence* (certainly not educationist or educationalist—expressions that were anathema to him). He taught and educated, in the widest possible sense, successive generations of students at Jerusalem who sat spellbound at his feet. His classes were by far the largest; at a time when there were some 500-600 students inscribed in all the faculties, about 150 of that total number would regularly attend his lectures. He would insist that students should be punctual and be seated in their places when he entered the lecture hall. He disliked the discourtesy of latecomers and the disturbance they caused to concentration on complex subjects. At some stage he decided to lock the lecture hall after he had arrived and put the key into his pocket. This measure certainly deterred the stragglers. On one occasion a student fainted during his lecture, and some of her friends ran forward to obtain the key from the professor, who reluctantly parted with it and exclaimed in his inimitable Hebrew: 'Is it conceivable that anyone can be ready for life at a university if that is what my philosophy does to him?'

At first I used to be astonished when Roth said, as he frequently did in his lectures or in reply to questions, generally with a slightly mischievous smile: 'I do not know' or 'I simply have no notion what this text could possibly mean'. This was unheard of; most professors at Jerusalem at that period were products of the continental tradition where professorial omniscience was axiomatic. In later years Roth and I often spoke about this, and no piece of advice has been more useful in my own career: confessions of ignorance, real or alleged, were always applauded— certainly above any pretence to all-knowingness.

Apart from the strength and independence derived from his English background—a great asset under the British Mandate—Roth also had the reputation (I do not know whether

it was justified or was an aspect of those mythopoeic qualities) of
being sufficiently wealthy not to draw his salary. In a country of
such scarce financial resources as Palestine was in those days, the
advantages, in terms of independence of mind and position,
which such assurance conferred were considerable. Moreover,
there was the ordered and tranquil background of a stable and
untroubled country of origin, an inestimable benefit to the few
immigrants from Britain and the United States. Roth also
possessed a fine house and an extensive library; his immediate
family and, as far as I know, more distant relations as well were
safe and, unlike those of so many others from central and eastern ·
Europe, out of Hitler's clutches.

   Although as an undergraduate I was primarily concerned with
oriental studies, I was naturally curious to see this famous
professor and university character and to savour his personality
at first hand. When, at the end of the first term, I presented my
registration and attendance book to him for his signature, he
pretended to be puzzled: 'Could you have mixed up philology
(which you are supposed to be studying) with philosophy, the
"love of words" with the "love of wisdom"? I was saved [he
added] from philology by the First World War, for when I
returned to Oxford after the war I had enough sense to turn to
philosophy.' I enjoyed his teasing and the twinkle in his eye.
During my first few weeks I had thought he was much too elementary and read Plato in Hebrew instead of in Greek, but that
was just a mixture of ignorance and youthful arrogance on my
part. The artistry of Roth's teaching method lay precisely in its
simplicity, in his ability to make the most complex matters
appear easy and clear. In his seminars (of which I attended only a
few) he employed his Socratic maieutic skills (the art of the
'midwife') with consummate ability. Students may have feared
him, for he could *appear* aloof, but most respected him greatly;
and more than a few (among whom, even as an outsider, I
numbered myself) revered him.

   The fact that Plato or Aristotle, Leibniz or Hume could be
read in Hebrew was entirely thanks to Roth who, soon after his
arrival at Jerusalem, set out to create a library of classical philosophical texts to be rendered into Hebrew. He shared this work
of translation with some of his disciples, with whose collaboration
he fashioned a vocabulary and syntactical receptivity in Hebrew

which allowed this process to be pursued successfully. The student body who congregated in his classes had widely differing educational backgrounds and aptitudes (much more so than in the more narrowly defined disciplines), which made the creation by Roth of the library of philosophical classics in Hebrew such an essential requirement.

I would suppose that the 1930s and the period of his Rectorship in the early years of the war were the best years of his professional career. His wife and children offered wonderful support to him; I have rarely seen such a united and contented family as his, over which he presided with quizzical humour and the true pedagogue's light touch.

During his Rectorship, Ben-Gurion (then Chairman of the Jewish Agency) and Shertok (in charge of the Agency's foreign department and later, as Sharett, the second Prime Minister of Israel) came up to the Hebrew University to urge students to join the army. When war broke out it became clear that, under the rules of the Mandate, the British Administration had no legal powers to introduce conscription. At first this appeared to be an unimportant restriction, as, in a war against the Nazis, Jews could scarcely fail to do their duty. However, with some of the young men the memory of the 1939 White Paper, which seemed to have placed severe limits upon the development of the Jewish National Home in Palestine (the official designation in terms of the Balfour Declaration and the League of Nations Mandate), was still too fresh. So, when Ben-Gurion visited the university, he declared that we must fight the war as if there were no White Paper, and we must fight the White Paper as if there were no war. This was no doubt the right spirit, but a somewhat greater emphasis on the fundamental distinction between political disagreement and genocidal mania would have been welcome. Ben-Gurion spoke for about an hour and was then followed by Shertok with a much shorter peroration. I do not recall that either speaker made a great impact on the student body on that occasion.

The meeting was brought to a conclusion by a brief 'footnote' (as he put it) from the Rector, Leon Roth. I can remember his speech in every detail, not least because my principal talent as an undergraduate lay in an ability to imitate two of my teachers, of whom Roth was one. It is, alas, impossible to reproduce in

English the flavour of his Hebrew, not being able to reflect on paper all the nuances and extra-linguistic concomitants of his brief address:

My brother and I were at Oxford during the First World War. Initially there was no conscription in England, and we thought to continue our studies. We thus found ourselves in much the same position as that in which you are now placed. But more and more of our fellow-students joined the forces, and we came to feel that we had to choose between being scholars or gentlemen. We chose to be gentlemen and not scholars. I know, of course, that all of you prefer to be scholars (*melummadim*) rather than gentlemen (*gentlemannim*).

It was powerful, humorous, and highly effective.

I recall another occasion, not long after the end of the war, when I briefly served in the Academic Secretariat of Jerusalem University and happened to see Leon Roth in action. It was, I think, December 1946, a dark period in the annals of Mandatary Palestine, with Jewish terrorist activities by Begin's IZL (National Military Organization) and by the Stern commandos at their height. The Government would intercept illegal immigrant ships and send them to Cyprus. The *Va'ad Le'umi* (Jewish National Council) would then declare a general strike, usually from 10 to 12 in the morning. Roth often lectured from 9 to 11 a.m. At 10 o'clock the students would leave the lecture hall, while Roth continued with his discourse before a virtually empty hall. It was not that he lacked sympathy for the hapless victims of Nazi persecution who wished to find refuge and a home in Palestine, but he did not believe that either terrorism or strikes were the best—or indeed a defensible—means of achieving these aims. On the occasion on which I happened to be passing his lecture hall, with the students banging the door to disturb his teaching, I heard him call out to them:

Gentlemen, listen to me for one moment, and then you can continue with your highly cerebral activity of door-banging. Let me just ask you what you think is more likely to bring about the end of British rule in this country—your noisy door-banging or my philosophy? Surely no reasonable man can doubt that it is my philosophy that will achieve those ends!

By that time Leon Roth was deeply troubled and unhappy. Developments in Palestine towards the end of the war and the following period, culminating in the murder of Lord Moyne, the Minister Resident at Cairo, the bombing of the King David Hotel, and the assassination of Count Bernadotte in Jerusalem as well as other acts of terrorism perpetrated by Jewish paramilitary organizations, led to his profound disillusionment and to ethical, moral, and ideological doubts which could no longer be suppressed. This was not how he and his colleagues, Magnes first and foremost, had envisaged the building of a Jewish commonwealth in Palestine. No doubt there was also some conflict of loyalties between his English birth and upbringing and his devotion to the Jewish National Home and its university which he had helped to create and to perfect.

So after twenty-five years of service, at the age of barely 56, he took his leave of Jerusalem, resigned his Chair, and returned to England. It was a profoundly traumatic decision, arrived at after prolonged heart-searching. It was said that the university was 'more than reluctant to accept his resignation' and that 'strenuous efforts were made to persuade him to remain in Israel', for the 'Government of Israel . . . appreciated what an asset to the country he was'. It was also reported that 'he was offered the Presidency of the University' and that 'his appointment as Minister of Education was mooted' (*Studies in Rationalism, Judaism & Universalism in memory of Leon Roth* (ed. R. Loewe), London, 1966, p. 5).

As an undergraduate and only occasional student of his, my personal acquaintance with Roth was fairly superficial. I admired him from a distance. When I served in Eritrea-Ethiopia during the war we had some occasional correspondence, and it was then that I came to develop the greatest respect for his pithy epistolary style, characteristically forceful writing, and sage counsel. During my brief service in the academic secretariat of the Hebrew University I saw a great deal of Roth, as I was associated with him, in a junior capacity, in the preparation of an international congress in Jerusalem. I observed him in his dealings with his Jerusalem colleagues and his confrères all over the world, his stewardship of the university press, and his relationship, always self-assured as well as humorous, with the leaders of the Jewish community in Palestine, particularly with the upright I. Ben-Zvi, the head of the Jewish National Council and, later, the second President of the State of Israel.

But I saw most of Leon Roth, and at close quarters, during the last ten years of his life, between 1953 and 1963, in London, Cambridge, Brighton, Manchester, and St Andrews. I was then teaching Semitic languages at St Andrews University, and he and Mrs Roth would come in the autumn for a week's visit to Scotland to savour the academic atmosphere of a small and ancient university city. During this last phase of his life, perhaps mellower and sadder, yet ever stimulating, wise, and witty, he would travel all over the world with his wife, lecture occasionally, and write books devoted to an interpretation of Judaism that was rational and humane.

When I was at St Andrews, and later at Manchester, he came to give a lecture that was entitled 'Some observations on useless knowledge'. It was a *tour de force* and greatly enjoyed by all who listened to it. It was a typical piece of Rothian wit and wisdom. Alas, it was hard to persuade him to consider another teaching post. Perhaps professional philosophy had become too insular and inbred, or perhaps he was too much out of sympathy with current fashions in the subject to feel sufficiently comfortable in a Chair of Philosophy.

To one particular suggestion by me to consider another university appointment he replied in characteristic terms:

I can claim acquaintance, I think, with the major trends of the philosophical tradition in the modern world, and, while not a Greek specialist, I have learned both to feel and to win respect for the thought of Plato and Aristotle. On the other hand, I know nothing about mathematical logic; I have doubts as to the final value of 'analysis', and I see no cause to believe that salvation is of the sciences. While having been faced from so near with so much wanton killing and destruction, I am more disturbed by the problem of evil than by that of induction.

In a sense, this letter embodies much of Leon Roth's credo and also affords a glimpse of his style and personality. It was a singular personality; and when he died, suddenly and painlessly, at the age of 67, I felt bereft and desolate. After nearly a quarter of a century I still mourn his premature passing. For so long he had been at the very centre of Jerusalem life and letters; and when he departed from that environment, which he had graced so elegantly, his moral stature still shone brightly—but something of his *joie de vivre* had departed. Present generations of students at Jerusalem have hardly heard of him; many of his own students have gone by now. And when I think of his fame and power and central position half a century ago, I am more conscious than ever of the inexorable truth of *sic transit gloria mundi*.

Martin Buber

Martin Buber (1878–1965) was an international celebrity from an early age. He headed Zionist Congress committees when he was 21, and two years later became editor of *Die Welt*. In works of reference he is described as 'philosopher and theologian as well as Zionist thinker'. Biographies were written about him before he was 50. He was guru, teacher, and prophet to successive generations of Jewish youth movements and to Christian theologians. And although he held Chairs at the universities of Frankfurt and Jerusalem, it is not as a conventional university scholar that he is renowned but as a man of vision, as the embodiment of Jewish ethics, as the tireless and courageous advocate (with Magnes and others) of Arab-Jewish understanding —even in the midst of an Arab–Israeli war—and as the friend, interlocutor, and correspondent of almost every man of letters anywhere in the world. Buber and his work and pervasive influence defy ready definition.

He was born in Vienna, but as a child lived in Lemberg at the home of his well-known grandfather, Solomon Buber, the Midrash (homiletic interpretation of Scriptures) scholar. German was the language in which he operated most easily, most commonly, and often most obscurely when he forced it into the mould of his own complex thought processes. His wife and lifelong companion was German and not Jewish, and the language of his home remained German. He was the mediator and rediscoverer of Hasidism, a mid-eighteenth-century movement of Eastern European Jewish mysticism characterized by religious zeal, joy, and prayer. His philosophy of dialogue, the *I and Thou* syndrome, is perhaps the basis of his world-wide reputation as a religious thinker. His translation into German of the Hebrew Bible (initiated with Franz Rosenzweig) was a monumental undertaking lasting from 1925 until 1961; and after Rosenzweig's early death, in 1929, it was continued and completed by Buber on his own. In conception and execution the work was, in my view, highly problematic: it was an important attempt, but the matching of Hebrew and German, so close to Buber's heart, could not prosper; and, additionally, the vicissitudes of the time militated against the success of the enterprise. The Hebrew scholarship in the narrow sense did not take account of the plethora of contemporary accretions to Old Testament research; and the German language was never free of an element of artificiality. Buber was, first and foremost, an aesthete (in the most favourable sense of that term—not for nothing had he studied art history at Florence), and his aesthetic conceptions would always hold sway over the mundane, boring, and pedantic requirements of strict adherence to textual minutiae.

Already before the First World War he had become a great cult figure to the Zionist youth movement, and, with Hitler's advent to power, Buber was made the focus of spiritual resistance to the Nazi evil by lecturing, teaching, and organizing Jewish education on a large scale. His comfortable home in Heppenheim, not far from Frankfurt, became a place of pilgrimage. The training of youth, of adults, and of teachers was at all times a primary concern to him. The three stout volumes of his correspondence bear eloquent testimony to the time and care Buber took over answering letters from the famous as well as the obscure, always in his fine, bold hand, equally characteristic of his Latin and Hebrew strokes.

Although he was one of the pioneers of the idea of a Hebrew University, he himself hesitated long and anxiously before committing himself to settling in Palestine and joining the university to whose original conception he had contributed. This hesitation was no doubt based on sound instinct, for Buber must have sensed that at Jerusalem and in the Yishuv, with its inward orientation and somewhat austere configuration, he would never attain the position or influence he had in the world at large. In 1925 he had begun lecturing on Jewish religion and ethics at the University of Frankfurt, and in 1930 he became titular Professor of Religion there, a post he held for only a few years owing to the events of the time. His negotiations with Magnes and the authorities of the Hebrew University were painfully prolonged over many years and, curiously enough for someone in Buber's well-nigh unique position, were accompanied by strongly felt reservations on both sides. In Scholem, S. H. Bergmann, and Magnes himself, Buber had strong advocates at court, but there was opposition to him in Senate. It was not clear what he was to teach. There were teachers of Bible already in post, men who could be trusted not to upset the theological applecart and whose close familiarity with the Hebrew text was held in greater esteem than Buber's real or alleged *Schöngeisterei*. Jewish mysticism and Hasidism were authoritatively represented by Gershom Scholem, whose competence in this field was uniquely powerful. Religion as an academic subject was frowned upon, and the religious complexities in the Yishuv at large were such that the study of Jewish religion in particular was not considered safe in Buber's hands. Comparative religion was, perhaps, not fashionable at that time, and Buber, though immensely knowledgeable in the field, was not able to read the Arabic, Indian, etc., sources in the original.

When eventually he settled at Jerusalem in 1938 at the age of 60, after endless, often abortive, and highly complicated negotiations, he was appointed not to the Chair of Bible he had coveted, nor to the Chair of Religion he had held at Frankfort (and for which, he had argued with unwonted asperity, the German professorship had established some legitimate claim in his favour), but to the Chair of 'Sociology of Culture'. That at any rate was the official Hebrew designation rather than the smoother English 'Social Philosophy'. His arrival at Jerusalem turned out to be a field-day for the wisecrackers: it was said that the entire traffic at Jerusalem had to be halted to allow the furniture vans with his property to pass through the narrow streets. He certainly moved into a fine, large, Arab-style house in the Talbiye suburb; the new home was elegantly furnished with the possessions from his Heppenheim house. And his splendid library reflected the width of his interests and the catholicity of his tastes; it was the largest and most variegated collection of books I had yet seen in private hands. They were housed in several intercommunicating rooms of large size and reached right up to the ceiling. There was a good deal of art history and of sociology, including amply filled shelves of the writings of Vico, Auguste Comte, Rousseau, Durkheim, Marx, Weber, etc.—quite apart, of course, from a vast array of works on Hasidism, theology, comparative religion, and the Bible.

I attended Buber's lectures during the first two years after his arrival at Jerusalem, not because I had developed a passionate interest in sociology, but because the man and the entire Buber phenomenon were fascinating and intriguing. I think most of my fellow-students in his classes were there for the same reason. He was always happy to be interrupted and to answer questions. He took great trouble over replying to the interventions of students. Dialogue was essential to him. He would stroll about the lecture hall in the authentic peripatetic manner. He was always meticulously attired in a markedly *soigné* way. He was quite small, and his full beard concealed a curiously lopsided mouth which became evident, however, when he endeavoured to pronounce something carefully and slowly. Altogether his appearance, demeanour, and background revealed the man of substance, in every sense of that word. The story was told, probably apocryphally, of a man who asked Buber how it was possible that a person of his spirituality, of his devotion to matters of the mind and the intellect, could be so interested in good food, good clothes, and all the other paraphernalia of a comfortable life. To which Buber was said to have retorted: and do you think that the Almighty has created all these fine things for fools only?!

Buber was a not untypical representative of professors at Jerusalem, in those early days of the university, who professed subjects that were not in themselves of central importance to the building of a well-balanced and integrated seat of higher learning. But it was the eminence or the availability of the person which sometimes determined the trend of academic development. This reflection is not proffered in any critical sense; rather the contrary: if the systematic evolving of basic and essential disciplines had always been the primary consideration, some of the greatest scholars would have been lost to the university. Buber would not have been there—nor would Scholem, the founder of the academic study of Jewish mysticism and one of the greatest scholars the Hebrew University has had in the sixty-odd years since its inauguration. The chance of the availability of a suitable incumbent determined that there was a Chair of Islamic Art before there was a Professorship of Arabic.

Another wisecrack that circulated widely at the time of Buber's arrival at Jerusalem was connected with the complexity, at times convolutedness, of his linguistic expression in German. It was said that his Hebrew was not yet good enough to be obscure in. There was a grain of truth in that witticism. Of course, Buber's knowledge of Hebrew as such was obviously not in question, but at first he lacked the fluency and ready command which he acquired in the course of time. In the early stages it was often painful to observe how he struggled to find the *mot juste*, but he would persevere, for the right expression of his thoughts mattered to him profoundly. Eventually he would do the same in Hebrew as he used to do in German: manipulate the language with some dexterity and fashion the *mot juste* he felt he had need of—except that in Hebrew that tendency was much more cautiously and less sweepingly pursued than had been the case in German.

Buber's international stature and fame, particularly among Christian theologians, did not consort easily with the limited parameters of the pre-war Jewish community of Palestine. While Christian theologians came to appreciate increasingly the manner in which Buber interpreted Judaism to the outside world, Jews regarded their religion essentially as a system of learning rather than as a faith that could be encompassed by the concepts of a systematic theology. By the standards of Jerusalem, Buber's Hebrew and Jewish scholarship was considered, rightly or wrongly, wide and extensive rather than specific or rigorous. He was at first thought of, not altogether fairly I believe, as an aesthete and dialectician rather than as the down-to-earth scholar needed at that critical time. While Buber and Scholem had great personal regard for each other, the latter's more rigorously based scholarship was thought to be more productive and more attuned to the requirements of the hour.

As a student I greatly enjoyed Buber's lectures and seminars and was particularly impressed by the enormous breadth of his general learning. At times he would arrange to hold small classes at his home, when the entire range of his wonderful library was available to us. Those were truly memorable occasions. In the early days he used to invite a few students, outside the official university framework, to work with him on some biblical text on Saturday afternoons. Here, too, it was a privilege to observe the Buber mind in full spate, but I must confess that for me his mode of exegesis was too divorced from the philological minutiae and methodology to which I felt more attuned.

In some connection which I cannot now recall I needed a testimonial from two of my teachers. Although sociology was scarcely a subject of major concern to me, I reckoned that Buber's name would carry some weight. He readily agreed to write such a testimonial and sat down in his study there and then, inviting me to browse among his books in the meantime. No invitation could have been more welcome, and I secretly hoped that he would take a long time to hit upon the right formulation, so that I might survey his treasures at greater leisure. Eventually he handed me a sheet of paper penned in purple ink in his lapidary writing. Still holding on to it, he warned me most earnestly not to believe the contents of the note which was written purely for the mundane purpose required and in no way reflected his genuine opinion of my prowess in the subject he professed. I assured him in all sincerity that his certificate would be used in that narrow context only and that I had absolutely no intention of allowing my head to be turned by his kind words—far less of switching in consequence from Semitic languages to sociology. He smiled benignly and suggested that I was, perhaps, making sport of him. He pronounced the word 'sport' in his delightful Viennese manner.

Although I saw Buber briefly at Jerusalem in 1961, my last long meeting with him was in the mid-1950s when he travelled to Aberdeen, in the company of his wife and grand-daughter, to receive an honorary Doctorate of Divinity there. At that time I held a Readership at St Andrews University and persuaded Buber and his family to interrupt their journey at St Andrews, so that he might lecture to the Theological Summer School. This he did with much aplomb, although by that time he was in his middle to late 70s. I had never before heard him lecture in English and was impressed with the ease of his performance. It was a typical Buber address, constantly endeavouring to make his audience participate in his discourse, asking them questions, and suggesting some English coinage of his invention when the accepted vocabulary appeared to him deficient for his purposes.

My wife and I had accommodated the Bubers at a large hotel, mainly frequented by St Andrews golfers, situated opposite our flat. His first question upon entering our home was about the 'purpose and rules' of the game of golf. He listened to my explanations and posed a number of theoretical problems with the same concentration and seriousness which he applied to concerns normally closer to his heart. The next day I took him to the large lounge of his hotel overlooking the last fairway and 18th green. He seemed fascinated and enquired whether it was a sort of 'ambulatory game of chess'. I thought it needed more brawn and skill than cerebral activity. This was the only time I saw a good deal of Mrs Buber (Paula Buber-Winkler, 1877–1958), whom M. B. had met when they were both students at Zürich. She was a writer, poet, and artist and a knowledgeable partner in her husband's general intellectual endeavours. Under the pseudonym of Georg Munk she had published novels and stories (Buber, *Briefwechsel*, Heidelberg, 1972, i. 34 ff.) which were highly thought of at the time. During their visit to St Andrews she was in her late 70s, but they looked after each other with touching concern. She was highly amused, but scarcely surprised, when one afternoon Buber appeared at our flat in a raincoat which was far too large for him. He had picked it up in the cloakroom of their hotel by sheer inadvertence and seemed a little uncomprehending at the sight of our amusement.

We went for long walks through the streets of St Andrews and he took great delight in the beautiful small university city. 'Here one could work', he told me repeatedly, an impression which I was able to confirm with emphasis. His pleasure and skill at teaching and imparting knowledge had not diminished, and I felt once more like the wayward pupil I had been twenty years earlier. We talked about the Aramaic background of the Greek New Testament, about the prospects of peace in the Near East, and remembered friends who had tirelessly worked for Arab-Jewish understanding, especially Magnes, Kalvaryski, and Senator. When he wished to stress a point, he would stop in mid-walk and face me for a minute or two and then suddenly march off. However, he had by then forgotten the direction in which we were going and would, in fact, retrace his steps by walking back whence we had come. It was an endearing eccentricity and an aspect of his total concentration on the subject under discussion.

On Sunday, 13 June 1965, I had to take the chair at a 'meeting of intellectuals' at University College, London, dealing with the moral problems posed by the existence and policies of the State of Israel. When the biochemist and Nobel laureate Sir Ernst Chain was speaking, a note was handed to me saying that Martin

Buber had died earlier that day. The meeting was interrupted, and I was asked to say a few words—alas, very inadequate ones—about my old teacher, the teacher and guide of several generations of students, youth leaders, and adults. If one had to select one single phrase to describe Buber's significance to the world, it would have to be 'teacher and sage', rabbi and mahatma.

Gershom Scholem

Martin Buber has said of Gershom Scholem (1897–1982); 'All of us have students, some of us have created schools, but only Scholem has created a whole academic discipline.' Indeed, Scholem was a unique phenomenon in the field of Jewish studies and almost certainly their greatest exponent this century. As the founder of the academic discipline of Jewish mysticism, until then far removed from rigorous scholarly inquiry and philological minutiae, Scholem established research in *Kabbalah* (the esoteric movements in Judaism, especially in the shape they assumed from the twelfth century onwards) on a firm and generally accepted basis. He was also a Hebraist and orientalist, as well as a student of the philosophy of language. His vast range as a polymath, reflected in his writings, in his conversation, and in the wonderful and truly unique library he had assembled, can scarcely be encompassed by any single person (and certainly not by the present writer) audacious enough to attempt to depict him. In my view, Scholem and Polotsky (about whom more later), in their very different subjects and attitudes, are the two great masters of genius in the annals of the Hebrew University of Jerusalem. Indeed, Scholem has become a vogue figure (and certainly not in the pejorative sense) in circles far beyond the study of Judaism or the Orient, seeing that the *Times Literary Supplement* and similarly prestigious journals of general literature and culture have devoted some of their principal articles to an assessment of his work. As the close friend and interpreter of Walter Benjamin, he has himself attracted widespread attention, interpretation, and exposition. Perhaps only Buber had aroused similarly extensive interest, but Scholem always remained more firmly within the confines of the academic world. In some ways Scholem had created, from an early age, a powerful persona which, in its fusion with his kabbalistic discoveries, may be reckoned his greatest achievement.

Scholem was born in Berlin into an assimilated German Jewish family, but to his parents' chagrin he turned to Zionism as a very young man. He came into contact with influential Eastern European Hebrew writers of the calibre of Bialik and Agnon, who resided in Germany before, during, and shortly after the First World War, and then began to acquire his prodigious knowledge of Hebrew and Jewish sources. At university he studied mathematics and philosophy, but eventually turned to oriental languages and wrote a doctoral dissertation, published in 1923, on the earliest and most complex kabbalistic text. He left for Palestine in the same year and joined the incipient university, first as a librarian, then, from its opening in 1925, as lecturer (later professor) in Jewish mysticism, a post which he adorned for the rest of his life.

By the mid-1930s he already had an international reputation as Kabbalah scholar, genius, and eccentric. As in the case of Buber and Leon Roth, I attended his lectures only occasionally, not because I was animated by a great hankering after mysticism, Jewish or otherwise, but because the man himself held a marked fascination for me. My curiosity about, and admiration for, Scholem increased rather than diminished over the years, and during the last ten or fifteen years of his life I felt he had become more impressive than ever. His eccentricities or idiosyncrasies, such as they may have been, seemed to me much less pronounced than people thought when he was 30 or 40. In 1977, aged 80, he published a short autobiography in German (Suhrkamp publishing house, Frankfurt) covering only the years up to his immigration to Jerusalem in 1923 and entitled 'Von Berlin nach Jerusalem'. It is a remarkable document, written, like his Walter Benjamin books (and indeed others), in a style and manner at once lucid and beautiful. But this particular work displays such wit and limpidity of narrative, as well as zest, that one can only lament profoundly that there is no sequel to take us close to the end of the story (at any rate this seems to be the case, as nothing has, to my knowledge, appeared since Scholem's death a few years ago).

In 1982 Scholem published a Hebrew version of his German book. This covers the same period but is an enlarged and much expanded text. He explained that the Hebrew reader was likely to take an interest in many details and episodes which were not thought to be of concern to those in the outside world. And, indeed, in its Hebrew form there are quite a number of additional facets which deserve to be more widely known. But the style, pellucidity, verve, and wit of the original are somehow lost. I trust I shall not be taken to imply that Scholem's Hebrew was not equal to the task, but I imagine that his dedication to the subject, so close to the end of his life (he was in his mid-80s), was flagging.

Wit and verve were always aspects of Scholem's personality, in speech and in writing. When someone remarked at a reception at Jerusalem (as, to my surprise, people not infrequently did) that there was a marked physical resemblance between Scholem and myself, he responded that that was scarcely unexpected, as we were both ugly and had ears that stuck out. On books or offprints sent to him he would always comment knowledgeably—however far they might be from his own scholarly concerns—and candidly, yet with genuine generosity.

While penning these lines I am browsing through some of his last letters to me, particularly those connected with a review I had written on a book by an American scholar about Scholem's work, entitled 'Gershom Scholem: Kabbalah and Counter-History'. My notice had stated that 'the chapter entitled "Counter-History" holds little fascination for me, partly because I find it hard to attribute any precise meaning to that notion and partly because I cannot discern any illumination in these thoughts . . . for an assessment of Scholem's scholarly work and position'. In response Scholem told me that at a recent congress in New York (May 1980) he had met the author of the book in question and was invited by the chairman to expound his views on its attitude to himself and to his work. Scholem did so in one sentence by picking up the three notions adumbrated in the book's title: 'Who Gershom Scholem is, I hope I know more or less; what Kabbalah is, I have tried to find out all my life; what Counter-History is, I frankly do not know.'

My review had also stated that the author was inclined to refer too readily to the Kabbalah 'according to Scholem' or to views Scholem 'ascribes to the Kabbalah'. Since Scholem was most meticulous about quoting chapter and verse, there really seemed to be no need for such coy circumlocutions. To these observations Scholem responded: 'We appear to be of one mind on this, for it seems never to have occurred to the author of that work that my main source of inspiration were the Hebrew books which I have studied for sixty years and especially the Kabbalists themselves. He has some difficulty granting the possibility that the Kabbalists actually said what I attribute to them! At any rate, I have learnt a lot about myself which I seem not to have known before the publication of the book.'

Even before I had ever set eyes on Scholem, as a student at Jerusalem, I had heard stories about his remarkable dealings with the German military authorities during the First World War. Most of these tales are now confirmed in the German and the lengthier Hebrew versions of his autobiographical 'From Berlin to Jerusalem'. Scholem strongly disapproved of the war, its conduct, and the militaristic fervour it engendered. He wanted nothing to do with that war and also deprecated the broadly favourable view towards those events which Buber and his followers had adopted. Scholem's attitude led to his expulsion from his school in March 1915. Later on he was twice rejected, or at any rate deferred, for military service on the grounds of neurasthenia. But by May 1917, when after nearly three years of war the general situation had grown more critical, he was declared suitable for service in the infantry. His military service turned out to be 'brief and stormy', in Scholem's own words. He rebelled against everything done in the army and, after two months, he was officially declared a 'psychopath', dismissed the service, and placed in the category 'temporarily unfit for military duty'. The doctors summoned his father and suggested that domestic conflicts with his parents, arising from his political views, were the cause of his psychological disorders. In January 1918 he received a last summons to another medical and psychiatric examination and was then declared 'permanently unfit for military service' as well as 'no longer controllable'. Scholem adds, in the Hebrew version of his autobiographical account, that never in his life had he been of sounder mind and clearer vision. It must have been a remarkable feat of acting to delude successive medical boards into believing that he was a genuine psychopath. Wiseacres would claim later on that his excessive preoccupation with Kabbalists and mysticism constituted excellent training for this astonishing performance.

Agnon, the great Hebrew writer and Nobel laureate, had been a friend and admirer of Scholem ever since the latter's student

days. He was the principal speaker at a reception in honour of
Scholem's sixtieth birthday and told us how Scholem had come
to him in Bad Homburg in 1923 to take leave of him before emig-
rating to Palestine (*Me'atsmi el atsmi*, pp. 276-7). But Agnon
was just about to depart in order to keep an appointment with
two of the greatest Hebrew writers then still living in Germany,
Ahad Ha'am and Bialik. He was embarrassed: he could not let
these two venerable figures wait and he could not send away his
young friend. So he took him along to meet these two sages, one
of them weak and old, the other weary of young lionizers in
search of a literary subject. But when Scholem began to speak
about his bibliographical discoveries in the field of Jewish
mysticism, they listened spellbound to this young man who was
so full of the most recondite knowledge and so eager to impart it.

The last time I saw Scholem was in the spring of 1980, less
than two years before his death, when my wife and I were invited
by him and Mrs Scholem to their home in Jerusalem. The centrepiece of their spacious apartment was the vast and priceless
library he had collected throughout his life and which now constitutes a special section of the Hebrew University Library.
Scholem was then 83, but physically sprightly and mentally as
alert as he had always been—indeed as enthusiastic, animated,
and witty as ever. He would jump up each time we challenged
him to find a certain book in that immense collection—and he
scored full marks on each occasion. My wife also raised a minor
query about his stimulating 'From Berlin to Jerusalem' where he
describes the scene at the opening of the university in 1925 with
'the aged and splendid-looking Lord Balfour standing *before* the
setting sun'; but with his back to the east he must have been
facing the setting sun. Two years later, in the Hebrew version,
Lord Balfour was standing 'in' the setting sun, which seems
more appropriate. It was a memorable evening of reminiscences,
of instruction, and of high spirits in which the two ladies played
their full part; but as usual Scholem was the heart and soul of the
party.

I am told by a young and very able lady colleague who is no
mean student of Scholemiana that now, half a decade after the
great man's death, the movement of revisionism has begun. This
is a common phenomenon: yesterday's toadies come crawling out
of the woodwork, but these epigones can rarely do serious

damage to the edifice they had hitherto striven to shore up. Revisionism for its own sake is an aspect of the *comédie humaine*—or, in its more serious guise, an agent of marginal progress. The sheer originality of Scholem's monumental *œuvre* is immune to such gnawing corrosion. This is not to say that, in the course of time, minor refinements, improvements, even some amendments, may not be needed; but the giant who bestrode the world of Hebrew and Jewish studies so confidently, so long, and so massively will not be toppled by a few pygmies scratching at the structure. I count it a great privilege to have been at the same university, to have shared some of the same intellectual experiences, and to have been acquainted, however superficially, with this great man and charismatic scholar.

H. J. Polotsky

It is difficult for me to write about H. J. Polotsky without a measure of personal involvement and indeed emotion. Of all the men of scholarship or affairs mentioned in this book he is, as my principal teacher, the one who has been and has remained closest to my interests and concerns. Only very recently I added a postscript to the proofs of an article of mine, on whose details H. J. P. had commented: 'At 80 Polotsky is as sprightly putting to rights this wayward pupil as he was half a century ago.' And as I set down these lines I receive H.J.P.'s review of my last book, on Tigrinya, the principal North Ethiopian language. In twenty-one typewritten pages he manages to attain recognitions more important and more profound than all those comprised in my entire book or indeed reached in several generations of Tigrinya endeavours. I have to confess that as an undergraduate, while recognizing H.J.P's remarkable learning, I did not necessarily consider him my favourite teacher. This was partly an aspect of what I then thought to be his scholarly austerity and, to a greater degree, a lamentable lack of academic maturity on my part. I think I have now, at the end of my own professorial career, reached the stage when I could most agreeably benefit from his teaching. It is a curious reflection, perhaps, that I have learnt more from H.J.P. and have felt myself a closer disciple of his *since* I ceased to be *in statu pupillari* to him in the formal sense. And although for only five of the last fifty years have we both lived in the same country, indeed the same continent, contact has been maintained by not infrequent meetings, by correspondence, and, over the last ten or fifteen years, by telephone.

As Egyptologist, Semitist, and linguist Polotsky is generally recognized as the supreme master. No one I have ever met or heard of possesses his command of language and languages in the widest sense. He not only knows how language works, how linguistic structures, sentences, are held together, but he has looked hard and deep into so many disparate language manifestations that the secrets of syntactical sinews and tendons (and all their complex inter-relationships) appear to have been revealed to him. While he is fully conversant with contemporary linguistic theories (and has himself operated with some of those techniques which promise to produce tangible results), he has shown little taste for theoretical frameworks or methodological processes *per se*. He is suspicious of those innovators who have neglected to read what some nineteenth-century scholars had already anticipated; and he does not care for those who are clever at devising systems rather than handling the raw material of language itself. H.J.P. will never cite a language for comparative purposes unless he has made a thorough study of it himself. Window-dressing with the mention of Japanese or Navaho or Tamil is anathema to him, though he is likely to possess a pretty good command of these as well.

His learning and its written expression are so perfectly matched that he has hardly ever had to unsay a single word which he has committed to print. How many other scholars could afford to give permission for the reprinting, without correction or qualifying remarks, of a collection of studies which they had composed in their mid-20s—as H.J.P. has been able to do, without loss of sleep or honour? In the half-century that I have known him I have, despite occasionally strenuous endeavours on my part, never found him to be wrong in matters within his professional sphere. Outside that area he can no doubt, like most of us, be wrong-headed, but his integrity and conscience as a scholar have not only earned him the respect and reverence of his pupils and of all those who have benefited from his pioneering writings, but have given him a (to my mind) unique place in the world of language study.

Polotsky was born in Zürich, in 1905, of Russian parentage. He studied at Berlin and Göttingen. His remarkable attainments in Egyptology and Semitic languages found recognition at an early age. Whether the bilingual background of Russian and German had an influence on his extraordinary gifts is a question which, in its general application, has often been pondered by linguists without reaching any clear conclusions. H.J.P. was soon attracted to the pursuit of grammar, and the singleminded quest for elucidation of syntactical interconnections and inter-lockings has occupied his capacious cerebral equipment ever since. At school he was considered to have very one-sided gifts, but, while in some senses this may have been true, his uncommonly wide reading and a self-education of very broad catholicity have wiped out all traces of such real or alleged one-sidedness. He is said to have claimed (in a book on philological precociousness to which he contributed a few observations about his youth) that he had a distinct aversion to mathematics and the natural sciences and was indifferent to music. I should regret it if the latter aspect were true, and, oddly enough, in all these many years we do not seem ever to have talked about music, despite my own interest in the subject. I can, however, vouch for the fact that H.J.P. used to be in good voice, for, when he and his wife visited us at St Andrews in 1957, I took a recording of our after-dinner singsongs which bear witness to a measure of musical enthusiasm and zest on his part.

The same book on philological precociousness also refers to an early inclination by H.J.P. to become a painter. I know little about these youthful ambitions, but Polotsky's handwriting in all the many scripts—hieroglyphs, Syriac, Arabic, Ethiopic, etc.—is extraordinarily beautiful; and he has a strongly developed sense of what is aesthetically acceptable in the graphic arts. In his own case, this sense of perfection would amount almost to vanity, were such a notion compatible with his essentially introvert nature, which would consider such strivings vulgar. Reticence, personal self-effacement, a good measure of reserve—even shy-ness (which may at times be taken for aloofness by those who do not know him)—are the hallmark of the Polotsky persona. It is not that he is unaware of his own merits (all the marks of inter-national academic acclaim, in the shape of honorary doctorates, fellowships of academies, dedicatory volumes, prizes, etc., must have inured him to that notion by now), but any form of ostenta-tion or self-advertisement is alien to his nature.

This self-effacement is evident also in his speech, which is halting and hesitant rather than fluent—in marked contrast to the stylistic felicities and elegance of his performance on paper and in print. Others may speak almost as many languages as he does and with greater fluency, but none, I am confident, can equal H.J.P. in the sheer range of languages covered and in the depth of his penetration into the functioning of the language organism. His talents are not those of the Levantine but eminently those of the greatest masters of nineteenth-century European philological scholarship. His command of most European languages is formidable, and so obviously is that of the languages that come within his professional orbit. There are well-documented instances of his contributions to Greek papyrology or to arcane layers of Arabic where those specializing in these fields failed to come up with the solutions and recourse had to be had to the 'non-specialist' Polotsky.

When, a few years ago, an international conference was held at Cambridge to celebrate H.J.P's achievements in Egyptology, the proceedings were to close with a lecture by the master himself. I was shown the lecture hall in the morning (since for the arrangement of the mundane things in life H.J.P. has a bevy of devoted disciples or admirers in tow wherever he goes) and, to my embarrassment, it turned out to be about the largest hall available. Yet I felt sure that, while the contents of the lecture would be splendid, the performance was unlikely to empty the punts on the Cam and bring in the masses. For Polotsky is essentially a scholar's scholar and not a popular orator. But I was doubly wrong: the hall was filled to the very last seat, and H.J.P. gave an enthralling performance full of gusto and wit. It had obviously been a number of years since last I had heard him give a public lecture, and half a century had elapsed since I first witnessed the young lecturer address a class on the refinements of Arabic syntax, with much humming and hawing.

The wit which is such a notable facet of the Polotsky style was not evident in those far distant lectures. He had come to Jerusalem in 1934 as an instructor, the lowest category of university teacher, and remained in that grade throughout my time at the university. Everyone knew that his singular gifts caused such grading to make a laughing-stock of the university or of the authorities which allowed this injustice to persist. I believe that it was thought—genuine financial stringencies apart—that he had not yet published the weighty tomes which were considered *de rigueur* for promotion. But H.J.P. is not the man to go in for heavy volumes; his thoughts are distilled in carefully directed forays which can express, in a few closely argued and generously exemplified pages, what lesser mortals set forth in lengthy tracts.

When I left Jerusalem for war service in Eritrea-Ethiopia, Polotsky gave me detailed instructions on what to look out for in the area of Ethiopian languages. It was then that our correspondence started, at first with hints and advice, on his part, and with queries, fumbling attempts at Tigrinya, and a supply to him of locally published books, on mine. When I became responsible for the publication of the first ever weekly newspaper in that North Ethiopian language of Tigrinya, H.J.P. received the full tally of this precious publication, while I, in return, got an earful of admonition and even more precious counsel and instruction. That correspondence, from the early 1940s to the present day (and, I trust, for a long while yet), running to some hundreds of pithily and candidly expressed letters, has been carefully preserved; it will in due course be inherited by my erstwhile pupil and friend, Simon Hopkins, of whom I have spoken in the opening part of this book. It is a formidable and precious legacy.

Every letter in this collection is not only instructive but also highly entertaining, for in whatever language H.J.P. may be writing he contrives to hit on the *mot juste*, the telling formulation, or the witty and ingenious turn of phrase. My wife, too, has become an addict to this genre, even though she started out with some serious reservations and handicaps. When she got permission from the military authorities to join me in Eritrea, I suggested that she should call on Polotsky before leaving Jerusalem. She did so, and she, very young and shy in the presence of my revered maestro, and he, awkward, at a loss for words, and shy as well, spent some ten minutes in virtual silence. Since then, they have been friends for many years, at ease with each other in jollity and banter; in fact, it was only quite recently that they recalled their first encounter, and H.J.P., with accustomed gallantry, said in his slow bass delivery: 'I still feel embarrassed.'

Before I left Jerusalem for Oxford, early in 1948, Magnes, the President of the university, suggested that I should get a testimonial from Polotsky. I assured him that H.J.P. did not indulge in such frivolities, but Magnes insisted and there was no defying his authority. I went to my guru with much trepidation, but he readily acquiesced. A few days later I called on him to collect the finished article, which read: 'Mr E. Ullendorff was my pupil from . . . to . . . I have no complaints against him.' There were not many occasions when I needed to have recourse to this fulsome assessment of my qualifications. But in 1954, when I shared a set of rooms at Pembroke College, Cambridge, with the great American orientalist W. F. Albright (during the International Orientalist Congress there), I showed it to him, for I knew he was a great admirer of H.J.P. He at once recognized the authentic Polotsky manner and thought no one could wish for a greater tribute, considering its provenance.

During the past half-century I have derived immense benefit from the instruction and from the friendship (if I may be so presumptuous) of H. J. Polotsky. Wherever we met, at Jerusalem or Rome, London or Manchester, St Andrews or Munich, Cambridge or Oxford, I have never left his presence without feeling enriched. Over the years he has much mellowed, but his cerebral cutting edge is as sharp as ever. Since I underwent a massive operation, two or three years ago, he has added solicitude to his other qualities. Ever since my student days he has remained *in loco parentis* (and not only intellectually), and I should find it hard to envisage a future from which his guidance and firm counsel were removed. Not to be able to appeal to the ultimate authority on language (and so many other things) would be deprivation indeed. Meanwhile I feel consoled that this contingency may not arise before senility has numbed the blow.

Other teachers and friends

N. H. Torczyner (later Tur-Sinai) was the most senior in age (1886–1973) and in status of those of my teachers who had direct supervision over my studies in Semitic philology. He also served as President of the Hebrew Language Council, later the Hebrew Language Academy. He was a very remarkable, highly individualistic, indeed passionate scholar. His contributions to the exploration of the Semitic languages and to the elucidation of the Hebrew Bible were nearly always hotly contested by others, yet everybody acknowledged the originality and the spark of (at times wayward) genius apparent in many of his numerous writings. From an early stage in his career he combined learning and acumen with a certain disdain for methodological rigour as well as a slight disinclination to temper originality with sobriety.

During his career he was at the centre of many scholarly controversies, for he believed in his discoveries with rare singlemindedness; but personally he always showed generosity even towards those who disagreed with him most. He was a teacher of remarkable power, enthusiasm, and persuasiveness. He took a deep and abiding interest in his students, who were always welcome in his hospitable home in Jerusalem. His wife was a most warm-hearted woman and cared genuinely about the welfare of her husband's students, especially those who had come from abroad and were without parental help and still very young. This interest would extend well into the future: when I visited them at Jerusalem in the early 1960s (having by that time been a professor for some years), she still asked me whether I could 'afford to eat as much as was needed for a growing man'.

Torczyner was possessed of a somewhat uncertain temper and temperament. Thus I was a little doubtful when we, his students, gave a party in his honour to celebrate the publication of his decipherment of the famous Lakhish ostraca and my fellow-students urged me to give a performance imitating our professor, a frivolous attainment in which I was said to have developed a plausible proficiency. Knowing his unpredictability and conscious of the imminence of my final examinations, I hesitated until the last moment. But when I saw his serene mood as the party proceeded, I took my courage in both hands and gave the most accurate impersonation I was capable of. I carefully watched his reaction, and when I saw that he was hugely entertained, I pulled out all the stops. When I had exhausted my repertoire, he insisted on further instalments and repetitions. By the end of the evening I counted myself very fortunate that things had gone so well; it could so easily have been otherwise. Thereafter, whenever I met him—often after an interval of years—his first remark would be: *bevaqasha haqe oti*, 'please imitate, impersonate me', until the time came when I had to assure him that I had lost my erstwhile talent to do so.

During the final period of his life two main spheres claimed his attention: the revival of the Hebrew language and an understanding (often a little idiosyncratic) of the text of the Hebrew Bible. His most concentrated energy was devoted to the Book of Job, to which he wrote detailed commentaries that appeared in a number of very different recensions over a period of some forty years. Each new version abjured its predecessor in the strongest terms. Many of his textual emendations have stood the test of time, while others were ingenious rather than generally acceptable. But it may be truly said of Tur-Sinai that even his errors or oddities of judgement had a grandiose quality about them and possessed all the marks of the whimsical genius with which this inspiring scholar had invested them.

* * *

It would be difficult to imagine a more contrasting personality than D. H. Baneth (1893–1973), Professor of Arabic. He was painfully shy, totally self-effacing, abnormally reluctant to speak about himself, yet a most exacting teacher and scholar as well as a severe examiner. His work was largely devoted to the religious philosophy of medieval Islam and Judaism as well as to the exploration of the character of Judaeo-Arabic. One of his closest colleagues has written of him: 'The fact that he, the master of so many languages, confined himself in his publications almost exclusively to Hebrew, is one of the manifestations of his striving for privacy. . . . In his published work he spoke to his colleagues and students only.' His standards of perfection and demands on himself were such that he wrote and published very little, generally only when circumstances and his respect for colleagues compelled him to do so. This means that most of his articles will be found in dedicatory or memorial volumes.

It was the custom of Hebrew in the past (it no longer is) to address one's elders and betters not in the second person but in the third person singular. This was so ingrained that in my student days it would have been unthinkable to speak to our teachers in any other way. But when one addressed Baneth in this mode, there invariably followed a determined abjuration (though delivered in his most halting and hesitant manner) of such deference shown to him. Our fellow-student Y. Navon, later President of the State of Israel, has rightly said in the memorial volume to Baneth that it was a true privilege to be numbered among his disciples: 'He was strict with himself and with the truth . . . pious and humble . . . obsessed by a supreme responsibility for every word he uttered, in case he might be guilty of error and thus mislead others; heavy-tongued yet producing pearls of wisdom.' We all remember him in precisely this way.

* * *

L. A. Mayer (1895–1959), Professor of Near Eastern Art and Archaeology, impinged on me only in a fairly remote and rather curious way. He had settled in Palestine as early as 1921 and, until he joined the university on its establishment in 1925, had worked for the Government Department of Antiquities. In my undergraduate days he was head of the Institute of Oriental Studies. He seemed remote, aloof, and slightly mysterious—at any rate to those who did not know him. He had a large black beard of a particularly ample and comprehensively framing kind. At first he made a Rasputin-like impression on me, with his sombre, but elegant, dark clothes, a high-pitched but exceptionally soft voice (one had to strain to hear him), his quick gait and silent steps which brought him so quietly into the centre of the oriental library that he was standing next to one before one had realized it. That library was, curiously, the only room in the building with a telephone. I do not remember that it ever rang or that anyone other than Mayer ever used it. He did so frequently, almost on every occasion he came into the library, but I was utterly fascinated that one never heard his voice when he was speaking on the phone. The fast movements of his beard were the only sign that his lips must be busy.

The American philosopher Brand Blanshard once told me at St Andrews that, as a young man, he had been a guest of the great John Dewey. In the course of conversation Dewey remarked that he hated a certain philosopher. Blanshard was surprised and said he had not realized that Dewey knew that scholar. 'Of course I don't know him,' he responded, 'if I did, I would not hate him.' When I heard that story I immediately thought of Mayer. One knew so little about him, he was so distant, also both so authoritarian and so authoritative, that one ascribed to him a character he probably did not possess at all. Everyone seemed to be in awe of him—for no precise reason one could identify—but he had that curious aura. At the same time he was polite, though in a somewhat studied manner. I had never

attended any of his lectures and knew no one who did until
during the war I met a former pupil of his in Eritrea who spoke
highly of him and, later on, himself became Professor of Near
Eastern Art (in the University of London). I think Mayer spoke
to me only once during my student days when, on a certain
occasion, he came into the oriental library where I was working
on some Syriac text, held an Arabic book in front of me and
asked me whether I would read a certain passage to him. I made a
thorough mess of it, and he just said: 'Oh, I had been told by
Professor Torczyner that you were good at Semitic languages.' I
think, though I have no real evidence, that this was some sort of
test for some minor job involving Arabic that was in his gift.

When during the latter part of the war I briefly came on leave
to Jerusalem, he was Rector of the university. To my surprise he
invited me to his home for tea. It was a fine flat, elegantly
furnished and with more than a few *objets d'art*. Mayer was un-
married and lived there with his mother. Indeed, I could not
have imagined him to be married or to have close friends. He had
many acquaintances in many parts of the world, but I never
heard of anyone who claimed to be close to him or to know him
well. His reputation outside Palestine/Israel was particularly
high: his *Saracenic Heraldry*, *Mamluk Costume*, or *Islamic
Architects* were widely respected. I was too ignorant of these
subjects to form an opinion. That afternoon over tea we mainly
talked about orientalists in Jerusalem and abroad and about my
service in the British Military Administration of Eritrea. He also
asked a few questions about Ethiopian archaeology.

He had travelled widely in pursuit of his career and was an
assiduous attender of professional conferences, even at a time
long before this epidemic of congresses had reached its present
proportions. I recall an occasion at Jerusalem, not long after the
war, when one of Mayer's professorial colleagues asked me for
his temporary Oxford address. When I told him that it was
Christ Church, he expressed some surprise that even someone as
agnostic as Mayer should take lodgings in a Christian Church!
The questioner was not, of course, one of the more sophisticated
members of the Senatus Academicus, but such innocence would
be unthinkable today. It is often forgotten how dramatically the
world has shrunk since the war, and how much closer contacts
have become as a result of the highly peripatetic existence of

academics everywhere and of Israeli scholars in particular. Mayer was certainly their primary precursor.

On a visit to Oxford in 1948 he came to see us in our modest and extremely run-down lodgings. Being acquainted with his own tastefully appointed home, I was impressed with his tact and composure in the face of such ugliness. He turned out to be an agreeable guest and was one of the few of our visitors who did not require a conducted tour of Oxford; he was well versed in its art and architecture.

One of the last times I saw Mayer was at the 1954 Orientalist Congress at Cambridge. We were staying at the same college, and one morning, when I was about to go for a walk before breakfast, I ran into an uncharacteristically distraught Professor Mayer, in his usual sombre, formal, and elegant attire. Did I know when tailors' shops at Cambridge opened in the morning? I said I supposed it would be about 9 o'clock. Well, he feared in that case he would have to do without breakfast. The causal nexus between those two propositions was not immediately obvious to me, but he explained that one of his jacket buttons had come off and he could not possibly go to breakfast in college in a state of virtual undress. My assurances that nobody was going to notice the absence of a button, especially one that was in any event redundant, did not put his mind at rest. However, he had the button in his possession and even produced needle and thread from his pocket—but no tailor until 9 o'clock! I volunteered to sew the button on for him back in college in good time for breakfast. He was cheered, but it had to be done there and then. So the great L. A. Mayer had his jacket restored to full splendour right outside King's College Chapel. He was immensely grateful, while I expressed the hope that my fiasco with his Arabic text fifteen years ago had now been redeemed by my prowess with the needle. He pretended not to understand, but he laughed—the only time such a relaxed gesture had occurred in my experience. I was sad when he died suddenly in 1959, aged only 64. I had long ceased to think of him as the Rasputin-like figure I had imagined him to be in the 1930s.

* * *

Norman Bentwich (1883-1971), though a part-time Professor of International Relations at Jerusalem (one of those posts created

entirely *ad hominem* and at that time wholly outside the range of
the university's curriculum), was known to me mainly as a man
of affairs and as a friend of remarkable innocence and purity of
character. He impinged on my interest in both Jerusalem and in
Ethiopia. A member of a well-known English Zionist family,
several of whom had settled in Palestine, Norman was active
throughout his life in the areas of law, philanthropy, authorship,
and good works generally. His wife was at one stage chairman of
the London County Council, and he fitted into the role of
husband and escort of the chairman of that (then) august body
with the same good humour and self-effacement with which he
discharged all his duties. Yet in Palestine, despite long service in
and to the country, he was always a little too English (as indeed
was his wife) and a trifle too distant from the Hebrew language
and milieu to be other than somewhat ill at ease in the rough-and-
tumble of the Yishuv. The title of his book *Wanderer between two
worlds* was a most telling description of his life and career.

Norman Bentwich was born in London. After practising law
there for only a short period, he went to Egypt in 1912 on
appointment as Commissioner of Courts and lecturer at the
Cairo Law School. During the First World War he served in the
army (he himself used to refer, with characteristic self-
deprecation, to his somewhat incongruous role in any military
organization) and saw action on the Palestine front. He stayed in
Palestine from 1920, when he was appointed Attorney General
in the new British Administration, until 1931, when the
Mandatary Government felt that his position in that crucial
appointment was no longer tenable. That view was understandable, despite the fact that Bentwich, like his friend Magnes, was a
keen advocate of Arab–Jewish accord. But there had been many
demonstrations against him and one attempt on his life. A
deputation of the Muslim–Christian Women's Association went
to see the High Commissioner to protest against Bentwich
remaining in office and declared that for the first time they were
unveiled in the presence of strange men and would not hesitate
to go further. (On this *Punch* commented; 'We hope not too
much further.')

In the following year N.B. was invited by the Hebrew University to fill the 'Chair of the International Law of Peace'. He
accepted, but stipulated that for half the academic year he need

not be resident at Jerusalem and would be free to engage in a variety of international activities. These included, among very many others, work on behalf of Jewish refugees from Germany, many missions in support of the Hebrew University, legal submissions on behalf of Ethiopia, and considerable endeavours to help the Falashas of Ethiopia (details will be given in the chapters on Ethiopia). It was in the last two contexts, as well as in connection with the Friends of the Hebrew University in London, that I saw a good deal of N.B. during the last thirty years of his life. And although we did not always see eye to eye on the subject of the Falashas, he was so lovable a character and motivated by such lofty ideals that not the slightest cloud ever disturbed our relations, even in the most contentious fields. We held many discussions, private and public, about the Falashas, the so-called Jews of Ethiopia, and disagreed in the most agreeable manner. He conceded that he knew little about the scholarly aspects of the subject but concluded our debates with the refrain, 'but I feel it in my bones'. The rejoinder that the seat of such knowledge was rather in the head made him chuckle.

On one occasion we happened to be in Ethiopia at the same time, he in pursuit of his Falasha work. He asked me to accompany him to an audience with Emperor Haile Sellassie, so that I could interpret for him. His Majesty was never enamoured of the idea of singling out the Falashas, one of His Ethiopian tribal groups, for special treatment. N.B. was prepared for that argument, both tactically and as an aspect of his universally applied philanthropy: 'Of course', he said, 'we shall offer help, educational and otherwise, to the neighbours of the Falashas as well. We want no discrimination.' To which Haile Sellassie retorted: 'But the Falashas' neighbours have neighbours, too!'

Norman Bentwich and I had met in Ethiopia on an earlier occasion. In 1943 he passed through Asmara, Eritrea (where I was then stationed), on his way to Addis Ababa to assist the Ethiopian Government in preparing legal drafts in connection with the Anglo-Ethiopian Treaty. On arrival at Asmara he asked my wife and myself to assemble at our home as many Asmara Jews, nearly all of Aden origin, as we could manage, as he wanted to give them a talk about the Hebrew University and then collect some money. We got quite a good number, but after the opening 'Shalom' N.B. spoke in English which none of his audience understood. I explained to him that they knew only Arabic, Hebrew, and Italian; but he continued in English quite undeterred by this information. When at the end he invited them to contribute to the Hebrew University, they hummed and hawed and said they would think about it and get in touch with me a little later. I knew they were not impecunious and approached them after a few days. Their chairman then told me quite categorically that they would not give money to a professor of the Hebrew University who could not speak to them in Hebrew. I explained that Professor Bentwich was a little out of practice, as he now lived mostly in England. The chairman then offered to assemble his friends at his home if I would give them a talk in Hebrew on Jerusalem and its university. In fact, he produced a large audience, and after my address he took me along the serried ranks of his minions (in both the English and the Hebrew sense of that word) and told everyone what he could afford to give. Eventually he transferred a few hundred pounds to Jerusalem.

N.B. gives a somewhat muddled account of his appearance at Asmara in his book *My seventy-seven years* (London, 1962) and also mixes up the reasons for my resignation, in 1946, from the British Military Administration. When I remonstrated with him about some of these inaccuracies, shortly after the book was published, he replied in his most disarming manner: 'Surely you know how bad I am about those boring pedantic facts!' He was a delightful man, so truly genuine, innocent, and good.

III

Hebrew and its Revival

The use of Hebrew as the principal language of the Jews of Palestine, and later of Israel, is of such paramount importance to the identity, indeed the creation, of a National Home that a few desultory observations on this subject must be included here. These remarks have, in the present context, inevitably to be of a general rather than a scholarly nature; and for this reason I do not propose to get involved in the semantics of the term 'revival', the appropriateness of which has at times been challenged in recent literature. For the same reason it is not my purpose here either to argue or to question whether Ben-Yehuda (to whose work I have briefly referred in the chapter on Talpioth) was the main agent of that revival or renaissance. What is not in doubt, however, is the fact that in the fourth quarter of the nineteenth century some very important changes affected the use and general circumstances of Hebrew, that is, it was transformed into the principal tongue of the main sector of the Jewish population in Palestine. Ben-Yehuda's role in that process was undoubtedly crucial, and his children were the first, for nearly two millennia, to speak Hebrew as their first and only language; in fact, it was in any meaningful sense also their mother tongue, for their parents never allowed any other language to be spoken in the home.

While Hebrew, in its various forms of Biblical, Rabbinic, and medieval, had of course always been well known to observant Jews as the language of prayer, first and foremost, as well as the vehicle of study and learning, it was not their everyday tongue of secular use. Some Jews had a ready facility for writing Hebrew, and in certain cases Hebrew was employed as a *lingua franca* when Jews met who had no other language in common. Until well into the second half of the nineteenth century those living in Palestine would generally continue to use the vernacular of their country of origin: thus oriental Jews usually spoke Arabic, while the Ashkenazi population (those originating mainly from Eastern

Europe) spoke Yiddish, an amalgam of Middle High German with Hebrew admixtures; and Sephardi families talked Ladino, a mixture of Spanish with Hebrew accretions. Both Yiddish and Ladino were normally written in Hebrew characters.

It is pointless to argue, as is often done, whether Hebrew was revived from death or merely from a moribund state. Of course, there had always been some people in Palestine who were able to use the language in some form, for some purposes, and with greater or lesser fluency. The revival, when it came, occurred in Palestine towards the end of the nineteenth century and was the result of a strong political, cultural, and social will and conviction. That will had existed, in part, also during the early years of the second half of the last century, some twenty years before the advent of Ben-Yehuda, but the latter proved to be the vital catalyst and the singleminded, indeed fanatical, agent in the process. And once the children, the younger generation, were Hebraized, the battle for Hebrew was virtually won.

From the time of Ben-Yehuda's campaign until the end of Ottoman rule towards the close of World War I (about 1881-1917), the struggle to establish Hebrew as *the* language of Jewish Palestine was hard and unrelenting. It involved the displacement of such 'indigenous' tongues as Yiddish, Ladino, and Arabic, and the restriction of German and French to relations with foreigners and as a key to European culture. I have already indicated that, despite the existence of a British Administration for close on thirty years, the influence of English remained relatively minor until its massive burgeoning after World War II when it became the principal foreign medium of communication, ousting German, French, and other once competing linguistic manifestations. Hebrew had first been used in an official, quasi-governmental context in General Allenby's proclamation upon entering Jerusalem in 1917, where Hebrew appeared together with Arabic and other languages considered important in Palestine.

But until that consummation Ben-Yehuda and others had to labour hard to fashion a medium that could respond to all practical everyday requirements. Of course, the fact that the various sectors of the Jewish population in Palestine had no common language at that time greatly strengthened the claims of Hebrew to universal acceptability. Not only did Hebrew stand above the rivalries between existing Jewish vernaculars, but above all it had a glorious literary past and was the vehicle of one of the great literatures of antiquity as well as being the language of the Book created by the Hebrews and spread across most of the civilized world in hundreds of translations. By its linkage with the Hebrew past in ancient Palestine it also established some sort of claim, or at any rate a clear marker, to continuity of language and presence in the Promised Land. No other tongue could have brought about a similar cohesion and a comparable fervour in the cause of Jewish renaissance in Palestine. This is also one of the main reasons why the *Sprachenkampf* ('language struggle') between Hebrew and German that raged just before the First World War in the schools of the German-Jewish *Hilfsverein* and in the Haifa Technical College was bound to be decided in favour of Hebrew.

The fashioning of a technical vocabulary to express the needs of science and progress in the modern world was, in most respects, one of the lesser problems for the language innovators and updaters. Ben-Yehuda has pointed out, in the long introduction to his multi-volume dictionary of Hebrew, that the filling of gaps in the vocabulary of everyday life, such as the concept of 'tickling', etc, was far more complicated. And very sensibly, when all the manifold resources of Hebrew, throughout the millennia, were unable to supply what was wanted, he would turn to Arabic, a sister Semitic tongue, and see whether it could help and a suitable term might be adapted from its ample means.

In the pronunciation of Hebrew by contemporary speakers we usually see their native tongue and its habits reflected in their phonetic realization. That was certainly predominantly the case in my time, half a century ago, when most people were immigrants of different vintages and different attainments, although even then there were, of course, those who had been born in the country or were the offspring of parents whose own parents were indigenous speakers of Hebrew. Those 'natural' native speakers had developed an 'accent', a distinctive mode, of uttering and pronouncing the language which is nowadays described as 'Israeli Hebrew'. It is curious how this distinctive accent has evolved without any traceable phonetic features of the particular European languages that were the substrata in the linguistic habituation of individuals or groups. Thus the prevalent Israeli accent can be discerned and identified even in the *foreign* speech patterns of native Hebrew speakers, that is, in the manner in which they produce English or any other language. It is not surprising that a foreigner speaking, say, English at once reveals his native tongue as being French, German, Italian, etc., but it is remarkable that in such a short time and from such disparate phonetic origins a unified and easily identifiable Israeli Hebrew 'accent' or speech pattern should have evolved so readily.

The area of syntax, sentence construction, is probably the linguistic sphere in which contemporary Hebrew has moved farthest away from its historical origins. The influence of European languages in this context has been remarkably pervasive, and in essence the shape of the average modern Hebrew sentence in an ordinary piece of prose or speech differs very little from normal European modes. In this area the Semitic prosopopoeia, the original face and garb, have all but disappeared. The exceptions are writers like Agnon who deliberately adhere to a particular type of traditional model or use a style of rhetorical and flowery phraseology (termed *melitzah*) that is (or was) highly prized in elevated writing in Hebrew.

Most resistant to change has been the morphology of Hebrew, the *système fermé* of verb formation in particular which is so central in all Semitic languages. It is only in very recent times that I discern the force of analogy making greater inroads, particularly as far as vowels are concerned, which seem to succumb more readily to analogical pressures. It may well be that more recent immigrants supplied the initial impetus in malformations and outright mistakes, but these forces of ignorance no doubt worked hand in hand with native pressures in the direction of eliminating 'aberrant' or 'irregular' forms. A situation may now be envisaged in Hebrew when quite marked problems of diglossia may arise —and the gulf between the common colloquial medium and the literary and literate as well as learned language may widen very considerably. In that case we might witness a position not all that far removed from that in Arabic.

From the outset the Hebrew Language Council (later Academy) has fulfilled an important function in word-creation and general advice, but in the nature of things language academies, however desirable their precepts may be in theory, will always be overtaken by events. Language develops in capricious ways and, although I am often irked myself by the fact that newcomers to Hebrew, ignorant of its history and habits ('rules'), should turn out to be arbiters of what is 'right' or 'wrong', in the end it is the 'mistake', the creative malformation, that rules—and determines language evolution. The day can easily be foreseen when children at school in Israel will no longer be able to read Genesis or Judges with fair ease, and the Hebrew Bible will be as strange to them as, say, Chaucer is to English-speaking people. And this is scarcely surprising, considering the very different time-scale. A normative grammar of contemporary Hebrew would have to be re-written at very frequent intervals and would be caught in constant pursuit of an extremely elusive and ever changing quarry. A fellow-student of mine in the 1930s, H. B. Rosén, has become the prophet (and a very learned and informed one, whether or not one agrees with him on all aspects) of the historical inevitability and indeed of the authentic right of natural linguistic growth, without constraint by any imposed authority (whose Canute-like labours would in any event be doomed to failure). Whether the wish of many (which I share) to strengthen the inherited and traditional components of Hebrew, perhaps through study of classical sources and extended education, at the expense of foreign accretions and distortion of the historical links, has any chance of success must now seem fairly doubtful.

Had English been adopted as the language of Palestine (as had sometimes been mooted by a few), it would naturally have opened all the lines of communication, in practical and cultural terms, which only a language with that unique prestige and power can achieve. But it could never have brought about the cohesion, national and cultural, for which Hebrew, with all its difficulties of acquisition (and possibly *because* of them), was fitted in a very special and exclusive way. Moreover, those of us who have seen the dichotomy in education in many parts of Asia and Africa, with the vernacular assigned to elementary teaching and English to the higher ranges of education, must be profoundly grateful to the founders of the Hebrew University who averted such a calamity. For bifurcation of this kind alienates the intellectuals from their native ambience and renders the indigenous language well-nigh useless for most processes of refined thought.

I have long considered the revival of Hebrew as the finest achievement of the Jewish renaissance in Palestine/Israel and, indeed, as one of the most genuinely creative accomplishments of our time.

IV

Return to Jerusalem

The University

The British Military Administration in Eritrea (where I had
served for most of the war) continued for fully seven years after
the end of hostilities in August 1945, because the United Nations
(by that time, alas, no longer united) had much difficulty in
deciding what to do with the former Italian colonies. The big
power game impinged even on so small a cog as Eritrea; and thus
this *colonia primogenita* (as the Italians used to call their first
colony) was not federated with Ethiopia, as an internally
autonomous unit within the ancient Empire, until the autumn of
1952. While my wife and I had come to love Eritrea and her
people (and indeed still do), shortly after the end of the war we
felt that it was time to think of a peace-time occupation and
return to Jerusalem. Apart from war service in Eritrea, which
had begun not long after my graduation from the university at
Jerusalem, I had obviously never held a regular job. I had,
perhaps rather unimaginatively, at no time thought of a career
other than within the framework of a university. I had greatly
enjoyed the good fortune of being able to work in the British
Military Administration of Eritrea and to learn a little about the
problems of administration, publishing, applied language work
of a quasi-academic kind, and, above all, I had benefited from
close contacts with Eritreans, Ethiopians, and many British
superiors as well as colleagues (as will be set out in greater detail
in Part Two). I did not at that time think of a career in the
colonial service, but I imagined that my experience with
Ethiopian languages *in situ* had fitted me for a minor university
post in that field. Of course, I was aware that openings in that
recondite subject were few and far between—if, indeed, they
existed at all.

In these circumstances I felt very lucky when Dr D. W.
Senator, the Administrator of the Hebrew University, wrote to

me early in 1946 and suggested that I might be interested in a newly created post in the Academic Secretariat of Jerusalem University, which might conceivably lead eventually to a transfer to the academic side. The latter possibility, vague as it was, constituted the greatest attraction to me. A few days after the arrival of Senator's letter I received, quite independently, a similar one from the Academic Secretary of the university, A. Ibn-Zahav, who had been in that post since the foundation of the Hebrew University and was soon to retire prematurely, partly for health reasons and partly to devote himself full-time to his literary activities. He was in those days a well-known Hebrew writer and had published several novels, particularly a well-regarded one on the theme of Shylock. I regret that his reputation as a writer is somewhat eclipsed now, and few of the present generation seem to have heard of him. There were two other gifted writers then working under Ibn-Zahav in the Academic Secretariat, Yisrael Zarhi, who died tragically young, and Haim Toren who became Secretary (later Managing Director) of the Magnes University Press.

· The new post about which Senator and Ibn-Zahav wrote to me was largely concerned with the 'foreign relations' of the university's academic secretariat. It appeared to involve the influx of American students, ex-servicemen, who came to Jerusalem on study grants offered by the Veterans Administration of the American Government to those who had served in the armed forces during the war. They knew little or no Hebrew, a hitherto unknown phenomenon in the annals of the Hebrew University, and some liaison officer was required to deal with their integration. Furthermore, with the end of the war it was hoped to expand the university, to recruit new staff, and to promote existing teachers whose advancement had been held up on account of the difficulties of establishing contact with experts abroad (quite apart from the scarcity of funds which had failed to arrive from the main centres of support during the war). These negotiations had to be conducted in languages other than Hebrew.

I felt that I probably ought to accept this post if a firm offer materialized. The university authorities now had the task of persuading the *Histadruth*, the trade union organization, to agree to the recruitment of someone who was neither *in situ* nor a member of any trade union. I, on my part, had to negotiate my release from the British Military Administration in Eritrea with my superiors, the Military Governor, the Chief Secretary, and the Chief Political Secretary. I think the latter task turned out to be the simpler proposition by a long chalk, and it was not until the autumn of 1946 that all negotiations were completed on both sides.

It was a great wrench to leave Eritrea and Ethiopia, and in the uncertainties of the immediate post-war period I was very anxious about the safety of the collection of precious books which I had assembled and acquired in my four-and-a-half years in the Horn of Africa. These books had to be left behind to await sea transport, if and when that became available, while my wife and I flew to Cairo and from there took the train, across the Suez canal and the Sinai peninsula, to Lydda (Lod), then the principal junction in the Palestine Railways network. For the first few weeks we stayed with my parents-in-law in North Talpioth until we could move into a small flat, opposite their house, on top of Dr Reiner's home. In the chapter on North Talpioth I have already spoken about Dr Reiner's personality and the wonderful panoramic views over Jerusalem from that small apartment.

The Jerusalem to which we returned was a very different place from the tranquil city I had left nearly five years earlier. At that time internal Palestine hostilities had been suspended for the duration; and although I had been back to Jerusalem two or three times for a week's leave, we were not entirely prepared for what we now faced. In the interval the Stern group, whose eponymous leader had been shot in 1942, had recommenced their misguided, indeed nefarious, activities and had assassinated Lord Moyne, the British Minister Resident at Cairo in 1944 (in 1948 they were to do the same to the UN Mediator, Count Bernadotte)—unspeakable perversions of nationalistic fervour. Also in the interval, the most sanguinary of all deeds had been committed by Begin and his *Irgun* movement, the blowing up of a wing of the King David Hotel, killing ninety-one Arabs, Britons, and Jews. Of course, during those same years the full horrors of the holocaust in Europe had been revealed, while the gates of Palestine remained barred to the survivors.

This seemingly irreconcilable conflict between Jews and the British Administration was now raging at its fiercest and was soon to be followed by a renewal of Arab–Jewish hostilities. The Palestine of the 1930s, of *havlaga*, 'self-restraint', had disappeared for ever. This was, perhaps, my first experience of the transitoriness of human affairs of which the young, in the nature of things, cannot be aware. Soon security zones were to be established everywhere, barbed wire was to become ubiquitous, as were identity cards and passes, body searches, bombs and machine-gun fire. The atmosphere was one of despondency and gloom, and it became inexorably clear that a violent denouement of the Palestine tangle could not be long delayed. It seemed to me then (and still does) that the Foreign Office under Bevin (for the nominally responsible Colonial Office played an increasingly subordinate role) and the Jewish Agency under Ben-Gurion were excessively suspicious of each other's intentions and highly unimaginative in their estimate of the long-term consequences of their respective actions. Personal vanities and dislikes by the decision-makers on both sides played an inordinately crucial part in those events, and petulance influenced the conduct of affairs, from which such unworthy elements ought to be absent, at any rate in an ideal world. I do not know whether students of politics have made a careful study of the importance of face-saving as well as of personal animosities at the apex of international relations; many instances can, of course, be adduced where such essentially extraneous sentiments have made a doleful and decisive impact.

* * *

This then was the atmosphere in which I returned to Jerusalem University in the autumn of 1946. Inevitably events in the country at large cast their shadow over the university as well, but coming back to my *alma mater* even in these circumstances was not without emotion. Five or six years earlier I had left as an impecunious student; now I came home, not to riches but to a position which afforded as much security as was needed at that stage of one's career. My wife, who had held senior secretarial positions (in status rather than salary) in Eritrea, got an appointment as personal assistant to one of the Under-Secretaries in the Palestine Government. In the university as well as in private life discussion of the Palestine situation was now all-pervasive, and the touchstone of personal and political views was everyone's attitude towards violence and terrorism. To the extent that it was consonant with one's integrity, one tried to avoid debate with the adherents of the school that believed 'history had to be written in blood', but it was not always possible to avoid such confrontations.

Work in the Academic Secretariat and in the university in general was as congenial as I had imagined. It was, of course, a fairly general experience of many of those returning from war service that they came back to positions of lesser seniority than those they had occupied in the exceptional circumstances of that long emergency. I was fully conscious from the outset that helping to govern an occupied enemy territory was headier stuff than trying to integrate American students or writing letters to famous professors abroad enquiring about the academic merits of university teachers proposed for promotion. Keeping in touch with the various offices of the Friends of the Hebrew University in many parts of Europe, particularly the United Kingdom, and in the United States was another of my duties.

The American students, men and women, who had come to pursue their studies at Jerusalem were clearly strongly motivated, for otherwise they could have had a very much more comfortable life back home. Only a small minority among them knew enough Hebrew to attend lectures. In the past, new immigrant freshmen either arrived with an adequate knowledge of the language or were absorbed at once into a Hebrew ambience that facilitated quick linguistic adaptation. The Americans were until then the first and only sizeable group to live as a self-contained unit whose social and private life continued to be conducted in English, a language and civilization of which they had no reason to be ashamed—unlike earlier waves of students who had been immigrants (which was not necessarily the case with these Americans) and were anxious to discard the language of their recent oppressors as speedily as possible.

The years 1946-8 were not a good period in which to see Jerusalem at its best, and I had great sympathy for the recently arrived American students having to find their way in such exceptionally difficult circumstances. No wonder they found comfort in their own tightly knit group and did not exploit all available opportunities of learning Hebrew expeditiously and smoothly. While research students were frequently better prepared than their local counterparts, this was not true of American undergraduates whose general education seemed to have more serious gaps than products of the European or Palestinian educational systems.

I was unfortunate as well as obtuse with the very first American girl I had to help with her registration. She had an accent to which I had not had any prior exposure. To the question about her father's occupation she replied that he was a 'rider'. 'Oh, a jockey?', I asked, 'No, an odour', she retorted. In my slow-wittedness I had not realized that he was, of course, a 'writer', an 'author'. Another student, to whom I had mildly complained that he was an hour late for our appointment, told me the allegedly true story of one of his professors in the States who was notoriously unpunctual. For his first lecture he had been half an hour late, and when finally he arrived he told his waiting class that the train from his rather distant home to the college had lost its way, and in the end it had returned to its point of departure. The following week he was almost equally late and reported that he had attended a university lunch, but when he got up towards the end of the meal and took his leave of his two neighbours on either side, he found that one of them was dead: 'Now, could I depart in these circumstances just because I might be late for my lecture?', he asked. On the third occasion he had decided not to entrust himself to public transport but to take a taxi all the way to the university. To make quite sure that he had adequate funds on him, he went to his bank early in the morning. On arrival there he found a large throng of people and police outside the bank; there had been a bank-robbery. The professor did not wish to get involved in this turmoil lest he be delayed once more, so he ran away. The police came after him in the belief that they had discovered the culprit. It took him a long time to establish his innocence and *bona fides*—too long at any rate to be on time for his lecture. On the next occasion he got his taxi and reached his destination on time, but when it pulled up outside the college, the taxi driver found him slumped in the back—dead! 'You see,' my American student friend added, 'it does not pay to worry over punctuality.' I had no convincing answer to that.

One weekend, at about that time, I took my wife to Kallia (Qalya) on the north-western shore of the Dead Sea. Kallia is situated only a very short distance to the north of Qumran, the site where the Dead Sea scrolls were discovered (in fact, at just about that time). The descent from Jerusalem (2,500 feet above sea level) to the Dead Sea, the deepest depression on the surface of the earth (nearly 1,300 feet below sea level), is spectacular. The climate, at any rate in the winter, is wonderfully balmy; and lying (for swimming is not required) on the surface of the salty water (ten times denser than that of the Mediterranean) is a singular experience. In those days the Kallia Hotel was one of the very best in the Near East, vying in comfort, luxury, and cuisine with the King David Hotel in Jerusalem and Shepheard's in Cairo. And its location in what was then the well-nigh complete seclusion of the Dead Sea region, away from centres of population and the turmoil of that period, was an added attraction.

During that particular weekend the hotel was fairly empty, no doubt an aspect of the disturbed times in which we were living. One of our fellow-guests was on his own and he made a rather forlorn impression. He looked very English, and one evening after dinner, as we were all sipping our coffee in the spacious lounge, we asked him whether he would care to join us. He thanked us very politely and came across to us, but there was an element of hesitation in his acceptance. He stayed with us for the rest of the evening and joined us again the next morning, this time on his own initiative. He then confessed that last night he had at first been reluctant, although he felt rather lonely, because these days 'so many of us' were lured into ambushes or trapped into revealing military secrets. It was a sad, indeed melancholy, reflection of the grim realities of the time. Curiously enough, I still remember that fleeting encounter and the initial look of apprehension in his eyes.

One of the most rewarding facets of living in Jerusalem again and being connected with its university was the chance of meeting one's former teachers, Polotsky, Tur-Sinai, Buber, Segal, Roth, and others. And, of course, some of these as well as Magnes, Scholem, and Senator also offered an opportunity of talking about the situation in Palestine, the seemingly hopeless cycle of violence in which we appeared to be locked. Roth and Senator in particular, though pessimistic themselves, offered comfort and at any rate small glimmers of hope. But I had the feeling, rightly as it unhappily turned out, that they were whistling in the dark. I saw a good deal at that time of both these men: of Senator in connection with the affairs of the university, and of Roth because we were engaged in organizing an international congress. There were many anxious discussions, both within the university and with Ben Zvi, the chairman of the Jewish National Council, whether this was an appropriate moment to bring hundreds of visitors to a country torn by strife, bombs, and bloodshed. Many took the view that we had to behave as if we lived in normal times. We also spoke to senior representatives of the Palestine Government who expressed willingness to issue visas to all *bona fide* members of the congress, provided Roth and I guaranteed their eventual departure. This was not a request which people like ourselves, with no powers of compulsion, could easily comply with.

* * *

One of my more interesting tasks was the drafting of letters to distinguished referees abroad who were to pronounce on the promotion of members of the teaching staff. They had to form a judgement that was principally based on the candidate's published work, but if they knew him personally they were also invited to say something about his suitability in general. Naturally his standing in the world of relevant scholarship was also an important consideration. The number of lecturers proposed for promotion was particularly large at that time, partly because of the blockage caused by the Second World War, and partly because the university had just introduced a new academic rank modelled on the American system, that of Associate Professor, intermediate between the grades of lecturer and full professor. Hitherto there had only been full professors and, in a few rare cases, professors *ad personam*; the latter were not inferior in attainments, but no established Chair was available for them. This grade was now abolished.

I attended a few meetings of the Standing Committee of Senate and listened with fascination to the consideration of the replies received from abroad. Of course, I merely went to those meetings in a secretarial capacity and had neither voice nor vote in the deliberations—except, perhaps, when the wording of the reply required a linguistic gloss. This was excellent training for my future career when in the Universities of Oxford, St Andrews, Manchester, and London I was a substantive member of such committees and had to make up my mind on similar questions which at times posed difficult as well as delicate problems. I recall vividly one particular case at Jerusalem which still causes much amusement. An elderly lecturer in history had been put forward for promotion to the new grade of Associate Professor. Among those consulted abroad was the Oxford Reader in Jewish Studies, the late Cecil Roth, brother of Leon Roth, the Jerusalem Professor of Philosophy. The letters of enquiry asked specifically in each case whether such promotion would be envisaged if the candidate were serving in the addressee's university; and letters to Britain also explained that the rank of Associate Professor corresponded to that of Reader in the United Kingdom.

To my letter (in English), addressed to Cecil Roth at Oxford, a one-line reply in Hebrew was received which read in translation: 'He is like a peg that is not to be removed from its place.' This cryptic rejoinder kept the committee in session for a whole hour. The members included some of the greatest Biblical and Talmudic exegetes of the day, concordances were consulted, and the discussion was animated as well as erudite, but they were firmly stymied. Did the writer of this cryptogram himself know what his one-liner was meant to convey? At one stage there was a suggestion to write back to him for elucidation, but then it was realized, justly, that some of the intellectual giants of the Hebrew University present at that meeting were in a much better position to form an opinion on the candidate's competence. After all, in some instances those enquiries abroad were sent out mainly to fulfil certain formal requirements and regulations. Whenever I met Cecil Roth in later years I was greatly tempted to ask him about the interpretation of that by then famous sentence and tell him about the hermeneutical crux he had posed to one of the most learned assemblies in the world, at any rate in this field, but I never summoned up the courage to do so.

One of the saddest and most pathetic spectacles during my brief period of service in the Jerusalem Academic Secretariat was the almost daily appearance of a scholar who had arrived in Palestine shortly after the war. His mind seemed very disturbed, but I was told that he had been a notable exponent in Europe of his extremely recondite discipline. He was under the impression that he had a professorial appointment in the Hebrew University and would try and persuade all and sundry to come to his lectures. He would go into a vacant lecture hall and hold forth to the empty room; occasionally someone would take pity on him and sit in the otherwise deserted hall. At the end of each month he would go to the Financial Secretary, hand him an envelope filled with money, and ask him to disburse it to him as his salary. It may all have seemed funny to us, but in reality it was a painfully disturbing and pitifully poignant scene, his mind unhinged by the cruel events through which he had lived.

* * *

When I prepared to return to Jerusalem from Eritrea, the Chief Secretary under whom I had served at Asmara, Colonel Gerald Kenyon-Slaney, gave me a letter for transmission to his erstwhile neighbour Sir Henry Gurney, the Chief Secretary of the Palestine Government. When I called on Sir Henry in Jerusalem, I found a quietly impressive man about whom I shall say a little more presently. Our conversation touched on my work in Eritrea-Ethiopia, on the situation in Palestine, and on mutual acquaintances. It was not a long talk, and I was therefore more than a little surprised when my friend and mentor Dr D. W. Senator told me, within two or three months of my return to the university, that Sir Henry Gurney had been in touch with him to enquire whether he would release me for service in the Palestine Government. Senator added that he would be in favour of such a move, but I think he somewhat overestimated what I might be able to achieve in the Secretariat, the Headquarters of the Government. I was attracted to this proposal in many ways, particularly as I had enjoyed the work of government in Eritrea, but I had no illusions either about my status within the much larger and infinitely more prominent framework of Palestine or, indeed, about the durability of the British Mandate. The latter view was shared by hardly anyone before the British Government announced its future withdrawal from Palestine. To me it had seemed, ever since our return to Jerusalem, that that outcome could not be long delayed.

I sought the counsel of both Magnes and Roth who had no doubt that I should accept the offer once it was properly confirmed. I knew I would leave the university with genuine misgivings, but at the same time I felt strongly that neither university nor government administration was my ultimate goal. Whether my ambition of becoming a university teacher would ever be fulfilled I had no means of judging, for I had not done enough in scholarship to justify an academic appointment, nor did those anxious and disturbed times seem propitious for the serious entertainment of such hopes. The general situation in Palestine was going from bad to worse, and in these circumstances it seemed to me marginally more sensible to turn to government, however lowly the level.

I was called to interview by the Civil Service Commissioner and was offered a post in the Palestine Secretariat, with the chance—but not the certainty—of transferring to the Colonial Service in the then still remote contingency (or so it was thought) of the Mandate being surrendered some time in the future.

My parting from my colleagues in the Academic Secretariat was sad, but I could never envisage a real severing of ties from my *alma mater* or from the professors who had taught me. My debt to, and affection for, the Hebrew University has never diminished, although the university has changed out of all recognition over the forty-odd years since then, and all my teachers, with the happy exception of Polotsky, have passed on. I feel confident that in an Israel and a Near East of well-nigh constant turmoil the University of Jerusalem has stood out as a beacon of enlightenment and as one of the great and non-controversial achievements of the Hebrew renaissance.

The Palestine Government

I can only speak of the Palestine Government in strictly limited and clearly defined ways: as a junior First Division Officer during the last year of its existence; as a citizen of Palestine throughout my years as an undergraduate at Jerusalem; and as one who has made some desultory study of the history of the British Mandate in Palestine and has had a little experience of colonial administration—in Eritrea in a practical sense, and later on at the Oxford University Institute of Colonial Studies in more theoretical ways. The few and rather superficial reflections which I offer in the following remarks are based on my own experience and observations. Anyone who wishes to look at a reliable, dispassionate, and readable account of the British

Mandate in Palestine cannot do better than study Christopher Sykes's *Crossroads to Israel: Palestine from Balfour to Bevin* (London, 1965).

When we returned to Jerusalem in the autumn of 1946, General Sir Alan Cunningham was High Commissioner. My wife and I were again living at North Talpioth and, as I explained earlier, the High Commissioner in his beautiful Government House was our nearest neighbour—yet socially and hierarchically a very long distance away. There was, however, one tenuous link: Cunningham had been GOC East African Forces in 1940-1 and had led the Ethiopian campaigns from the south, culminating in his entry into Addis Ababa in May 1941. Ethiopia was probably his greatest military success, and I had been told by my chief in Eritrea, General J. M. Benoy, the Military Governor, that Cunningham cherished his memories of Ethiopia and was likely to welcome an opportunity of exchanging reminiscences with someone who had served in that country for several years. But it was only when Sir Henry Gurney, the Chief Secretary of the Palestine Government, told me that I should sign the High Commissioner's visitors' book that I walked the short distance to Government House and signed the book. A few days later I received a summons to call on His Excellency. This was the first time that I entered this fine building, which I had admired from a distance throughout my student days and from which I had seen Sir Harold MacMichael's Rolls Royce issue almost daily. Government House turned out to be even more impressive than I had imagined, and Sir Alan Cunningham was even finer-looking than I had gathered from the many photographs of the Commander-in Chief that were published during the Ethiopian campaigns.

The audience lasted barely more than twenty minutes, and the conversation touched, predictably, on Ethiopia and the Emperor, my thoughts on returning to Jerusalem after such a long absence, and the sort of work I was expected to do at the university. After I joined the Palestine Government my wife and I saw the High Commissioner only on two or three social occasions. But twenty years later, when I was chairman of the Anglo-Ethiopian Society in London, I invited Sir Alan and Lady Cunningham (he had since married, at the age of 64) to be our guests of honour. By then he was 80, still good-looking and sprightly, and we had a chance of a longish talk on Ethiopia and Palestine.

I mention General Cunningham, the last High Commissioner of Palestine, mainly because I wish to say a few words about the seven High Commissioners who governed the country during the twenty-eight years of the British Mandate and whose individual style of administration is connected with distinctly marked periods in the history of that time. Of the seven British governors of Palestine, one was a professional politician and a past and future Cabinet Minister, two were lifelong colonial civil servants, and the remaining four were professional soldiers (two of them Field Marshals). It has always been said that the soldiers were by far the most successful of the British rulers of Palestine. On the surface this judgement appears to be accurate, but it does not allow for the incidence of fortuitous factors; and the two colonial governors had a bad press even before they arrived, almost as a matter of principle.

By a curious fluke I had been personally acquainted, albeit superficially, with the first and the last High Commissioner only. This was due entirely to their longevity, for Lord Samuel was 93 when he died and Sir Alan Cunningham 95. As will be seen later, I knew the first Viscount Samuel's son and heir, Edwin, fairly closely; and it was he who first introduced me to his father when he gave a lecture on British institutions at the Schocken Library at Jerusalem. After the war I met him fairly regularly, though always briefly, when he took the chair at meetings of the Executive Council of the Friends of the Hebrew University in London.

Sir Herbert Samuel's appointment as the first British High Commissioner was greeted with unbridled enthusiasm by Jews in Palestine and elsewhere. In his governorship of the Holy Land, the first Jew in such a position for two millennia, they saw the fulfilment of Messianic hopes. In many respects the reality turned out to be somewhat different. Samuel's policy of even-handedness and fairness, of 'equality of obligation' (in the official terminology), though scrupulously adhered to, was not appreciated by either of the two principal communities of Palestine. It became increasingly clear that, whatever line might be adopted, one or other of the main sectors of the population would feel aggrieved. Today, while Samuel's name may still be known in Israel, it is not held in any particular esteem. Yet in most senses he was by far the most experienced and probably also the ablest man to govern Palestine.

There are two principal grievances laid at Samuel's door by the Jewish population. Both go back to 1921. It was in that year that the Mufti of Jerusalem died, and Samuel sanctioned the succession to that office of the late Mufti's half-brother Hajj Amin el-Husseini, although the latter had a well-known record of political agitation and violence. No doubt it was the High Commissioner's aim to placate the Arabs by this gesture, and his expectation that senior office and responsibility would cool the anti-Jewish ardour of the new Mufti was not entirely unreasonable. I do not think that Samuel can in fairness be blamed for not foreseeing the terrible future antics of this violent and unscrupulous man. Nor did the Jews of Palestine react with indignation at that time, though voices of warning were heard, and with hindsight this remains no doubt the most criticizable act of the first High Commissioner.

This is not the place to rehearse the complex history of the greater Syrian area in the immediate aftermath of the First World War. By virtue of the San Remo decisions conferring upon Britain the Mandate over Palestine, both sides of the River Jordan came under the rule of the new British Administration. The territory to the east of the Jordan was sparsely populated, and no ordered authority was exercised over it. Samuel had promised it some form of self-government, and when the Amir (later King) Abdullah ibn Hussein arrived with an army to claim the country of Moab, Transjordan, there was no one to impede him. The 1921 Conference on Palestine, dominated by two pro-Zionist statesmen, Churchill and Samuel, ratified this *fait accompli*, confirmed Abdullah in his fiefdom, though under the authority of the High Commissioner, and established the separate status of Transjordan. Samuel was later to be blamed for detaching the territory to the east of the Jordan from the Palestine to which Jewish immigration was permitted under the terms of the Mandate. But at the time the Zionist organization, including the revisionist leader Jabotinsky, acquiesced in this arrangement without demur.

Samuel's governance of Palestine was criticized by Arabs and Jews in about equal measure; it was punctuated by periods of Arab unrest, riots, and the occasional suspension of further Jewish immigration. In 1925 the first (and only Jewish) High Commissioner left the country which he had entered five years earlier amidst such extravagant hopes on the part of the Jewish population. He was succeeded by Field-Marshal Lord Plumer, whose three-year rule is generally regarded as the golden period in the annals of the British Mandate in Palestine. The quiescence of the country during his High Commissionership no doubt owed something to Lord Plumer's personality, but there were also many external as well as fortuitous factors which made this period so uncharacteristically peaceful.

His appointment, the advent of a 'simple' soldier, was not welcomed by the Yishuv, who imagined that a more intellectual governor would have greater sympathy with the aspirations of the National Home than this conservative man of the Empire. No assessment could have been more awry. Lord Plumer was simple in his mode of life, but he was so patently straightforward and honest, as well as so decided in what he expected of the two sectors of the population, that he soon became the most generally respected of the British proconsuls in Palestine. He was the only High Commissioner who could afford, thanks to the improved security situation, to go on sightseeing walks through Jerusalem entirely unescorted; yet his ultra-Englishness, in attire and general bearing, made him a well-recognizable potential target.

The politicians in both communities soon appreciated that it was Lord Plumer's very simplicity of manner that was proving so effective. To a Jewish delegation who questioned him about his policy he replied that he had none, since his only duty was to carry out the instructions of His Majesty's Government. And when an Arab deputation complained to him that he had stood to attention during the playing of the Jewish national anthem, he invited them to get a national anthem as well and he would then stand up for theirs in the same way. He was equally unperturbed when told by another delegation that in certain circumstances they could not be responsible for law and order in Jerusalem. He assured them that there was no need for them to trouble, as it was for him to shoulder that responsibility.

Lord Plumer's successor as High Commissioner was Sir John Chancellor, whose period of office, 1928–31, was a time of considerable unrest and turmoil. His background as a colonial governor, with experience in Africa and the West Indies, has often been blamed for the turbulent events during his administration, but this is far too simplistic an explanation and takes no account of the constantly changing and highly volatile situation in the country. When, in 1931, the Prime Minister, Ramsay MacDonald, and Dr Weizmann were seeking a replacement for Sir John Chancellor, they were both thinking of someone in the image of Lord Plumer. The choice fell eventually upon General Sir Arthur Wauchope, whose term of office from 1931 to 1938 turned out to be the longest during the British Mandate.

When Wauchope was appointed it could not have been foreseen, despite all the ominous portents in Central Europe, that his administration would have to cope with a sudden and very significant increase of Jewish immigration, following upon Hitler's advent to power, and a concomitant growth in Arab restiveness and indeed violence. The number of immigrants rose from about 4,000 in 1931 to 62,000 in 1935. Surprisingly, those entering Palestine from Europe during the years 1933-5 did not come predominantly from Hitler's Germany (only about 12 per cent) but continued to issue from Poland as in the past (about 43 per cent). Christopher Sykes, in his excellent book on the British Mandate, thinks that 'this puzzling state of affairs . . . was in part due to the fact that most of the Jews in Palestine were Slavs and, as the choice of immigrants was democratically controlled, it followed . . . that the Slav majority saw to it that Slav preponderance was not lost in the suddenly changed circumstances of the Nazi era'. But he adds, justly, that 'Zionism had never meant as much to Western Jews, with their long tradition of assimilation, as to Eastern Jews with their long tradition of escape from persecution'.

These then were some of the grave problems with which Sir Arthur Wauchope's stewardship of Palestine was faced almost from the outset. The new High Commissioner had reached the conclusion that Palestine needed some quasi-parliamentary framework and he worked hard to bring about the creation of a Legislative Council. After some initial hesitation the Arabs saw in such an institution a device to prevent further immigration, and the Mufti made no secret of his wish to destroy the National Home altogether. The Jewish Agency, equally naturally, was firmly opposed to a scheme under which the Jewish sector would always be outvoted and thus condemned to perpetual minority status. At the same time, immigration continued to accelerate, and by April 1936 the Arabs were in open revolt, leading to widespread bloodshed, which lasted for three years. In the summer of that year the British Government appointed the Palestine Royal Commission, under Lord Peel, in the hope that it would find a solution for a problem that seemed as insoluble as that of Northern Ireland—and was not all that dissimilar in character.

The Jewish leadership—and even Weizmann himself—had turned against Sir Arthur Wauchope. Future events were to show that this antagonism was neither well-founded nor in the long-term interest of Palestinian Jews. The time would come when the *Yishuv* longed for a High Commissioner of Wauchope's broad sympathies. His successor, Sir Harold MacMichael, was at first abused by the Arabs for his energetic suppression of their rebellion, and soon afterwards, with added vigour, by the Jews for the 1939 White Paper whose true architect had been the Colonial Secretary, Malcolm MacDonald. Sir Harold MacMichael was a fine classical scholar with a long record of distinguished service in the Sudan and a short spell as Governor of Tanganyika. His command of Arabic was good, and he was said to favour the Arabs, with whose language and habits of mind he was familiar. I do not think that this charge is altogether fair, but he had the tragic misfortune of having to administer the policy of the ill-fated White Paper, of having to refuse entry to Hitler's victims, and of being required to turn back the flimsy and unseaworthy boats on which some of those hapless people came to seek refuge in the only country which might yet open its gates to them. The wrath of the Yishuv knew no bounds, while the British Government reckoned, correctly, that the Jews, unlike the Arabs, had no choice of allies in the war that was now raging. If blame has to be attributed, then it probably attaches not to the High Commissioner but to his masters in London, for the gravity of the hour required not a colonial civil servant, however distinguished, but a statesman of international standing. That HMG, at that fateful stage in the fortunes of a war whose outcome still hung perilously in the balance, did not give priority of thought to Palestine must surely be reckoned a venial sin in the light of the cataclysmic events of the time. For if Britain had been vanquished, her people would have survived, but Jews everywhere would have perished.

When Sir Harold MacMichael's six unhappy years in Palestine drew to a close in 1944, London returned once more to the

Plumer formula and appointed another Field Marshal to the office of High Commissioner, with equally felicitous results. Lord Gort's reception at Jerusalem was rapturous, at any rate by the Yishuv. At the same time, fair-mindedness compels one to hope that one day soon a dispassionate assessment of his predecessor and his Palestine period will be written.

Lord Gort, like Plumer before him, came to Palestine from Malta, where he had governed the George Cross Island during its long siege. His High Commissionership lasted only a year, from the autumn of 1944 to the end of 1945, when cancer forced him to leave the task on which he had set out so auspiciously. He died a short time afterwards. During his period of office the atmosphere in Palestine was transformed and personal relationships with the leaders of the two communities were resumed, but in terms of policy Lord Gort had no more leeway than his predecessors, except in the removal of some minor pinpricks. Yet his outgoing personality, his genuine sympathy with both sectors of the population, and his eminence as soldier and man helped to defuse a dangerous situation. Where MacMichael had, perhaps, been scholarly, austere, aloof, and awkward in presenting himself in a favourable light, Gort's fame and great popularity helped to alleviate the tensions that had built up. However, there is no reason to suppose that, had his term of office lasted its full span, the basic situation would have been materially altered and that events would have taken a different turn.

* * *

I now return to the last phase of the Palestine Government, to the High Commissionership of Sir Alan Cunningham and the Chief Secretaryship of Sir Henry Gurney, with which I began this chapter. I had left my job at the Hebrew University and was now (early 1947) installed in the Palestine Government Secretariat at the King David Hotel. The destroyed south wing had only just been shored up, and we were accommodated in the rest of the large building. The Arabs were still mourning the deaths of relatives and friends killed in the outrage, and Britons and Jews were very conscious of the loss of colleagues. When in the summer of 1947 the Government held a memorial service on the first anniversary of this dreadful deed, the large foyer of the building was crowded with mourners, colleagues, and relations;

and, despite the lofty address by the Bishop of Jerusalem, the atmosphere was heavy with emotions that seemed vengeful rather than forgiving.

My arrival at the Secretariat fell within the political, though by no means military or terrorist, hiatus between the stalling at Whitehall that followed the report of the Anglo-American Committee in 1946 and Mr Bevin's announcement in February 1947 that the Mandate of the now defunct League of Nations was to be referred back to UNO. This led in May 1947 to the appointment of the United Nations Special Committee on Palestine (UNSCOP). Meanwhile acts of terror and occasionally counter-terror continued and had a most brutalizing impact. It was against this desperate background that the routine work of government continued within the walls of the King David fortress—at any rate until the United Nations vote on Palestine in November 1947.

There were several heavily fortified security zones at Jerusalem, and ingress into, as well as exit from, these was carefully controlled. I remember one particular Palestine policeman who usually formed part of the King-David-complex guard. He was small of stature, authoritative in manner, well-spoken and educated. We would occasionally have a chat and I was sufficiently impressed with him to recall his face and conversation for many years afterwards. When in the 1970s and 1980s Sir Kenneth Newman appeared on television, I felt sure that I recognized in him that friendly policeman, especially as *Who's Who* confirmed that he had served in Jerusalem in the Palestine Police at the operative time. I then wrote to him to enquire if my memory served me right. In a charming reply he said he could not remember having the specific duties at the King David security zone to which I had referred, although he was, of course, in Jerusalem at that time. On the very day I received his letter I saw a television programme on Scotland Yard in which Sir Kenneth figured prominently; and I now felt even more certain that he was that impressive young policeman. Or could memory, stretched over forty years, play such tricks on either of us?

Of course, life in Jerusalem and elsewhere in Palestine continued somehow—despite curfews, bombings, and executions (on both sides). There were 100,000 British troops in Palestine at that time, many of them war veterans who deserved a more peaceful life after their long exertions. Most of my colleagues and friends, in government and in private life, did not believe that Britain was in earnest about handing back the Mandate and quitting Palestine. I had endless discussions on this subject, for I felt convinced that, despite my low opinion of the delicacy of Mr Bevin's much vaunted statesmanship, he did mean what he said on this particular subject, whether from mere spite or from a cool assessment of Britain's best interests.

Every First Division Officer in the Secretariat had a clerk in the Central Registry. Most of these clerks were Arabs. The one assigned to me was a pleasant middle-aged man with whom I got on well. We never spoke about politics and confined our conversation to the business in hand, although there were very few issues in Palestine that were devoid of some political angle. In the initial stages my work was concerned with financial compensation for the victims of terrorist attacks. Even these delicate matters could be discussed between us without rancour and without getting overtly involved in current politics. It was only after November 1947, in the violent aftermath of the UN decision, that the general atmosphere was apt to become sullen; and I suspected that my clerk was prevented by his more militant colleagues from coming to my office as often as he used to.

During the summer of 1947 UNSCOP visited Palestine and also looked in on a few administrative officers in the Secretariat. I recall that the Swedish chairman of the committee asked me what I was by profession. When I told him that I was an orientalist, he retorted smilingly that his experience of British practice had taught him that no one was ever engaged in the area in which he was an expert, 'no doubt to prevent people knowing too much about any particular subject', he thought, 'one might call it experto-phobia'. I suggested that the all-rounder, trained in classics, appeared to have done well in the British overseas services. The visit lasted scarcely more than two minutes.

I came to form a high opinion of the senior echelons in the Palestine Secretariat, from the Chief Secretary downwards. Most of them were endeavouring to remain genuinely impartial in very difficult and trying circumstances. Many of them became colonial governors themselves in the years after 1948. In the middle ranks there were some whose training and colonial experience predisposed them to greater sympathy for the Arab cause. This seemed to me entirely natural, for their proficiency in Arabic and service in Arabic-speaking countries almost inevitably had that effect. Moreover, the Jews in Palestine, with their autonomous institutions and intellectual outlook, were scarcely typical colonial subjects. I do not think there was any British official with a real knowledge of Hebrew; nor is that fact surprising, for Arabic was of use in other colonial territories as well, while Hebrew could only be employed in Palestine. And very few colonial civil servants remained in Palestine long enough to make a study of Hebrew worth their while. Personally I never encountered any British official in Jerusalem who revealed overt anti-Jewish sentiments, though I am obviously in no position to assert that such officers did not exist.

It so happened that my wife and I had arranged to give a party for some of our senior British colleagues and a few of our neighbours at North Talpioth on 29 November 1947. When these arrangements were made it could not have been foreseen what a fateful date this would turn out to be. The corridor in the house of my parents-in-law, where the party took place, was lined with heavily armed policemen to protect the British officials, but by the end of the night we were not certain whether in their state of merriment their arms were not a greater danger to the guests than to any potential terrorist. Fortunately this contingency never arose, but at the close of the proceedings one of our guests, Esther Herlitz, a future Israeli ambassadress, received news of the UN vote in favour of the UNSCOP plan of partition.

The next day there were heavy Arab attacks on Jews in most parts of Palestine, with serious loss of life. From now until the surrender of the Mandate on 15 May 1948, the security situation went from bad to worse. Christopher Sykes, in his impartial account, writes that

British police and troops in the area of conflict looked on . . . only intervening after the rioters had wreaked damage and injury which prompt British action could easily have prevented. In trying to carry out an incomprehensible and impossible task even the best of the British troops began to be demoralized, and the daily abominations of the Jewish terrorists had embittered thousands of them against the whole Yishuv.

As an eye witness of these events I can only confirm the accuracy of this assessment. Government in all its manifold forms suddenly disintegrated and collapsed. Most aspects of normal civilized life, postal services, police protection, transport, and communications—all seized up, abruptly and frighteningly. Yet we sat in our offices in the Secretariat and circulated files and reached decisions which everyone knew had not the slightest chance of being implemented. No one has been able to comprehend how this unprecedented and positively eerie state of affairs had arisen. I am convinced that it was not ordained by the High Commissioner, the Chief Secretary, and their most senior advisers. If it was decreed by Mr Bevin, then his executants in Palestine must have been endowed with acting talents worthy of an Olivier or a Guinness. From my knowledge of these humane officials I find this very hard to credit. I have no explanation, but the situation on the ground continued to deteriorate quite alarmingly.

Sir John Glubb, who was not renowned as a Zionist sympathizer, summed up the situation neatly and succinctly: 'With the machinery of the Palestine Government still in position, with officials still going to their offices every morning, with the police still in the streets and a considerable army still in its barracks, raging battles were going on in the country almost unhindered.' Christopher Sykes speaks of the 'mischievous incompetence' of the British in Palestine from November 1947 to May 1948. I find it difficult to apply these words to the principal British administrators in Palestine, but as a description of the situation they are entirely true. Mr Bevin had said that the British Government would have no part in the implementation of the United Nations' decision, and somehow he and perhaps the army saw to it that this promise was carried out even while the Government was still the responsible authority between November 1947 and May 1948.

In the meantime, Sir Henry Gurney as Chief Secretary was the very embodiment of British sang-froid; he was invariably calm yet firm, approachable as well as sympathetic. 'His imperturbability was proverbial in moments of recurring crises', in the words of his entry in the *Dictionary of National Biography*. By January 1948 the general situation was one of well-nigh total chaos, and First Division officers, British, Arab, and Jewish alike, were expecting to hear of the Government's 'abolition terms', a scheme of compensation for officials who were not offered employment in other overseas dependencies. When Sir Henry Gurney called a meeting in January of all senior members of the Secretariat, in the conference room on the top floor of the King David Hotel, we were certain that an announcement of those terms of compensation was about to be made. The Chief Secretary then made a short speech, somewhat along the following lines:

Gentlemen, the High Commissioner and I have been much disturbed about two aspects of the work of the Secretariat. Some of you, in draft despatches to the Secretary of State, have been referring to the High Commissioner as 'His Excellency'. As you know, the High Commissioner has this prefix only within Palestine and not in communications with London. Secondly, I have observed that some of you construe the 'Palestine Government' as a plural. Again as you know, only His Majesty's Government is to be pluralized, i.e. 'HMG *have* decided', but 'the Palestine Government *has* decreed'.

Thank you, gentlemen.

There was some anger among my senior colleagues at this excessive display of British cool, but I was full of admiration for Sir Henry's performance at a time when all governmental functions were crumbling fast, and few of our inland letters, at any rate, were reaching their destinations.

Some days later he called me to his office and apologized for having persuaded the Hebrew University to release me for service with the Palestine Government, but nobody could have known at the time how soon the Mandate was to end. In these circumstances he had arranged for me to have an interview at the Colonial Office in London with a view to employment elsewhere. I thanked Sir Henry for his thoughtfulness and said that, while I would be glad to be interviewed, I had, in fact, received an invitation, subject to interview, from (Dame) Margery Perham to join her Oxford University Institute of Colonial Studies. He counselled me to go to both appointment boards, which I did. I accepted the Oxford post, although its remuneration was about one third of the other offer. I have never had cause to regret that decision.

Some time in the summer of 1948, when I had been installed at the Oxford Institute for a little while, there was a knock at the door of my office and, to my great surprise, Sir Henry Gurney entered. He asked a few questions about my job and about the work of the Institute in general and then told me that he was interested in the post of Director of the Institute which Margery Perham was about to resign. I was pleased at the thought of having him as my chief again, but unfortunately (in so many senses) a week later the Prime Minister appointed him High Commissioner of Malaya, another prominent trouble spot. I understand that Sir Henry accepted that assignment only after some hesitation, for the Oxford post had attracted him (thus also the *DNB*). Gurney's tragic death in Malaya is common knowledge (and has quite recently again been described in a *Times* obituary of Sir Michael Hogan, a most charming Solicitor-General in Palestine and later Attorney-General of Malaya): in an ambush of the High Commissioner's car, outside Kuala Lumpur, Sir Henry was killed when he deliberately and gallantly stepped out of the car to draw the fire away from his wife. I imagine that Lady Gurney must often have regretted that her husband had not followed his instinct and accepted the Oxford post.

The man next to Gurney in seniority in the Palestine Government was the Financial Secretary, Duncan Stewart. He was subsequently appointed Governor of Sarawak, and while distributing prizes at a school ceremony he was stabbed and, insisting on continuing with the ceremony, bled to death. The tragic passing of these two devoted proconsuls was deeply saddening to all who had known them in Jerusalem.

No less tragic and saddening was the manner in which the British Mandate in Palestine ended, a charge accepted with such high hopes and acclaim at the close of the First World War and surrendered amidst such bloodshed and recriminations not long after the end of the Second, during which Britain had saved Palestine and its inhabitants from a fate too cruel and unspeakable to contemplate.

PART TWO
THE SECOND ZION

I

From Jerusalem to Eritrea

When, not long after the outbreak of the war, I volunteered for
military service, the Hebrew University arranged that those
prepared to join up should be excused one semester. As I had
already studied one semester abroad before coming to Jerusalem,
the university had only to recognize that term, which, in peace-
time conditions, it had not been prepared to do. Soon after my
final examinations I was approached by the Hon. Edwin Samuel,
the son and heir of the first Viscount, who was at that time in
charge of censorship operations in Palestine. He suggested that I
join his office for a while for training as well as substantive work
on some of the languages within my competence, with a view to
being recruited for similar tasks by the British Military
Administration about to be established in Eritrea. Eritrea was at
that time an Italian colony and, after its conquest by British and
Commonwealth forces, was to be governed as an occupied enemy
territory under British administration for the duration of the war
or until its fate was determined by the eventual peace conference.
   Historically Eritrea and its highland region, together with the
Tigre province of Northern Ethiopia, had been the cradle of
Ethiopian civilization, but in 1889 it came under Italian colonial
administration and in 1935 served as the springboard for
Mussolini's conquest of Ethiopia. Linguistically and culturally,
as well as historically, it was thus an inalienable part of
Abyssinia-Ethiopia, with its people speaking two Semitic
languages, Tigrinya and Tigre, which are direct descendants of
classical Ethiopic, Ge'ez. As we have seen in an earlier chapter,
Eritrea was federated with Ethiopia in 1952 by a decision
of the United Nations, and ten years later was incorporated as a .
province of the Ethiopian Empire by a shortsighted decision of
the Ethiopian Government.
   When Edwin Samuel first spoke to me, there was very little I
knew about Eritrea—except that it formed the northernmost area

of Ethiopia, that its capital was Asmara, and what Semitic languages were spoken there. Until then I had met Samuel only socially and superficially, and at that initial encounter at his office we spoke in Hebrew—but never thereafter. In referring to my likely future duties in Eritrea he stressed repeatedly that the *misrad* (office building) was not very high. I found this a little odd, since in Palestine we were not used to skyscrapers either. It dawned on me only gradually that he had confused Hebrew *misrad* (office building) with *misrah* (office = position).

At that time he was very much the boss and was held in some awe at the office. He was tall and walked in a remarkably erect manner; on his way to and from the office he was followed by an Arab boy who carried his briefcase, which at no time seemed particularly heavy. Even a decade-and-a-half after his father had ceased to be High Commissioner he was still widely regarded as the Governor's son, a role he did not find uncongenial. Yet when one came to know him more closely (as my wife and I did, until his death in 1978), one recognized that these foibles were only skin-deep and that essentially he was very conscious of being less weighty than either his father or his own sons. He was justly proud of his distinguished parent and of his children, particularly of his elder son who attained a professorial position at the Weizmann Institute at Rehovoth at an early age. In later years he came to visit us at Manchester, London, and Oxford, frequently for breakfast when he stipulated that it had to be of a kind 'not readily obtainable at Jerusalem'. Occasionally, after his succession to the viscounty, he would give us lunch at the House of Lords and then ask us to stay for a debate in which he proposed to speak.

But back during the war he ran his censorship and kindred offices with exemplary efficiency, though never appearing to be wildly profligate of his energies. I cannot aver that the contents of the material I had to scrutinize were ever particularly interesting or exciting, but linguistically they offered many challenges, especially in the early stages. The decipherment of either a highly practised or a very poor hand could of itself present problems; and fathoming the significance of a passage, perhaps not intended for the eyes of a stranger, could involve many hours of contemplation. And as far as Amharic and Tigrinya were concerned, there were no dictionaries available outside the

University Library, and I am not sure now whether even the latter possessed such aids for Tigrinya at that time. Moreover, dictionaries could not be removed from the library; and since it appeared reasonable to assume that such *instruments de travail* were even less likely to be found in Asmara (an assumption that proved to be inaccurate, but there, too, works of this kind were strictly confined to the Government Library for consultation *in situ*), it was agreed to photograph Guidi's famous *Vocabolario Amarico-Italiano*. Alas, in those days the photographing of a very large book was a laborious and costly process. Facilities of that nature were not then provided by the University Library, and a commercial photographer had to be engaged to experiment with this job—in the end successfully. Edwin Samuel's position opened all doors that might otherwise have been barred.

A year or so later I discovered and purchased a copy of Guidi's great opus in Eritrea; but when the War Department, to which I had returned the photographed book, prepared to sell this dictionary which was now surplus to their requirements, they found that, while they could expend money, there was no rubric under which they could receive funds. I cannot now remember what the army did with this unwanted item. More serious was the absence of a dictionary of Tigrinya, the principal language of Eritrea. When eventually I reached Asmara, this turned out to be a sensitive lacuna. So there was no other way but to copy by hand the 1308 columns of the only extant book of this nature, available at the Government Library in Asmara. The scholarly Director of that institution, the late Gavino Gabriel, gave me permission to come in every morning from 6 to 8 a.m., in company with the cleaners, to engage in this task. But from my immediate chief I got only criticism for my pains. He wrote to complain to HQ in Cairo on the grounds that this might be interpreted as scholarly work and that my matutinal labours might sap my energies for the rest of the day. He was, however, sufficiently fair-minded to show me the reply he received from Cairo, which opined that my activities were 'unlikely to undermine the war effort in a manner that could attract serious opprobrium'. Six months later, when less than a quarter of the work had been done, I was fortunate enough to acquire a copy of this rare Tigrinya dictionary which remains a treasured possession. The 280 handwritten columns of text that had been completed I presented to the Chief Censor.

Meanwhile, during my training period at Jerusalem, Edwin Samuel was more broad-minded and encouraged everything that rendered intelligence work more effective. Occasionally I was despatched to Latrun or Sarafand for instruction in other aspects of training and in different processes that might be useful in my future sphere of activities. At the censorship offices in Jerusalem the atmosphere was highly congenial. Among my colleagues were several graduates of Jerusalem University as well as a close neighbour of ours at North Talpioth, the daughter of Kalvaryski. At the same time I read up everything I could find on the subject of Eritrea and Ethiopia, mostly written in Italian. I also went back to the Ethiopian Church and community in Abyssinian Street where I discovered several speakers of Tigrinya. But my progress in the spoken language was not impressive; advances in this area proved to be much easier once I had reached Asmara. H. J. Polotsky, my teacher, was also very helpful by reading with me some relevant texts in Amharic and Tigrinya.

At the university such work on Ethiopia as I had done was almost exclusively confined to study of the languages. The historical and cultural background was not part of the curriculum. In the course of my intensive reading now I found out that Ethiopia considered itself the 'Second Zion', a claim adumbrated in their national saga, the *Kebra Nagast* ('glory of the kings'), which embodies the narrative of the Queen of Sheba's visit to King Solomon at Jerusalem and the birth to them of a son, Menelik, who went to visit his father, abducted the Ark of the Covenant, and brought it to Axum, the ancient capital of Ethiopia. Throughout historical times Judaized nuclei were among the waves of immigrants who crossed from Arabia into the Horn of Africa and imbued pre-Christian as well as Christian Ethiopia with more than just a veneer of Jewish customs, practices, and religious observances. Ethiopian Christianity is suffused with a significant leaven of Hebraic and Jewish elements which give the country its peculiar syncretistic cultural and religious appearance.

When the time came to leave Jerusalem for Eritrea, it was a great wrench to part from the city, then so uncharacteristically peaceful, and from my girlfriend and her family. The war situation at that time was very serious, and it was by no means certain that the enemy would not be able to push into

Palestine either from Egypt or from the north—or even both. I had stipulated that no one was to come to the railway station to see me off, but not long before the departure of my train for Lydda and Cairo my future parents-in-law appeared. It had not occurred to me that they might come, and when, just before the train pulled out of the station, my future mother-in-law kissed me (then an unheard of manifestation of familiarity—or so it seemed to me), I felt from that moment that I was in honour bound to consider myself engaged to her eldest daughter, my long-time girlfriend. By the railway crossing at Bak'a, close to the barrier, the latter and her two sisters stood waving, long and energetically, until the train was out of sight. It was an emotional moment.

I shared the compartment with two Jewish Palestinian medical officers. One of them had just taken leave of his wife and was still visibly upset; the other was a bachelor and seemed very cheerful. When the first one asked his colleague, 'Aren't you at all *émotionné* or excited?', the latter replied, with a deliberate eye to the notoriously slow pace of the Palestine Railways, 'Do you think I have never been on a faster train?!' At Lydda, where we had to change for the Cairo train, one had to report to the RTO (Rail Transport Officer). These officers were ubiquitous at every junction between Lydda and Khartoum, and we reached the conclusion that a significant proportion of the army were concerned with the smooth running of rail transport.

On arrival in Cairo I had to report to HQ for instructions and onward travel warrants. I was not sorry that there was no train to Aswan in Upper Egypt for another three days, for this was my first visit to Cairo and I hoped to see as much as possible of this metropolis which seemed so vast compared with any city in Palestine. The Italians and Germans were at Tobruk at that time, and Egypt was full of troops on their way either to or from the front. Accommodation was at a premium, and I was quartered at some billets whose location I cannot now recall—anyhow a far cry from the luxurious Shepheards hotel where I was lodged some years later when I passed through Cairo on leave for Jerusalem, long after the Axis powers had been expelled from Africa. But meanwhile I went for all the obvious tourist sights, the Pyramids, the Cairo Museum, Groppi's, etc. Even a ride on a tram, an unknown mode of conveyance in Palestine, was exciting.

The train from Cairo to Aswan-Shallal (nearly 600 miles), where we had to board the Nile steamer, was very full and had standing room in the corridors only. It was not a comfortable night, and I was glad when day began to break and one could observe the *fellahin* tilling the fertile soil along the shores of the Nile. There was no opportunity of catching more than a glimpse of Aswan. The two days and nights on the Nile boat might have been romantic in normal times, but the steamer was extremely crowded and we got stuck, grounded, several times, as the rainy season in the Blue Nile area of Ethiopia had only just begun and its waters had not yet filled the shallow stretch of the river which we were navigating. I always hoped to return there in better times, but all my journeys in the later stages of the war and in all the years until the Ethiopian revolution in 1974 had to be made by air. Even from a great height it was, however, easy to observe the green and cultivated strips along the banks of the longest river on earth.

Then followed a protracted train journey from Wadi Halfa to Khartoum, this time in reasonable comfort. The Sudan Railways had been renowned for their excellent amenities, and these had not completely disappeared even in wartime conditions. I remember in particular the remarkably ample breakfasts of kedgeree followed by liver and eggs, and the first real coffee we had tasted in a long while. Khartoum, at the confluence of the Blue and White Nile, was our next stop and impressed us with its orderly appearance. We had to obtain onward travel warrants from Army HQ, which was temporarily situated in the Gordon Memorial College. The journey from Khartoum via Wad Medani and Gedaref to Kassala, on the Sudan–Eritrea frontier, was very slow but afforded the first real impressions of Africa, as distinct from the Near East. The train was mostly so leisurely (largely, we were told, because the track was in poor condition) that one could leave the front carriage, walk along its length, and board the rear coach as it caught up. From Kassala, with its giant rock formations, one could see across the vast plain into the foothills of Eritrea (Ethiopia). Kassala is the principal town of the homonymous Sudanese province, a picturesque place situated on the Gash river which rises, in the highland province of Hamasien in central Eritrea, under the name of Mareb, and is called Gash as it reaches the plains of Tessenei (the border station on the

Eritrean side) and Kassala—until it peters out in the direction of Atbara.

Kassala had just seen heavy military operations. The Italians had occupied the town shortly after entering the war in June 1940. But by 19 January 1941 it had been reconquered by General Platt's forces which reached Tessenei, forty miles on, the next day, Barentu and Agordat on 1 February and, after the heaviest battles of the Ethiopian campaigns, took Keren on 26 March. Thereafter it was relatively plain sailing: Asmara, the capital, surrendered on 1 April and Massawa, the principal port, about a week later. Our progress from Kassala to Agordat, a distance of some 160 miles, was largely during the night and by a succession of rickety buses along roads partly washed away by a heavy rainy season; it seemed to us almost as perilous, though infinitely less bloody, than General Platt's recent push into Eritrea. We reached Agordat at 4 a.m. and were able to rest there until the evening and the departure of the slow overnight train to Asmara. At that time we saw nothing, during the night, of the difficult terrain over which the battle of Keren, the first major British victory during the war, had been fought, nor of the town of Keren and its beautiful situation. But in future years I showed many visitors over the battleground there and also spent one or two local holidays in these surroundings.

With our arrival at Asmara I had not only reached my destination but had also found the area, viz. Ethiopia, which was to become the principal focus of my subsequent life and academic career. I remained there, in three very different posts within the British Military Administration, for the next four-and-a-half years.

Asmara is situated some 7,500 feet above sea level on the mountain plateau of Northern Ethiopia. At first sight it looked like a typical small Italian town. It still had some 40,000 Italian inhabitants and double that number of Eritreans, carefully segregated in separate quarters; but the prominent sight of many half-castes showed that that segregation was frequently more honoured in the breach than the observance. It had fine wide avenues, a palace, parks and gardens, and good colonial-type houses; also an Italian cathedral, a fairly modern (1917) but not unattractive Italian-built Ethiopian monophysite church, modelled on traditionally styled rectangular structures of this type, and a fine mosque, also Italian-designed (1937). The climate of Asmara and of all highland regions of the Ethiopian plateau is excellent, with a mean annual temperature of 17° Celsius, the highest levels of 25° in April and May and the lowest recorded temperature being 6°. The main rainy season is in July and August, with lesser precipitation from April to June and in early September. The rains are usually confined to two or three hours after midday. Altogether Asmara was physically a fine place and full of interest in many spheres. When I arrived, water was scarce, and taps produced only a tiny trickle; but the situation improved greatly over the years.

The Italians, the recently conquered enemies, were at first apt to be sullen, though ruled with a light hand. Fraternization was forbidden by the British military authorities, and by and large this remained the guiding principle up to the end of the war. Until the fall of Mussolini in 1943 and the recognition that they had lost the war, the Italian population could be awkward and recalcitrant, with the Fascist salute still shown on occasion. The indigenous population, on the other hand, now had a markedly enhanced measure of freedom. Education was greatly expanded, and the general limitation to elementary schooling only for Eritreans was gradually removed, but the abolition of the colour bar proved to be a troublesome problem, for under international law the occupying authority could not change the existing legal structure, except where the exigencies of war demanded it.

II

Eritrea under British Military Administration

A military administration

The framework under which the Italian colony of Eritrea, occupied by British forces since April 1941, was governed was at first called OETA (Occupied Enemy Territory Administration). The head of the administration was initially styled Deputy Chief Political Officer (the Chief Political Officer at GHQ Cairo being responsible for all occupied enemy territories), subsequently Military Administrator and, from 1943 to the end of the British administration in 1952, Chief Administrator. He was the *de facto* Military Governor who, acting under the authority of the Commander-in-Chief, was empowered to govern the country on a 'care and maintenance' basis in accordance with the existing Italian legislation, supplemented by proclamations required by the exigencies of war or by essential local developments. The garrison forces in Eritrea, mostly members of the Sudan Defence contingents, were under the command of another senior officer, a Brigadier, who held ultimate authority for the military security of Eritrea.

One of the first acts of the new administration was to restore the *status quo ante* 1935-6 when the Fascist conquest of Ethiopia had re-drawn the provincial boundaries of Mussolini's short-lived East African Empire by enlarging the area of Eritrea through incorporation of much of the Tigre province of Northern Ethiopia. Once Emperor Haile Sellassie had re-entered his capital, Addis Ababa, on 5 May 1941, the Tigrean enlargements of Eritrea, effected as a result of the Fascist occupation, were handed back to Ethiopia, and Eritrea itself reverted to its 1889-1935 boundaries, prior to Mussolini's Abyssinian adventure. This was, of course, without prejudice to the ultimate post-war disposal of Eritrea which was energetically claimed by the Emperor as an integral and historic part of his realm. In 1943 the designation OETA was changed to BMA, i.e. British Military Administration.

That administration, though composed of military personnel, was not very different from an ordinary colonial government. Quite a number of the more senior administrators, civil affairs officers as they were styled, had been colonial civil servants in civilian life before the war. They were drawn from territories such as Northern Rhodesia, Nyasaland, Tanganyika, Kenya, Sudan, Palestine, etc. The first Military Governor of Eritrea and his Chief Secretary (the two most senior government officials) were conveniently and most suitably recruited from the neighbouring Kassala Province of the Sudan. Brigadier Brian Kennedy-Cooke was Governor of that province when in 1941 he was appointed to establish and head the military administration in newly occupied Eritrea. He did so most effectively, with the assistance of his friend and colleague Duncan Cumming (1903-79) as Chief Secretary. Both left Eritrea within a year, the former to return to the Sudan and later to senior appointments in the British Council, while Duncan Cumming went to govern the recently conquered Cyrenaica and later became Chief Civil Affairs Officer, Middle East, in ultimate control of all occupied enemy territories in that area. In 1951-2 he was the last British Governor of Eritrea, handing over the administration of that country, for whose original establishment in 1941 he had toiled so hard and knowledgeably, to Emperor Haile Sellassie. For these services he was knighted in 1953, and for the remainder of his life he engaged in research and the collection of much valuable material on some of the areas and personalities he had been concerned with in the course of his career.

At the time of my arrival at Asmara I met Kennedy-Cooke and Cumming only fleetingly, partly because they were just about to depart from Eritrea and, more importantly, on account of the vast hierarchical gap between us. After the war I encountered the former, most agreeably, on one or two occasions and later corresponded a few times with his widow, while Duncan Cumming became a dear and much respected friend. The man who took over from Kennedy-Cooke as Military Governor of Eritrea was Brigadier Stephen H. Longrigg who had administered Cyrenaica (where Cumming was just going) during the two brief spells of British military occupation in 1941 and early 1942. Longrigg was by far the most important and successful of the six Governors who ruled Eritrea during eleven years of British administration.

Stephen Hemsley Longrigg (1893-1979) was a scholar, Arabist, oil diplomatist, and proconsul. He served in Iraq for thirteen years and rose to become Inspector General of Revenue. He then joined the Iraq Petroleum Company (with which he remained for twenty years) and was principally concerned with delicate negotiations in various parts of the Arabian peninsula. His books include standard histories of Iraq, works on Syria and the Middle East, on oil, and a short history of Eritrea. His style in speech and in print was fluent and effortless; he was an exceptionally good public speaker. His command of Arabic was excellent. He could appear arrogant to those who did not know him; if he was convinced of his friends' loyalty he could be introspective and even self-depreciative. He was pompous only with those who themselves suffered from that affliction. He was always dissatisfied with what he had achieved, and he was unlucky at crucial junctures in his career. He had done remarkably well in his Governorship of Eritrea, but just as he was about to depart from Asmara a corruption scandal in one or two departments of the administration was revealed. There was, of course, no doubt in anyone's mind that he had nothing whatever to do with it, but he was the head of the government in which those peccadilloes had occurred and as such he had to take the blame. It was very unfortunate and very unjust. In his long retirement he did a great deal of valuable academic work. Above all, he was a steadfast friend.

These were some of the men who put their stamp on the new military administration of Eritrea. It was a humane government which treated the defeated enemy with leniency and did much to liberate the Eritreans-Ethiopians from the many restrictions by which their lives had been hemmed in. The currency now introduced (after a brief experiment with Egyptian money) was the East African shilling: 20 shillings = £1 = 480 devalued Italian lire. Overtly Fascist institutions were closed, and known propagators of fascism were either interned or sent to other parts of East Africa. Even within the constraints of international law and the requirements of careful accounting in those perilous days of war, many improvements and reforms were introduced which brought about enhanced standards. All aspects of administration, police, postal services, health, railways, trade, printing, education, etc., were supervised by the new administration who usually put one or two British officers in charge of those departments. Italian and Eritrean personnel were generally retained, unless the former were politically compromised and untrustworthy. British Overseas Airways established a major repair base in Asmara, and, after the American entry into the war, US army and airforce installations operated in various parts of the country. Local industries were encouraged, and by 1944 Eritrea seemed a relatively prosperous and certainly well-ordered country.

My own duties were at first rather limited and unexciting, for the needs of correspondence on the part of the Ethiopian-speaking population were somewhat restricted and thus imposed similar limitations upon the requirements of censorship. However, I was soon also concerned with traffic in Italian and Arabic which offered a richer field of general interest and importance, certainly within the terms for which censorship was exercised in the first place. I was fortunate that the head of an adjoining office, concerned with similar wartime activities, was a man of wide education and interests. He had bought a number of local artefacts, inscribed Ethiopian crosses, etc, and it was in connection with the decipherment of these inscriptions that I first made his acquaintance and was impressed with his knowledge and civilized pursuits. His name is Marc Fitch, and although we overlapped in Eritrea for less than a year, I never forgot his kindness to me and the illumination he brought to what was initially (though not later) a rather bleak intellectual atmosphere. We met again after the war and have been close friends ever since. In the 1950s he established the Marc Fitch Fund which has offered generous support to many scholarly projects. Beyond that he has been a Maecenas who has promoted many enterprises in the arts and in scholarship which would not otherwise have materialized. In the 1970s he was elected an Honorary Fellow of the British Academy, an honour only rarely bestowed.

He and I were also friendly with a man who was in charge of the Department of Education. H. F. Kynaston-Snell served in that crucially important post virtually throughout the entire period of the British Administration in Eritrea and created, almost *ex nihilo*, an educational service of high standards and achievements. He was totally and single-mindedly dedicated to this task, which he discharged with wonderful devotion, integrity, and genuine sympathy for all Eritreans. His name, above all others, is still remembered in the country today and held in high honour. But in those initial stages of the administration he impinged on us mainly as the spirited organizer of a series of weekly gramophone concerts of classical music.

Of a very different character was a man connected with another branch of the security services, S. Reich (later, as D. S. Rice, Professor of Islamic Art in the University of London). He had been a pupil of L. A. Mayer and possessed an uncanny flair for languages, disguise, and the decipherment of epigraphic material. Of the last accomplishment I had vivid demonstrations when we visited the Dahlak islands in the Red Sea, not very far from Massawa. He had organized our little expedition. It was then only my second visit to Massawa, a spectacular drive, either by car or rail, along sharp bends descending steeply from 7,500 feet to sea level over a distance of less than sixty miles. The scenery is starkly beautiful and changes rapidly from the cool highlands to the lush vegetation of the intermediate zone and then to the steppe and desert of the plains. And with the changes of climate and landscape one encounters entirely different human types, from the Ethiopian Christian sedentary and agricultural population of the highlands to the Tigre-speaking nomads spanning all three zones and to the Muslim, somewhat Arabicized, inhabitants of Massawa and its surroundings. Reich-Rice had arranged for a police launch to take us on the two or three hours' crossing to the Dahlak Islands. In the well-known Arab cemetery there he read the Arabic Kufic funerary inscriptions with remarkable ease and competence. Outside the area of his scholarly concerns he was thought to have a somewhat cavalier attitude to strict accuracy, and his penchant for highly imaginative embroiderings of his recent past made those in authority a little wary of him.

I also met, soon after arrival at Asmara, the anthropologist S. F. Nadel who, as Major Nadel, was Secretary for Native Affairs (as it was then called). He was already a well-known scholar with an impressive array of published work to his credit (especially his *Black Byzantium*). I found him a bit austere and humourless and, for someone of his profession, more than a little edgy and ill at ease with the Eritrean-Ethiopian subjects of his anthropological inquiries. At that time he was just setting out on four pieces of work which he completed with remarkable speed and efficiency. They were a booklet on the Races and Tribes of Eritrea, a Glossary of Tigrinya terms relating to customary law and land tenure, a study of land tenure on the Eritrean Plateau (which is equally applicable to Northern Ethiopia), and a pamphlet on Eritrea and her neighbours, mainly Ethiopia and the Sudan. He enlisted my help for some linguistic work in connection with these writings as well as for his contacts with his informants. It was certainly instructive for me to be associated with these researches, and I learnt a good deal about the area in which I was now stationed.

In the evenings, during the first few months of my stay in Eritrea, I would usually work with an informant in order to gain a reasonable command of, and fluency in, Tigrinya. On Sundays I generally went on excursions to explore the countryside, to see the neighbouring villages and their inhabitants, and to practise my Tigrinya on them. I also began to collect and buy books on the languages, civilization, and history of Ethiopia. Books that were in print and could be purchased from the Catholic and Swedish Evangelical Missions were usually fairly inexpensive, but others of a more recondite character and not of local production could at times impose a heavy burden on my budget.

Apart from Kynaston-Snell's weekly concerts, entertainment was at first confined to two or three Italian cinemas and to one reserved for Allied personnel showing films in English. A fairly good meal could be had at the CIAAO (Compagnia Italiana Alberghi Africa Orientale) Hotel and at two or three Italian restaurants. A very different and extremely hygienic repast (accompanied by water imported from the States!) was offered by the American Officers Mess to which Marc Fitch invited me on some occasions. Compared with the scarcities experienced in Palestine, the availability of local produce, especially meat, was at first quite startling. The so-called native quarter, with its various and colourful markets, silversmiths, and other crafts, was another source of entertainment as well as instruction.

In 1943 I had my first direct experience of the vicissitudes to
which the aristocracy are prone: Lieutenant-Colonel Gerald
Wellesley, at that time a senior administrative officer in Asmara,
suddenly and unexpectedly succeeded his nephew and woke up
as Duke of Wellington. It seemed to me very romantic to be able
to speak to a direct descendant of the Iron Duke.

Looking at Eritrea-Ethiopia

During the first few months of my service at Asmara I spent most
of my spare time trying to look at country and people. Thus I
travelled as much as possible throughout Eritrea and Northern
Ethiopia. But the impressions I am setting down here derive, of
course, from the totality of my experience of the Horn of Africa.

I endeavoured to attend Ethiopian church services as often as
possible. These services are conducted in the classical tongue,
called Ge'ez, fairly closely related to Arabic and Hebrew. The
number of churches all over Ethiopia is immense, and their sizes
vary from the little round village churches to the large rectangular and octagonal buildings or modern cathedrals constructed
at Addis Ababa and Asmara. The rectangular churches are
generally older, while the round ones are considerably more
numerous. The most famous rectangular sanctuary is St Mary of
Zion at Axum, the ancient capital of Ethiopia, situated in the
north of the country.

All the churches have a threefold division which is undoubtedly modelled upon that of the Hebrew Temple. The
outside ambulatory of the three concentric parts of the
Abyssinian church is called *kene mahlet*, the place where hymns
are sung and where the Debteras or cantors stand. This outer
part corresponds to the *haser* of the Tabernacle or the *ulam* of
Solomon's Temple. The next chamber is the *keddest* where
communion is administered to the people; and the innermost
part is the *makdas* where the *tabot* (Ark of the Covenant) rests
and to which only priests and the King have access. The form of
the Hebrew sanctuary was thus preferred by Ethiopians to the
basilica type accepted by early Christians elsewhere. Similarly,
churches throughout Ethiopia are usually built upon a small hill
overlooking the village, or at any rate at the most elevated place
available. Jewish writings mention the same requirement for the

site of a synagogue which is to be erected at the highest point of the town.

Culturally, religiously, and in all other aspects of their civilization Ethiopia and Eritrea are hewn of the same block (as I have already indicated) and my remarks in the following pages apply generally to both. At the same time, I ought to stress that I can only speak with first-hand experience of Ethiopia as it existed until the Marxist revolution of 1974—i.e. the traditional Second Zion.

Physically, the Hamito-Semitic union in Ethiopia has produced a handsome race, elegant, subtle, and nervous. It is more difficult to generalize about the Ethiopian national character, for all such pronouncements are of necessity purely impressionistic and subjective. Yet most observers would agree that the Abyssinian is exceptionally intelligent, mentally agile, and extraordinarily eager to learn. His quick absorption of knowledge is at times stupefying, but profundity is not, perhaps, greatly esteemed. Ethiopians are proud people, yet at the same time they display a courtesy and humility towards each other as well as towards strangers that can be deeply moving. Their low bow and their kiss are not an expression of obsequiousness but an aspect of politeness and considerateness in manner. Most of them are born diplomats, some of them are unduly suspicious, but all are generous and quick to forgive. Many Ethiopians are given to litigiousness, but their sense of honour and justice is satisfied once the matter has been properly argued out; thus they will present a case with great dexterity and a distinct flair for oratory. Of Ethiopian hospitality—generous and uncalculating—one cannot speak too highly; it retains something of a Biblical and patriarchal flavour. Friendship is greatly prized and willingly offered, though often there remains, perhaps, a residue of reserve. Few of those who have come into contact with Ethiopians have been able to resist their compelling charm and the abiding interest of country and people.

While indigenous housing in Asmara (or, for that matter, in Addis Ababa and most of the larger towns) retains little of the traditional mode of building, the situation is different as soon as one leaves these urban centres.

The elaborate architecture depicted on the Axum monoliths or exemplified in some of the great ancient churches was, of course, exclusively that of a number of ecclesiastical and royal prestige-buildings. Even in the heyday of Axumite power and prosperity the ordinary Abyssinian lived in a modest hut—as indeed he still does today. The usual type of house in Ethiopia is the round *tukul* with a cone-shaped roof. It appears that circular structures and conical thatched roofs stand up more successfully to winds and heavy rain, and the roof in particular can more easily be made watertight. In smaller houses the roof is supported by a big pole, while larger buildings usually have an inner concentric circle of props. The round skeleton of such huts is made of tree trunks and branches tied together with bundles of straw and then frequently cemented and plastered over. The interior is usually similarly treated with a mixture of mud, clay, and ash. There is one fairly low door and no windows or other openings; light and air have to enter by the door. The 'hearth' either consists of a hole in the ground or is made in the form of a small earthen elevation. The beds, placed by the walls, are similarly built of a ridge of earth on which hides and blankets are spread out.

That is, of course, the simplest and humblest type of dwelling, without any internal divisions—except, on occasion, a small compartment for animals. Larger *tukuls* of more prosperous owners can be a good deal more elaborate: the cylindrical wooden structure is often strengthened by stones either inserted or super-imposed in layers; but the large amount of wood needed for the building and not infrequent reconstruction of these huts has, incidentally, caused serious deforestation of the Abyssinian uplands, especially in the north. As prosperity increases, internal divisions, generally of wood, sometimes of stone, become more common. These internal walls are concentric, so that little round corridors enclose the central part of the house. In such cases we would also be likely to find one or more windows placed fairly high in the outer wall.

The villages of the Tigre province and Eritrea are of a less uniform type. Houses may be either round or rectangular (the latter kind is, perhaps, more common and is called *hedmo*) and are at times of substantial size. They are usually built of stone, rough blocks, in some cases held together by a sort of mud-mortar and in others ingeniously stacked without any such binding sub-stance. As rainfall in the north is somewhat lighter, roofs here are almost invariably flat—as is, of course, also the case in the adjacent and sun-baked regions of Semitic Western Asia. These flat roofs usually protrude a few feet and are supported by large poles which are secured in the ground in front of the house and form a sort of portico. The roof itself consists of layers of twigs, branches, and earth. Very frequently whole villages are perched along the slopes of hills (called *ambas*), at times so steep that the mountain forms the back wall of the house. This type of building is so perfectly adapted to the landscape, with its mud-coloured contours, that it represents the most effective kind of camouflage and is scarcely visible from the air. The interior of the humbler houses is marked by haphazardly distributed wooden columns which help to support the roof. There is ordinarily no walled division, but frequently grain jars separate the living quarters from the 'kitchen' and stores. The space near the entrance serves throughout the rainy and cold seasons as a sitting-room during the day and by night as a stable for animals.

The lay-out of the villages is generally irregular and quite haphazard, yet at times the overall effect is far from displeasing. Village and district chiefs and other important personages usually live in larger and more elaborately constructed houses (at times with an upper storey) which often possess a sizeable reception hall. In towns, officials, ministers, and other well-to-do people live in European-type houses, often of great spaciousness, which are in every way comparable to dwellings in the materially more advanced countries.

Furnishings in the majority of huts are extremely limited and usually consist of a couple of low stools, a large stone serving as a table (sometimes baskets or wooden tables are available), and kitchen utensils. Hooks are liberally distributed all over the interior of the houses to hang up clothes, hides, water-containers, knives, and anything else that need not occupy the restricted floor-space.

The national dress of the Ethiopians is the toga-like white *shamma*, which is a rectangular shawl, exceeding three yards in length, hand-woven and made of cotton. Both men and women wear the *shamma*, but the manner in which it is draped by the women differs from that of the men. If this garment has a wide red stripe not far from the hem, it is worn on feast days; it is then also differently folded. Underneath the *shamma* men will be dressed in cotton trousers or white jodhpurs which are tight-fitting from knee to ankle, while women have shirt-like dresses with very full skirts of ankle length. These dresses are often made of beautifully coloured materials.

Men of distinction wear a silk tunic (*kamis*), magnificently embroidered and coloured according to their rank. Both men and women may wrap a cloak (*barnos*) over their shoulders, especially in the cool evenings. These garments are often richly ornamented and lined with leather. Most of the people walk barefoot, but some wear sandals. Very few Ethiopians cover their heads, though a hood is ordinarily attached to the *barnos*, and recently European headgear has been gaining ground among men. Small umbrellas, woven from grass or reeds, are sometimes carried as protection against rain or sun. At church ceremonies highly colourful or intricately ornamented brocade umbrellas are carried by the great dignitaries. In the towns European dress has been spreading at a rapid pace.

The Ethiopian national dish is *injera* (bread) and *wat* (*zegeni* in Tigrinya), a kind of curried stew made of beef or chicken, often with some hard-boiled eggs, and liberally seasoned with red pepper (*berbere*) and other spices. It is an excellent and delicious dish, but the uninitiated foreigner will at first suspect that his alimentary channels have been set on fire. He will therefore have generous recourse to the extremely tasty and potent *tedj* (*mies* in Tigrinya), a sort of honey-mead, or *talla*, the Abyssinian beer.

Injera is a type of unleavened bread made of *teff* (millet) or barley. It is circular, generally 18 inches in diameter and less than a quarter of an inch thick. It is baked in a large earthenware or iron pan over the open fire. The meat (beef or mutton) is either eaten raw (*berundo*), especially at large (and usually most colourful) banquets, or in the form of *wat* (or *zegeni*), and also as *fetfet*, small pieces of meat cooked in a sauce of butter and pepper.

Tedj or mead is made of honey and water and then fermented with the leaves and bitter roots of the *saddo* (*Rhamnus saddo*) or *gesho* (*Rhamnus pauciflorus*) tree. It is not only a delicious but also a highly inebriating drink, and is invariably kept in an attractive round-bellied bottle with a very tall neck of decanter shape (called *berille*). While *tedj* is prepared by men, *talla* or beer is usually made by women. The main ingredient is barley, and the leaves of the *gesho* are used for fermentation. *Talla* is drunk out of horn-shaped vessels.

Except by the well-to-do, fruit is not widely eaten, nor are sweets or sugared dishes. The excellent Ethiopian coffee is usually drunk bitter; it is served in double-handled pottery jugs of carafe shape. In the major towns European cuisine is gaining ground.

Women wear their hair in numerous narrow plaits, with the strands of hair, waxed by means of rancid butter, fashioned into those thin plaits from the forehead down to the nape of the neck where they end in a frizz. Boys have generally close-shaven heads, but with banana-shaped tufts of hair on top of the head.

Three forms of marriage are current in Ethiopia:

(1) A limited and 'salaried' (*damoz*) matrimonial arrangement by which a woman agrees with a man to cohabit for a specified time (a month or longer), renewable or terminable at the wish of either party, and at a specified remuneration. This is a purely contractual arrangement, and unless her salary has been in arrears the woman has no claim against her partner's estate. On the other hand, any issue from such a union is regarded as legitimate with the same rights of inheritance as children born in full and lawful wedlock. Neither the Church nor the 'Establishment' look with favour upon such temporary unions.

(2) The most common form of marriage in Ethiopia is a binding civil marriage contract entered into by the parents of the prospective bride and bridegroom. This is usually, though not invariably, preceded by a long engagement until the bride reaches the age of puberty and is declared by her parents to be fit for marriage. During the period of the engagement the bridegroom is not supposed to meet his betrothed or any of her female relations. When the marriage is finally celebrated, without any ecclesiastical intervention and purely as a civil ceremony, there are several days of feasting on a very lavish scale which usually far exceeds the financial resources of the two families. After the wedding the bride follows her husband to his parents' house, but in many cases she returns again to her own home for a limited period. Upon consummation of the marriage the young couple will join the household of the husband's parents, and only after about two or three years will they request a plot of land from the village community and build their own

house on it. Modern practice, especially in the larger urban centres, may vary perceptibly and increasingly follows the European pattern.

(3) The civil marriage does not require, and in the majority of cases does not receive, the additional sanction of the Church. A small number of people prefer, however, to celebrate their marriage in a religious ceremony as well, which consists of joint communion. Such marriages are, strictly speaking, indissoluble and are therefore frequently chosen by elderly people who have long been united in civil marriage and now feel sure that divorce can safely be ruled out. Church ceremonies are customary also among the ruling classes and are compulsory for the clergy.

Death is followed by the most vigorous manifestations of mourning. Men and women will lament and cry, recite dirges, and sing the praises of the departed. All this will be punctuated with the shrill notes of ululating women. Relatives will tear their clothes, throw themselves to the ground, and appear in sackcloth and ashes. The body of the deceased is then washed, wrapped in a white sheet, and taken to church where it receives the blessing of the priest. The burial, usually in a rather shallow grave, takes place a few hours after death has occurred.

Similar to Hebraic customs is the daily assembly of relatives and friends in the house of the deceased throughout the first week of mourning, when prayers are said, laments are recited, and (as in some parts of Europe) generous hospitality is dispensed to all and sundry. On the twelfth, fortieth, and eightieth day after death memorial services (*tezkar*) are held in church: these are frequently followed by sumptuous banquets which may at times impose a heavy financial burden on the bereaved.

The canons of Ethiopian etiquette are strict and well-regulated, and there exists a good deal of punctiliousness in Ethiopian life which is far removed from empty cere-moniousness. When people meet on the road (apart, of course, from the larger urban centres), they will enquire after each other's health even if they are strangers. While the formulae employed in this elaborate exchange of greetings are stereotyped, it would be wrong to infer that they are meaningless or insincere. A low bow is *de rigueur* in almost all instances. If the *shamma* covers one's head, hood-like, it will be lowered, and at times also the shoulders may be uncovered. Frequently the ground is touched with the right hand which is then brought to the lips. Children will often prostrate themselves before their father or grandfather and kiss his feet.

On encountering a friend or acquaintance the exchange of the formulae of greetings may take fully a minute or two, and if neither has time or occasion to stop, the pronouncements will continue long after the two persons have passed each other and are some distance apart: 'How are you?' or 'How have you passed the night?'—'Thanks be to God. I am well; how are you?' —'Thanks be to God. I am well.'—'How are your sons?' And this will be followed by enquiries after other members of the family, animals, harvest, etc. It is only after this unhurried exchange of courtesies (and the same, incidentally, applies to epistolary etiquette) that one speaks of matters of substance. And convention demands that the replies to all the questions during the initial interchange are in the affirmative: 'Well, thanks be to God', whatever the real position may be. Bad news is communicated only later on, after the requirements of etiquette have been satisfied.

By far the most important form of land tenure is family or group ownership (*rest* in Amharic, *resti* in Tigrinya). *Rest* is 'hereditary' possession of the land and is deeply rooted in the social structure of Abyssinia. It refers more commonly to ownership by a kinship group rather than by an individual, but historically *rest* is conceived as being derived from an originally clearly defined single notion of ownership—that founded on the first occupation of land by an individual family. With the natural growth of the family of the original occupants the title of the land changed from an individual to a collective right. The council of elders of each village group will assign the land to individual families and lay down a strict system of rotation. The ideologically inspired land reforms which have been carried out of late, overdue in the non-traditional south of the country, have also swept away much of the socially advanced and desirable system in the north, and have contributed to the recent famines in those northern regions.

*   *   *

While Christianity in its monophysite form (belief in the one and undivided nature of Christ) has been the predominant and state-sanctioned religion of the country, Islam has made considerable inroads over the past half-millennium. This is particularly true in all areas outside the central or core highland regions which have constituted the traditional homeland of Abyssinia-Ethiopia.

But in the present context I would like to refer briefly to a sector of the Ethiopian population that has been much in the news of late—the Falashas, who have been dubbed the Jews of Ethiopia. They live in North-Western Ethiopia, to the north of Lake Tana, and are Ethiopians of Agaw (non-Semitic) stock practising a peculiar kind of Judaism. The Falashas usually refer to themselves as the 'House of Israel' or by the Cushitic term of *kayla* which is of somewhat uncertain interpretation. This has to be compared, however, with the traditional claim by Christian Ethiopians that they are the 'Children of Israel' and their kings the 'Israelitish kings' or 'kings of Zion'.

Their cult embodies a curious mixture of pagan-Judaic-Christian beliefs and ceremonies, but the Falashas are neither the only non-Christian and unconverted tribe nor the only sector of the Ethiopian population that has clung to so strange a religious amalgam. Similar claims have been made for the Gafat, the Kemant, and others. The Falashas do not know of any religious prescriptions outside the Pentateuch; Mishnah and Talmud are unknown to them. They have no knowledge of Hebrew, and the language of their prayers is Ge'ez—as is the case with their Christian compatriots. The feasts mentioned in the Pentateuch are observed by the Falashas in a manner often materially different from that of Jews elsewhere. Post-exilic feasts are not celebrated by them. The Sabbath is observed with considerable strictness, and the prescriptions regarding ritual cleanness are practised with great zeal—both features which exist among very many other Ethiopians. In common with their monophysite neighbours the Falashas carry out circumcision on boys and excision (a kind of clitoridectomy) on girls. Monkery plays an important part in their community (and here, surely, is a fundamental distinction from Judaism), and their literature, though it includes some works peculiar to them, is mostly derived from general Ethiopian sources.

A dispassionate appraisal of the ethnic and religious position of the Falashas has generally been vitiated because—as many scholars have pointed out—reports about the Falashas have been incomplete and characterized by a Christian or Jewish missionary tendency, which appreciably diminishes their usefulness and objectivity.

In common with those who have undertaken a careful and unprejudiced study of this remarkable sector of the Ethiopian population I have long held that the evidence available points to the conclusion that the Falashas are descendants of those elements in the Axumite Kingdom which resisted conversion to Christianity. In that case their so-called Judaism is merely the reflection of those Hebraic and Judaic practices and beliefs which were implanted on parts of South West Arabia in the first post-Christian centuries and subsequently brought into Abyssinia. If this opinion is correct, then the religious pattern of the Falashas—even though it will have undergone some change in the past 1,600 years—may well mirror to a considerable extent the religious syncretism of the pre-Christian Axumite Kingdom. It is in their living testimony to the Judaized civilization of the South Arabian immigrants and their well-nigh complete cultural ascendancy over the Cushitic and other strata of the original African population of Ethiopia that we must seek the value and great interest of the Falashas today—and not by imputing to them the status of a long-lost tribe of Israel (which is historically quite unwarranted). Like their Christian fellow-Ethiopians, the Falashas are stubborn adherents to fossilized Hebraic–Jewish beliefs, practices, and customs which were transplanted from South Arabia into the Horn of Africa and which may here be studied in the authentic surroundings and atmosphere of a Semitized country.

Recent developments have brought nearly half the Falasha population to Israel. This is not the place to consider either the wisdom of this move or the question whether the Falashas can be regarded as Jews in any real sense. The former is now a *fait accompli* and as such the new immigrants deserve to be treated with considerateness and respect, while the latter would involve one in the unprofitable conundrum of speculating on who or what is a Jew or constitutes Jewishness. What remains important, however, is the integrity of scholarship and respect for historical truth. The anthropologists, comparative religionists, and students of kindred disciplines who have now descended upon the Falashas in Israel present a grave danger to the survival of genuine knowledge of the factual and traditional background and the historical antecedents of these hapless people. In the first place, nearly all these questioners are innocent of the Ethiopian languages spoken by these recent immigrants. The use of interpreters or enquiries by means of a smattering of recently acquired Hebrew are wholly unsatisfactory *per se* and do not inspire confidence either in those questioned or in the results as such. Secondly, such studies conducted away from the traditional habitat of the Falashas are virtually useless. And, thirdly and most importantly, the Falashas have very quickly learnt that full acceptance as Jews requires them to give an account of their former life in Ethiopia that approximates as closely as possible to normative Judaism—yet is far removed from reality. Some such enquiries and studies, carried out by researchers unfamiliar with Falasha languages, their original native ambience, and their religious configuration, have already appeared and constitute a grave disservice to historical truth. Moreover, no study of this nature can have any hope of genuine success, unless it takes into account what those members of the community remaining in Ethiopia have to contribute to the picture. And, above all, since the Falashas can only be understood as a segment of the population of Ethiopia as a whole, it is futile to examine the truncated parts without investigating the place and position from which they were severed.

As a tailpiece to the Falasha story I might here add a word about an experience during my early days in Eritrea. J. Faitlovitch, the Jewish missionary (in itself a very unusual phenomenon) to the Falashas, arrived in Asmara not very long after the liberation of Ethiopia from Mussolini's conquest. He intended to travel to the Falasha region. Having recently visited the area, I suggested to him that such a journey might be dangerous, since the Falashas' experience under Fascist rule had shown them that there are apt to be grave disadvantages connected with Jewishness, and especially as that Jewish consciousness had only been stimulated by Faitlovitch himself in the course of his visits to Ethiopia early this century. He thought these fears were groundless and that 'his' Falashas would receive him with open arms. Alas, this did not happen, and the wrath of many of the Falashas against the man who had unwittingly placed them in such a perilous situation was strong. In fact, he needed to be rescued. Falasha anger did subside, however, in later years, and Faitlovitch was able to go back to his erstwhile disciples. He was, perhaps, the only one of the Falashas' Jewish missionaries who had acquired a thorough knowledge of the country and people and of their languages.

A personal interlude

After some months in Eritrea I had got accustomed to my daily work and had seen a little of the country and people, as described in the previous chapter. I had also embarked on a project, conceived under the auspices of the Public Information Officer (who was in charge of the local office of the British Ministry of Information), to establish the first ever regular newspaper in Tigrinya as well as some other journals in various languages spoken in Ethiopia. This activity was eventually to become one of my main concerns and will be described in some detail in the next chapter. In the meantime I had come to love the great beauty, often stark and overpowering, of highland Eritrea and Ethiopia. In later years the highlands of Scotland were to remind me of that awesome scenery of mountains and lakes. I had also greatly taken to the people with their fine looks and manners, their villages perched along the slopes of the hills, and their churches and solemn services—all so reminiscent of the world of the Old Testament.

In the course of my work I also had a good deal of contact with the local Italian population. Those with whom I had any official dealings were careful to conceal their Fascist past (or present, in some cases) and endeavoured to be as co-operative as possible. I for my part enjoyed speaking Italian, and this rather minor attainment generally eased relationships. I can only recall one spot of trouble when a fairly lowly post-office official, whose duty it was to carry postal bags to and from the censorship offices, was caught withholding letters from the Italian ladies to whom they were addressed until they agreed to offer sexual favours. We also had some successes in areas of greater consequence to the war effort when we discovered one or two local spies or, more significantly, firms in the East African and Red Sea region trying to trade with the enemy. On one occasion the *Queen Mary*, then a troop carrier, anchored just off Massawa.

Any references to her presence in the Red Sea were, of course, strictly prohibited. But some enterprising Italians tried to pass on the information to contacts in the Near East by referring to the mighty shadow darkening the entire town of Massawa—or similarly veiled allusions.

But by and large the situation was relatively peaceful (at any rate at that time), the position as regards the water supply was beginning to improve, and most items of food were plentiful—or so it seemed to me, coming from Jerusalem. Rommel was still in the Western Desert and remained a serious menace. But I felt I had by now enough experience of Eritrea to think of applying to the Military Administration to be permitted to bring my girlfriend to Asmara. There were at that time very few British or Allied women in this area, which was still considered a war zone; and those who were given permits to enter the country were required to undertake some kind of work connected with the War Office or the Military Government, usually as confidential secretaries. But before submitting such an application I thought it might be proper to write a formal letter to my future parents-in-law to press my suit—or whatever it is that one does in these circumstances. I felt woefully ignorant of the correct procedures and, in the nature of things, inexperienced. At the same time, I have to confess that, in the light of earlier conversations, I faced the likely outcome of this *démarche* without undue trepidation. My (now) fiancée's father sent an entertaining reply and her mother added a cordial postscript, both of which seemed to suggest that their eldest daughter's foray into unknown Africa did not fill them with serious forebodings.

I was now ready to submit my formal application to the Administration, together with my fiancée's assurances that she would be willing to undertake any duties assigned to her by the authorities. In due course I was interviewed by Junior Commander Adamson of the ATS, a white-haired and rather stern lady. She promised a decision within the next few weeks. My own boss, the Chief Censor, was strongly opposed to the idea that I might get married: 'This is no time for marriage, and in any event you are much too young!' I did not think he had any *locus standi* to enforce that view—nor did I know whether he would despatch another complaint to HQ Cairo (as he had done, it will be recalled, in the case of my pre-dawn copying of the

Tigrinya dictionary, which he feared might sap my energies).
Arguably, marriage might constitute an even greater danger to
my wholehearted devotion to the affairs of censorship, but I had
the utmost trust in the good sense of Cairo Headquarters who
had acquitted themselves so well on the previous occasion; and
I also supposed that they would be more concerned about
Rommel's presence along the fringes of Egypt than over this
minor cog's marital plans.

In due course I received the Military Administration's reply
over Junior Commander Adamson's signature. It was negative.
But she did sugar the pill most charmingly and encouraged me to
return to the charge once the war situation in the Middle East
had improved and it was less hazardous to admit women into this
occupied enemy territory. The only advantage of this delay was
that my fiancée's typing and shorthand proficiency would
meanwhile improve and that my prospects of promotion might
be enhanced in the interval. For the time being, however, we had
to be content with correspondence, which took about ten days to
reach Asmara from Jerusalem and vice versa. I thought it right to
warn my fiancée about the rigours of the journey, the shortage of
water (which made it, at first, virtually impossible to have a
bath), and the long distance from her family and friends. She
pooh-poohed these words of caution and wrote that she would
wash in fruit-juice if there were no water. While this particular
resolve was never put to the test, I can confirm, after forty-five
years of marriage, that such resourcefulness and loyalty have
never been wanting. The Chief Censor at Asmara was
meanwhile very concerned that courtship was being conducted
in what he termed 'the holy tongue of Hebrew employed for
secular purposes'. I suspected, however, that he was more than a
little miffed that he was unable to examine letters in that
language and had to pass them on to the Jerusalem censorship for
inspection.

My first Christmas at Asmara I spent in hospital. The
Palestinian Jewish Army doctors with whom I had travelled to
Eritrea were unable to diagnose the nature of my illness and
referred me to Professor Giovanni Ferro Luzzi, an authority on
tropical diseases and director of the local 'Regina Elena' hospital
(later 'Empress Mennen'—goodness knows what it might be
called in these revolutionary days!). Ferro Luzzi gave me one

look and decided (entirely correctly as it turned out) that I had *itterizia*, jaundice, and confined me at once to his hospital. This was not a wholly unpleasant experience. Jaundice and all diseases of the liver are very prevalent in Ethiopia, and Ferro Luzzi and his colleagues were knowledgeable about their treatment. The hospital—like everything else in wartime—was under military control, but that control was exercised very lightly, and the Italian doctors were able to get on with their work. The British medical officer in charge came to see me occasionally, but he wisely trusted Ferro Luzzi and the devoted nursing staff who were nuns. The food consisted almost entirely of barely luke-warm spinach and a nice white fish which tasted like cod. I am still surprised that I never enquired why the food could not be hot. On the first evening a young Sicilian priest appeared to offer me 'conforto di anima'. I assured him that my illness was not serious and that I did not think I stood in need of his professional attention. He came back every evening for a chat and was pleasantly free of all missionary zeal. I was much taken with his very strong Sicilian accent, and he was as surprised at my knowledge (quite secular and purely linguistic and historical, I fear) of the Bible as I was at his almost total ignorance of it. Many years later I was told by my Italian colleagues in Rome that such ignorance was not uncommon in certain parts of Italy. But on my last evening in hospital the priest felt he had to do his duty, pointed to the crucifix over my bed and asked me whether I knew who this was. I assured him that I did, for after all Jesus and I had both lived in the same city. He expressed surprise: 'But you told me that you had come to Asmara from Jerusalem, while *He* lived in the Vatican City!' I do not know to this day whether he could possibly have been serious—even though he sounded so—or was just having me on.

Early in 1943 the northern shores of Africa were being cleared of Axis forces, largely as a result of the victory at El-Alamein in October-November 1942. I think it was in February 1943 that Junior Commander Adamson wrote to me to say that the Military Administrator of Eritrea was now willing to authorize the issue of a permit for my fiancée to enter the country, on condition that she was willing to work for the military government or local branches of the War Office. So I sent a cable to Jerusalem, 'No further obstacles on the road to Eritrea', which the Chief Censor felt might be liable to be misunderstood if it were to fall into enemy hands. Although I thought that that contingency was unlikely to arise, I readily acquiesced in his amended wording, 'Entry permit to Eritrea available now.'

Preparations and arrangements were at once put in train in both Jerusalem and Asmara. The journey between these two places was infinitely complicated for a civilian in wartime. Edwin Samuel was helpful and also wrote me a charming letter of congratulation after my fiancée had called on him. In general she was to follow the same route as I had taken some time earlier. There was no question of a trousseau, but suitable clothing and equipment for life in Eritrea-Ethiopia were required. I had also been told by some friends that wedding rings were unobtainable at Asmara (this intelligence, I was later informed by my wife, was quite inaccurate), so she had to bring her own. The scale of preparations was such that she had to give up her secretarial course midway and concentrate on all the intricate logistics of the journey.

In Asmara things were less hectic but almost equally time-consuming. The first priority was to find a flat or house and, despite the endeavours of the officer in charge of accommodation, nothing could be had until about two months after my fiancée's scheduled arrival. I settled for that and meanwhile got rooms in an Italian boarding-house whose sanitary facilities, largely on account of poor plumbing and of the water restrictions at that time, left much to be desired. Perhaps I may anticipate here and say that the house, when we eventually obtained it, proved to be very satisfactory. It was adequately large for our purposes, was partly furnished with PWD standard issue, and was situated in a very pleasant part of Asmara. Some years later, when my wife had risen to the dizzy heights of being the Military Governor's Private Secretary, we were given an excellent flat in a fine tree-lined avenue with a centre promenade, opposite the palace gardens and library, that was at first called 'Viale de Bono' (after Mussolini's general who initiated the Ethiopian campaign in 1935), subsequently, after Mussolini's downfall, 'Viale Roma', and later still re-christened by Emperor Haile Sellassie 'Queen Elizabeth II Avenue'. I shudder to think after which member of the Communist pantheon it might be named now. It has always struck me how sensibly things are ordered in Britain, at any rate in this respect, where streets names do not generally have obvious or recent political connotations, whilst in so many countries they are subject to frequent changes in consonance with fluctuating political fashions and fortunes.

To revert to the chronological sequence: the principal problem at the Asmara end was posed by the actual mechanics of getting married. At first it seemed quite straightforward: the law officers advised that the Military Governor was authorized to perform marriages. There was, in fact, a recent precedent when his own ADC had got married. But some unexpected delays during my fiancée's journey complicated matters in a rather curious way. GHQ Cairo had decreed that the governors of the various newly occupied enemy territories were to be re-styled, that is, from Military Administrator to Chief Administrator. But the seals of office, which were required for the solemnization of marriages, had been surrendered and the new seals were not expected in the immediate future. We, however, were anxious to get married as soon as possible, as we could not afford to maintain two separate establishments. Moreover, Junior Commander Adamson had not so far been able to find a suitable secretarial post for my fiancée, since—not unreasonably—no one wished to commit himself without interviewing the lady concerned.

Meanwhile that lady, having arrived in Cairo from Jerusalem, at the end of March 1943, was stuck there. It had been arranged that, on reaching Cairo, she would be met at the station by an acquaintance of mine, Mr Nathan Marein, at that time Legal Adviser to the Ethiopian Government. Marein, on his return trip to Ethiopia, was to travel by the same trains and boat from Cairo to Asmara and had promised to act as protector and guardian to a young girl embarking on a week's journey, alone and in wartime North-East Africa. When they met in Cairo, Marein suddenly disclosed that he preferred travelling by air and suggested that she join the same flight to Asmara. My fiancée doubted that she would be able to obtain the necessary priority allocation on a flight. When they made enquiries, the officer in charge assured them that she would be accommodated on the Asmara plane. On that clear understanding and not without some hesitation she surrendered her surface transport tickets to Messrs Thomas Cook who informed her that the actual cash could only be refunded at the point of issue, i.e. at Jerusalem. Meanwhile Marein lent her £20, to be refunded by me in Asmara, for her air tickets.

In due course I received a cable from Marein that he and my fiancée would reach Asmara next Saturday and would I meet them at the airport. Marein arrived—but without his female charge. At the last moment the priority allocation for air travel had not been forthcoming. I was less than pleased at being saddled with Marein and with £20 of debts—at that time quite a large sum, about a month's living expenses. Meanwhile my hapless fiancée was abandoned in Egypt and had some difficulty in retrieving the air fare in order to pay for fresh overland transport. Moreover, another passage could not be obtained immediately, and the delay in arriving in Asmara would be at least ten days. It was during this interval that the change in the Military Governor's designation occurred which made it impossible for him to perform the marriage ceremony himself. In later years, when Brigadier Longrigg had become a good and trusted friend to both of us, he always expressed regret that he was deprived of 'that privilege', as he put it. For fully thirty-five years thereafter, whenever we saw Stephen Longrigg, the subject of that missed opportunity would always be referred to.

However, eventually she did arrive—at dawn on Tuesday, 13 April 1943, on the overnight train from Agordat. In fact, she had not been all that lonely; there had been a certain amount of competition among a number of officers to act as her protectors. At that dark hour, however, in the cold dawn of an altitude of 7,500 feet, Asmara must have seemed rather forbidding. But two hours later, in the beautiful spring-like sunshine, things looked more cheerful. And at lunch she had a splendid Italian-style meal at a restaurant, of a quality and quantity quite unobtainable in wartime Palestine. But the boarding-house, with its dicey sanitation and less than satisfactory fellow-guests, was somewhat of a shock. It was a great relief when eventually our house became available.

The day after her arrival I presented my fiancée to the Chief Censor, as a matter of courtesy, and to a smiling Junior Commander Adamson, as a matter of duty. Within a week of her arrival she had to start work at the War Office's Department of Claims, as Private Secretary to the Major in charge of the office, at a monthly salary of £6.

Meanwhile the problem of the legal mechanics of our nuptials seemed a little closer to a solution when the law officers advised

Brigadier Longrigg that, under the powers vested in him as Military Governor, he should direct the Italian mayor of Asmara to marry us. The mayor, Gaetano Inserra, readily consented. He was in fact a senior colonial official of the old school, quiet and perhaps a little colourless. But his secretary-general, dottore Melodia, made up for that deficiency by a high degree of boisterousness. Alas, now fresh problems arose: as members of the occupying power we were, by definition, unknown to the local population; and without banns no marriage could be solemnized. Then the Procuratore del Re (Italy was still a kingdom at that time), the senior Italian legal officer, stepped into the breach and declared that he was willing to authorize the marriage if we could each produce four witnesses (i.e. eight altogether) willing to declare on oath that we were both single. I might just be able to manage, but how could my fiancée do so, having arrived only two or three days ago? However, she looked so young and innocent that four American servicemen of my acquaintance volunteered for the task without undue compunction.

While all the documents were being prepared, I was approached by the Abuna Kerillos, the Ethiopian Orthodox Deputy Bishop of Eritrea (the substantive Bishop, Abuna Markos, was at that time temporarily resident in Addis Ababa). We had met a number of times, and he had claimed to be impressed with my knowledge of the liturgical language of Ethiopia. He had heard of our plight and now offered to marry us at his church—'Tomorrow if you like'. It was a tempting offer—and romantic into the bargain. It was also impolitic, in the circumstances then prevailing, to rebuff so senior a dignitary. But the next day I informed him that neither of us had the spiritual maturity and preparation for so grave a step. He seemed to appreciate that and repeated several times the word *manfasawi*, 'spiritual', which I had used.

Finally, all the formalities were completed and the day, 27 April 1943, was fixed. The Chief Censor agreed to be present at the short ceremony at the Asmara Municipio (offices which, incidentally, I was later to occupy myself when I joined the Ministry of Information and it subsequently moved to those spacious premises), and he and a close colleague of mine acted as witnesses. I was allowed two hours off work (from noon to 2 p.m.), while my wife was permitted to stay away from her office for the whole day. The Chief Censor obviously reckoned that my absence during the entire day might prolong the war. Commendatore Inserra, however, was festively attired and wore the colourful regalia of his office. He was supported by the cheerful dottore Melodia and a bevy of uniformed attendants. For the benefit of my bride they had thoughtfully laid on an interpreter who translated the Italian version of the ceremony into what he conceived to be English. In fact, they were English words in a fluent Italian pronunciation, and I had to nudge my wife-to-be whenever he reached the words 'tay breeday' (i.e. 'the bride'). At the end we were handed a certificate, in duplicate, signed by Messrs Inserra and Melodia, which confirmed, in Italian, that we had been properly married according to law. It was dated 'Era Fascista XXI', no doubt one of the last documents to bear such a political imprint, for a few months later Mussolini was toppled and the Fascist era came to its inglorious conclusion. There were not many occasions subsequently when we needed to exhibit this marriage certificate, but once or twice its accurate translation into English puzzled or impressed British official-dom.

In the months and years after the wedding I encountered the dignified Inserra only a few times, usually at official functions, but the colourful Melodia was part of the Asmara street scene. And whenever he caught sight of us he produced the same leering 'come va' (how goes it!?).

A year or two after the event the new Legal Adviser to the Military Administration questioned the legality of the pro-cedures leading to our marriage. Both my wife and I were delighted at this news, for in the meantime we had acquired many friends in Eritrea, British as well as Ethiopian, and had also advanced up the hierarchical ladder. The then Military Governor, General J. M. Benoy, was looking forward to performing the marriage of his Private Secretary to his Assistant Political Secretary and to arranging a large party at his residence, the Vice-Regal Lodge in Asmara. To us, the thought of having lived in sin for some time seemed to have a somewhat piquant thrill which, in this day and age, must appear positively antediluvian. It was, therefore, a genuine disappointment when eventually the combined forces of the Legal Department reached the unanimous conclusion that the original marriage had been lawful after all.

Asmara was a fine place in which to start married life. The war had left Africa by now, and we often felt a twinge of conscience at our relatively comfortable life at a time when people in Europe were dying and the fiercest battles were yet to come. Paradoxically, when the situation on the war front was beginning to improve and, in the end, victory was won, the local position gradually worsened. The conflicts attendant upon the future disposal of Eritrea were intensifying apace.

In our private life, however, we were extremely fortunate in finding an excellent home-help for our house. As we were both working, we needed someone to look after our home. Hagossa was a Swedish-Mission-educated married woman, utterly dependable and a most congenial person to have about the house, which she looked after with care and devotion. In later years we often dreamed of having another Hagossa, but we never found anyone like her. In contrast to most Ethiopian women she was rather plain, but we both grew fond of her. She did not cook, but all else she did to perfection. She could read and write, and every Thursday I brought her the Tigrinya weekly newspaper which she studied avidly. On one occasion she was utterly overwhelmed when the Military Governor, my wife's chief, came to dinner. Hagossa had seen his photograph in the paper almost every week, opening schools, making speeches, taking parades, etc. But the living image, the real person represented by those pictures in the newspaper, was almost too much for her. The exclamation of wonderment, *gway*, was all she could utter. When we eventually left Eritrea, the parting from Hagossa was sad. We tried to find her another job, and I wrote to her from Jerusalem. When I came to Asmara ten years later I brought her some presents from my wife, and on one occasion Leon Roth, on a journey to Eritrea, took some pieces of jewellery to her. But since the mid-1960s we have been unable to find her: all attempts to trace her whereabouts have been unsuccessful. We remember her with fondness.

We made good friends among Eritrean-Ethiopians and among our British colleagues. All who served there consider that period among the best in their lives. I dedicated a recent book of mine, on the Tigrinya language,

TO THE MEMORY OF MY COLLEAGUES
BRITISH AND ERITREAN
IN THE BRITISH MILITARY ADMINISTRATION
OF ERITREA DURING THE SECOND WORLD WAR
WHO HAVE SINCE DIED
AND TO THE FEW
WHO ARE STILL WITH US AND CHERISH MEMORIES
OF ERITREA AND ITS PEOPLE

Alas, most of them have by now gone to their Elysium, but I hope to say a few words about some of them, and about the few survivors, elsewhere in this book. The enduring quality of the friendships made at that time and in that place has been a source of great pleasure and comfort to us.

One of those friendships, though initiated and cemented at Asmara, was with someone who was only an occasional visitor to Eritrea's capital and who was, in fact, stationed at Gorgora near Lake Tana. Dick Luyt was (and happily still is) a South African with sanely progressive views. He had been a Rhodes Scholar at Oxford shortly before the war, had served in Ethiopia with Mission 101, had won a DCM, and had remained in Ethiopia with the British Military Mission in which he rose to the rank of Lieut.-Colonel in a remarkably short time. He was an ideal companion and faithful friend, and we spent a most agreeable Christmas with him when he came to Asmara in 1943 during the festive season. After the war he advanced rapidly in the Colonial Service and finished that part of his career as Governor-General of Guyana (and as Sir Richard Luyt). He then embarked on a new career as Vice-Chancellor of Cape Town University. Nowadays we do not meet often, but the friendship survives in good repair. In fact, during his Vice-Chancellorship he was able to offer the Chair of Hebrew at Cape Town to my erstwhile student and young friend Simon Hopkins, and in this way another link between us was forged.

Towards the end of 1943 we were entitled to a few days of local leave which we decided to spend at Keren—a belated honeymoon. We had both been working hard, and, in addition, since my marriage social life had increased considerably. Women were in short supply in wartime Eritrea, and I found that my popularity had suddenly grown—for reasons not far to seek. My wife greatly enjoyed the unaccustomed whirl of social activity, parties, dinner dances at the Officers' Club, etc, while I would often have preferred to stay at home and continue with my work on Tigrinya and Amharic. I was trying to become as proficient as possible in these languages, for I was never thereafter likely to find equally propitious conditions in which such study could be pursued. Thus in the evenings I would frequently have informants come to the house with whom I could work on these Ethiopian tongues, or I would sit alone and write up my material. These studies were eventually to mature and lead to an Oxford doctorate on the relationship of the modern Semitic languages of Ethiopia to the classical language called Ge'ez. But in Asmara it was often a struggle to concentrate on scholarly pursuits. I vividly remember one particular occasion when the Military Governor wished to spend a weekend on the Red Sea coast at Massawa. He invited us and his personal assistant, a lady, to accompany him. My presence was only required to act as chaperon, as he could scarcely turn up there in the company of two young ladies. He was more than a little taken aback when I begged to be excused, as I felt I had to do some of my own work.

But our 'honeymoon' at Keren was also needed because my wife appeared to be suffering (as quite a few people did) just a little from prolonged and unaccustomed exposure to an altitude of 7,500-8,000 feet. The descent to Keren (4,300 feet) was bound to be salutary. We went by train and returned by road, an extremely winding road with some spectacular bends, by the side of which one would see the wreckage of cars and lorries that had failed to heed the warning signs. The closer one approached to Keren the lusher the vegetation became. It was a garden city situated in the valley of the Anseba river, with a wonderful climate and the most beautiful flowers and exotic birds. My wife was quite enchanted with this luxuriant vegetation and the amazing colours, especially electric blues and greens, of the birds. We had never seen anything like it before; unfortunately we were both so ornithologically illiterate that we could not identify any of them. Twenty years later, when I travelled in those regions with my colleague Charles Beckingham, I received some instruction in that sphere—alas, since then long forgotten again. Keren was a centre of Italian agricultural settlements (*concessioni agricole*) and large-scale plantations: coffee, tobacco, agave, fruit of all kinds, but particularly bananas, papaya (pawpaw)—and, of course, vegetables in great profusion. The entire vast valley was surrounded by a mountain chain which had been the scene of the last serious Italian resistance to the British and Imperial onslaught in 1941.

We put up at the small and comfortable hotel and had a few days of blissful rest in this paradisiac spot. On one of those days we lunched with the Senior Civil Affairs Officer (District Commissioner) and his wife who were profoundly aware of their good fortune in being stationed in such marvellous surroundings. One of our fellow guests was the chairman of the Imperial War Graves Commission who had come to inspect the impressively beautiful and sadly extensive war cemetery sheltering the remains of the many fallen in the battles of early 1941.

At our hotel was a young British sergeant whom I had met occasionally at the Croce del Sud Café before my wife's arrival. He was extremely well spoken and educated and worked for the local branch of the Ministry of Information as a journalist on the *Eritrean Daily News*, the official English newspaper which also had an Italian edition. Soon we were to become colleagues in the same establishment. I never knew George (Sutherland) Fraser well and have always regretted that I did not manage to get closer to him. He was shy and awkward, and he seemed untidy and ill at ease in his uniform. I was told that his general demeanour made it impossible for him to receive a commission and that he was perfectly content to remain a sergeant. I was acutely embarrassed that I could not invite him to the officers' club and that I was technically senior to him. Yet he was in most ways superior to nearly all of us.

George Fraser was born in Glasgow in 1915 and, so he told me, moved to Aberdeen as a child when his father was appointed Town Clerk Depute of the granite city. He retained a firm loyalty to Aberdeen and to St Andrews University where his resolve to become a poet and writer was formed. I think he was the first to speak to me of St. Andrews where, later on, my wife and I were to spend some of our happiest years. Fraser had come to Asmara in 1942, after a spell in Cairo. He had already published some poems and was even then the literary man *par excellence*. It must have been agony to him to churn out a daily avalanche of trivial prose, either sub-editing the war news as it came in or, much worse, going in search of local stories with pseudo-local colour. He did it manfully and without complaint, yet his heart was not in it. He said he envied me editing a Tigrinya newspaper which was at least of real linguistic interest and meant converting the trivia of the day into thought categories accessible to Tigrinya-speaking readers, a challenging task.

After the war I lost touch with him, to my lasting regret, but I saw his poetry reviews in the *New Statesman* and recognized his style in some (then still anonymous) reviews in the *Times Literary Supplement*. He did some work for the British Council and for the BBC, and also lectured and translated. His output as poet, travel writer, translator, literary critic, and biographer made his name widely known. In 1959 he became, successively, Lecturer and Reader in Modern English Literature in the University of Leicester, specializing particularly in poetry, both as practitioner of the art and as critic. His subsequent publications add up to a very considerable *œuvre*. He died in 1980 just after his retirement from Leicester University. In 1983 a posthumous autobiographical fragment was published, under the title *A Stranger and Afraid, the autobiography of an intellectual* (Carcanet New Press, Manchester), that takes us up to 1949, the year in which it was written. In many ways it is a sad book, conceived before his achievements became widely known, but the ten pages about Asmara are a gem and show what a real writer can accomplish. His vignettes of our Italian colleagues are particularly successful, and the poem 'A Native Girl in Decamere' is strongly evocative of that deserted town, some twenty-five miles south of Asmara, which simply died when Mussolini's conquest of Abyssinia was completed. My wife and I once cycled to Decamere, but on our way back we grew so tired that we could not carry on. A passing bus took us and our bikes back to Asmara. On that bus was Sgt Fraser. Had he just written that poem on the girl in Decamere?

Publishing for Eritreans and Ethiopians

In the summer of 1942 I had some discussions with the then Public Information Officer of Eritrea, Major David C. Cousland.

It seemed to us that the time was ripe to found a regular newspaper in Tigrinya, for, apart from some occasional information sheets issued over the years by the Italian Colonial Government of Eritrea, there had never been a newspaper in that language, published either weekly or at stated intervals. Not only was Tigrinya the principal language of Eritrea, it was also the indigenous tongue of the eponymous Tigre province, just south of the then artificial Eritrea-Ethiopia frontier. With some four to five million native speakers it is thus, next to Arabic and Amharic, the living Semitic language with the largest number of native speakers—comfortably outstripping the figures for Hebrew. Cousland acted with great speed and efficiency and produced the necessary technical equipment and finance for this new enterprise. We recruited an excellent Swedish-Mission-educated teacher, Ato Waldeab Waldemaryam, as the effective editor, and the first issue of the Tigrinya *Eritrean Weekly News* appeared on 31 August 1942. It continued without interruption, under the same executive editor, until the end of the British caretaker administration in 1952.

When, late in 1943, Cousland was succeeded as head of the local Ministry of Information by Philip Mumford and his wife Margery, both proved to be very interested not only in the continuance of the Tigrinya paper but in its strengthening and consolidation as well as in an extension into the field of publishing in Amharic and Arabic, the other main languages spoken and read in the wider Ethiopian area. They discussed these plans with me and, as a result, offered me the post of Editor of the Ministry of Information's African Publications—subject to the approval of Mr C. N. Ryan, the head of the British Information Services in the whole of the Middle East. After some initial hesitation Ryan agreed, and I set out on a job which proved to be infinitely more rewarding than the essentially negative aspects of censorship. The new post also opened up vistas and offered scope and opportunities beyond all my initial hopes. The Mumfords and Ryan became great friends to us.

Before I come to describe the substance of my new and greatly enhanced sphere of life, I must first say a few words about Margery Mumford. She was the daughter of Major H. Rayne, soldier and colonial administrator, a man of a highly adventurous bent of mind, famed in East Africa where he took part in the campaigns to capture the 'Mad Mullah'. Her mother was the sister of (Dame) Margery Perham whose personality and writings had for so long exercised a great influence on British colonial policy, particularly in Africa. When Margery Mumford arrived in Asmara she seemed to transform the social milieu. She was as efficient and as hard-working as she was beautiful. Her gaiety (I trust one can still safely use the noun!?) was truly infectious, and everyone was charmed by her entirely natural, outgoing, and unpompous manner. Half the male population of Asmara was a little in love with her. She treated the lowliest Eritrean messenger boy with the same regard for his dignity as she would the Military Governor. In the office she smoothed friction and ironed out problems; no one could resist her. She was highly imaginative rather than being an intellectual, but she wrote and spoke beautifully and had a mind remarkably open to all new ideas.

My wife and I thought she was wonderful and we spent many happy hours with the Mumfords. On some occasions we would hire bicyles and roll down the Massawa road with its steep descent and hairpin bends. If you could have confidence in your brakes, it was an exhilarating sensation. If we went down too far, we would get a lorry to take us back, but at times we would push the bikes on our return and have the most entertaining conversations on the long steep climb up the mountain. The Mumfords stayed for less than eighteen months in Eritrea, and after their departure we had to console ourselves with their dog which they bequeathed to us. Much later Margery suggested to her famous aunt (Margery Perham) to give me a job at her Institute at Oxford and thus provided the initial impetus to my academic career. We have remained close friends.

The Tigrinya *Eritrean Weekly News* (*EWN*) became my main responsibility, and it was a truly exciting assignment to be closely associated with a journal that was not so much a newspaper, rather the repository of Tigrinya intellectual life and the springboard for the creation of a literary tradition in that language. Hitherto Tigrinya had been principally employed for all oral purposes and for brief written communications, announcements, etc, as well as in very limited literary contexts such as the translation of the New Testament (the whole Bible had to wait until much later). But now there was a regular weekly instalment of good Tigrinya prose (and occasionally even poetry) which contributed immeasurably to the enrichment of the vocabulary and to the development of more sophisticated syntactical means. In the wake of the birth of the *EWN*, the thirty years from 1942 until the early 1970s witnessed the greatest flowering of Tigrinya writing hitherto encountered. In an anthology of Tigrinya literature which I published early in 1986, literary pieces from the *EWN* occupy an important place.

Of course, the wartime Ministry of Information was not primarily concerned either with Tigrinya literacy or literature but with the creation of a medium in which news of the war and the claims of democracy might be conveyed to a people which had not until now been exposed to such heady stuff. In the long run, however, the concomitant and incidental features to which I have referred have proved to be of the greatest consequence. During the ten years of its existence the *EWN* not only became a vehicle for genuinely good Tigrinya writing but constituted by far the most weighty body of written material in that language— running to some 520 issues, each of four (occasionally six) pages of very large format. This represents a total of nearly 2,500 pages or some three million words. It is difficult to overestimate the role of the *EWN* in helping to evolve a style of Tigrinya writing in many disparate branches, such as war news, political discussion, religious and edificatory literature, humorous and general literary essays, Ethiopian history, simple announcements and advertisements as well as official legal proclamations, and many other themes—not least among these a lively correspondence column. I would argue that these cultural gains—together with Kynaston-Snell's devoted work for Eritrean education—represent some of the principal achievements of eleven years of British rule in Eritrea. That an essentially short-lived military and caretaker administration should have done so much must surely tip the scales in its favour when the definitive history of the period comes to be written. 'The establishment of this indigenous medium of Tigrinya expression (I wrote in the introduction to that recent anthology of Tigrinya literature),

coupled with the new-found freedoms concomitant with the military successes of the democracies, led to a heightened sense of Tigrinya national consciousness which was further enhanced by the educational and political prestige gained during the period of federation from 1952 to 1962. Subsequently, the pressure exerted upon Tigrinya by the institutions of the central Ethiopian Government and its gradual replacement, in many official contexts, by Amharic played a not insignificant role in the genesis of the Eritrean independence movements—which, since the 1974 revolution, have spawned similar bodies in the neighbouring Tigre province, and indeed elsewhere in Ethiopia.

Of course, we distributed the *EWN* only within Eritrea, but it was inevitable that it should also be read avidly across the unguarded and arbitrary border in the Tigrinya-speaking Tigre region of Northern Ethiopia. The circulation figures for this paper were excellent and impressed even the hard-nosed financial criteria of Mr Ryan on his visits of inspection. For Curteis Ryan was never content to direct affairs from his Cairo headquarters but would frequently descend upon the many territories under his control, when all our activities would come under the most searching scrutiny. In the course of one such visit to Eritrea and Ethiopia he insisted, on the spur of the moment, on climbing, by mule and on foot, to the medieval Bizen monastery, perched over 8,000 feet up on a well-nigh inaccessible mountain ridge. There, to our surprise, he discovered several copies of the *EWN*. It was not until he had satisfied himself that nobody could have had prior knowledge of his visit to plant copies of the paper in that remote spot that he expressed his pleasure and commendation.

As a considerable proportion of the population was illiterate, we appointed a number of public readers in some of the key areas. On Thursdays, when the *EWN* was published, I would often travel to different parts of the country and observe those public readers, standing in market squares or other prominent assembly places, reciting the contents of the paper to a large and attentive audience. Thursdays, after the *EWN* had been distributed, were usually relaxed days that could be used to visit outlying districts to inspect the efficacy of the Ministry's various activities. Thus in this job, as well as in my future appointment as Assistant Political Secretary in the Military Administration, I had ample opportunities of visiting most parts of Eritrea and many regions of Ethiopia. The beauty of the highland scenery and the graciousness and warm hospitality of the people were a constant source of pleasure.

While Thursday was thus an easy day, the rest of the week could be very busy with collecting and writing up the material, not only for the *EWN* but also for the other publications for which I was responsible. Wednesday was the heaviest day, putting the paper to bed. That day was usually spent with the compositors and printers. They taught me a good deal about the processes of printing and publication. The Tigrinya, Amharic, and Arabic papers were composed by hand, while publications in English and Italian were set on then fairly modern linotype machines—no doubt a far cry from current processes of newspaper and magazine production.

The linchpin of our Tigrinya activities was the aforementioned Waldeab Waldemaryam, with whom I developed a most congenial working relationship. He also became a good friend and in many respects my principal Tigrinya teacher and informant. Waldeab was some twelve years older than myself, in his mid-30s then; he was born at Adwa, the famous place just south of the Eritrea-Ethiopia frontier, but had spent most of his life as alumnus and teacher at the Swedish Evangelical Mission in Asmara. His manner of writing Tigrinya was liked and appreciated by his readers, and most Eritreans spoke of him as the father of contemporary Tigrinya writing. As far as I know, he never engaged in any imaginative writing, and his name will always be associated with the *EWN*, a monument of which he may be justly proud.

Waldeab had a wife and children who lived in Addis Ababa and whom I never met. I do not recall that he himself ever went there to visit them. He could be stubborn and was inclined to be impetuous; he seemed to be deficient in the diplomatic skills of which so many Ethiopians are masters. After I left Eritrea he became the co-founder of a party advocating the independence of Eritrea. As such he became the focus of enmity on the part of the large and powerful organization striving for union with Ethiopia, led by Tedla Bairu who became the first Chief Executive (= Prime Minister) of Eritrea under the Ethiopian Federation in 1952 (and about whom I shall have more to say in the next chapter). There were no fewer than six attempts on Waldeab's life between 1947 and 1952, and after Tedla's accession to power he left for Cairo. It was in the early and mid-1950s that I last heard from him direct, in some long and moving letters from

Egypt. Thereafter I lost touch with him, but I was told in the late 1960s that at that time he was still at Cairo. Since then the trail has gone cold. I am sad to have lost such a good friend.

There was an interesting venture directly connected with the *EWN*. The absence of a literary tradition posed questions and problems in at least three areas. First, writing in Tigrinya required a measure of standardization in its modes of spelling. Secondly, Tigrinya needed some adaptation to contemporary demands (the vocabulary of war and modern martial equipment necessitated the fashioning of suitable technical terms). Thirdly, the limited experience of writing Tigrinya entailed that means of expression as well as syntactical and stylistic conventions and patterns had to be devised which were likely to meet with fairly general acceptance. I therefore thought it would be useful to establish a limited pilot scheme which might perform, on a modest scale, what the Hebrew and Arabic Language Academies did in their grander spheres. We thus set up a Tigrinya Language Council, composed of some representatives of the churches and of a few of the most experienced practitioners of the language. At first, for a year or two, the experiment worked reasonably well, but later on political considerations began to enter the picture, the initial enthusiasm flagged, and the committee became moribund. But I feel that, short-lived as it was, the Tigrinya Language Council has its modest niche in the history of Tigrean cultural endeavours.

Many years later, Emperor Haile Sellassie spoke to me about the pros and cons of establishing an Amharic Language Academy; and not long before his deposition and death a law was enacted to create such a body, of which my friend, the Amharic poet and playwright Mangestu Lemma, was a prominent member. I do not know whether this Academy survives in present circumstances and, if so, in what form.

Next to my responsibility for the already existing *EWN* was the initiation of a paper in Arabic. We hired a sub-editor who was quite satisfactory but in no way of Waldeab's calibre. The problem was that Arabic is not indigenous to Eritrea or Ethiopia, although it was liked by all local or immigrant Muslims and read by some. Thus it was virtually impossible to achieve a consensus as to what sort of Arabic should be employed in this new paper. Most of those consulted opted for Sudanese Arabic but, they emphasized, 'in a less literary form'. When a few issues had appeared, I received a letter from A. J. Arberry, then at the Ministry of Information, later Professor of Arabic at Cambridge and a much admired senior colleague and friend. In that letter he complained, in characteristically civilized and felicitous terms, about the quality of the Arabic we were using. In reply I could only assent to every one of his politely worded strictures, but I had to say that it was our duty to put our message across and be understood. Regrettably we were not an organization charged with the teaching of Arabic and the improvement of its local variety. We did, however, experiment with a number of different types of Arabic that might be understood in our region. None proved to be entirely satisfactory, largely because those who spoke or understood Arabic in this area originated from various countries with differing, narrowly localized patois and because the resultant speech forms represented an amalgam of so many disparate components.

The new Arabic paper started out as a weekly and was called *Al-Usbu'*, 'The Week', but we soon found that we could neither afford nor justify a weekly publication, and 'The Week' became *Ash-Shahr*, 'The Month'. In this form it survived for several years. When the British Administration was succeeded, in 1952, by an autonomous Eritrean Government within the Ethiopian Federation, their Information Office published a daily paper of four pages which was half in Tigrinya and half in Arabic.

More interesting as well as more important were our activities involving Addis Ababa. The situation there was fairly delicate. The Emperor had returned only recently to his country and taken charge of the administration of his realm—with certain restrictions connected with the conduct of the war. These restrictions, limited as they were, were perceived by him and by many Ethiopians as an irritant. The British Minister, (Sir) Robert Howe, and his Legation (this was, of course, at a time before all Ministers and Legations were upgraded to Ambassadors and Embassies, respectively) had to tread warily in order not to offend Ethiopian susceptibilities, still in a vulnerable state as a result of their recent experience with the Italians, on the one hand, and of the awkwardness of feeling beholden to (and simultaneously slightly resentful of) the British liberators, on the other.

In these circumstances it was extremely fortunate that our opposite number in Addis Ababa was a man in whom the Ethiopians had the utmost confidence. He was the Press Attaché at the British Legation, H. D. Molesworth, who had held (and was to occupy again after the war) senior posts at the Victoria and Albert Museum. Molesworth had precisely the right temperament: he was unworried by delays and procrastinations, for he was himself no mean practitioner of this art; he was informal in his manner and did not have even the remotest feeling of colour discrimination; he was outspoken and possessed a vocabulary singularly rich in expletives (unrecorded in my *Concise Oxford Dictionary* at that time); he was an artist and a widely educated man; he was fun, though he could be irritating in his conduct of business. It was usually much more expeditious to take the plane from Asmara to Addis Ababa than to wait for an unequivocal written reply from Molesworth.

Those flights, over a distance of about 650 miles, were at times fairly adventurous. The direct route over the Semien mountains had to maintain an altitude of at least 18,000 feet, and in pre-pressurization days flights in those small but reliable DC3s could be very painful to one's ears. More often than not such heights were avoided by flying over the Red Sea and stopping for refuelling either at Aden or on Kamaran Island, a tiny (then British-administered) island close to the Arabian coast, some 180 miles north of the Bab el Mandeb. Kamaran was taken from the Turks in 1915 by British forces and was subsequently under the control of the Governor of Aden. Its administrator since 1935 was Major D. Thompson, who seemed to enjoy the loneliness and seclusion of the twenty-two square miles and two thousand inhabitants of his barren but not unromantic dominion. He played the customs officer when we landed at his small airstrip, then drove us to his residence, and shortly afterwards re-appeared as the Governor and gave us a most delicious as well as ample breakfast.

In Addis Ababa Molesworth was an excellent host. Things rarely worked out as originally arranged, but he was never put out. It was at once obvious that the Ethiopians took to him greatly. He had had the excellent idea that our first joint publishing venture should be a translation into Amharic of Dr Johnson's *Rasselas*. For this not uncomplicated task he had

recruited the ideal person who possessed almost equal
competence in English and in Amharic. He was Sirak Heruy
Walda Sellassie, an Oxford graduate and proud Brasenose man,
son of the Emperor's late Foreign Minister, Blattengeta Heruy
Walda Sellassie, who had himself been an Amharic writer of
note. Sirak was of slight build and frail-looking, often in ill-
health, with a noble head and a neat turn of phrase. I at once
formed the impression that nobody then available could
discharge this task as well as Sirak, but he worked at his own
sedate pace. I was apt to be impatient, mindful of the likelihood
that at his rate of progress there would probably be no Ministry
of Information in existence to publish the finished product in
which it had invested a fair amount of money. The combination
of Molesworth's tact and patience with Sirak's wayward genius
did produce something excellent in the end—but nearly two
years after the end of the war. Sirak's Amharic rendering of
Rasselas was published at Asmara in 1947. A second, slightly
corrected, edition appeared at Addis Ababa in 1974.

We also produced, for distribution in Ethiopia, an Amharic
illustrated magazine, usually published once a month and
intended for a highbrow audience. It carried some reflective
articles about the war, essays on China, Russia, Britain, and
Ethiopia, as well as some pieces of more general cultural interest.
It was called 'Towards Victory' (in Amharic). Its progress was by
no means smooth, for Amharic is not indigenous in Eritrea,
though quite a few educated Eritreans, even at that time, could
speak and understand it. We found someone in Asmara who had
lived most of his life in Addis Ababa and seemed a suitable
translator of the articles that were to appear in the journal. I
scrutinized his Amharic as carefully as I was capable of and also
submitted specimens to competent judges at Addis Ababa—
including the then Prime Minister of Ethiopia, Bitwodded
Makonnen Endalkatchew, who was more renowned as an author
than he was as a politician. Everyone seemed to be reasonably
content with the quality of our translator's Amharic, except
Molesworth as advised by Sirak. The latter had neither the time
nor the strength or inclination to do the work himself (and, in
any event, he would have transformed a monthly publication
into an annual one); but he felt that nobody else could write
decent Amharic. His stylistic idiosyncrasies coupled with his

dog-in-the-manger attitude led to some friction in correspondence, though never when we met in person.

My first visit to Molesworth was also the first occasion on
which I was received in audience by Emperor Haile Sellassie. I
had seen him once before when I stood in a large crowd as he
emerged after delivering his memorable speech to the League of
Nations at Geneva. He did not seem to have changed in the
intervening seven or eight years. His slight figure was in marked
contrast to the overpowering impact of his personality. In the
course of the following thirty years I was to be received by him at
fairly frequent intervals, usually in Ethiopia but occasionally also
in Britain. And though my Amharic may have improved over the
years and there may have been more give and take in our
exchanges, the indefinable aura of his regal presence never
changed, never diminished—even when he was very old, sated
with days, and we were already several months into the 1974
revolution.

Addis Ababa in the early and mid-1940s was not so much a
town as a vast conglomeration of hovels, houses, compounds—all
encompassed by the ubiquitous groves of eucalyptus trees. After
the Italianate and orderly Asmara, Addis Ababa was distinctly
African with an attractive profusion of formless, primordial
dishevelment. It had character—a far cry from the modern city of
the late 1950s and 1960s with its wide avenues and contemporary
buildings.

*   *   *

In 1944 Sylvia Pankhurst, the suffragette leader and tireless
campaigner on behalf of Ethiopia and of Emperor Haile
Sellassie, passed through Asmara on her way to Addis Ababa.
The Mumfords gave a dinner party in her honour, and my wife
and I entertained her at our home. She met Eritreans of all
persuasions, but she was apt to dismiss those whose views she
did not share. I was impressed with this prominent member of
the Pankhurst family and with her fighting spirit. Alas, she was
very unimpressed with me and found it difficult to understand
that, as a member of the British Military Administration, I was
not free to express partisan views on the future of Eritrea.
Members of the caretaker government were strictly enjoined to
observe the most scrupulous neutrality on contentious subjects

of this nature. On her return to England she described me in her newspaper *New Times & Ethiopia News* as 'whimsical'; to this day I am not sure which of the three definitions of the word (in the *Concise Oxford Dictionary*) she had in mind: 'capricious; odd-looking; fanciful'—perhaps all three? I sincerely regretted that we did not reach a better understanding, for I admired her endeavours in the Ethiopian cause, although I found it hard to agree with some of her methods. In 1979 her son Richard published a beautiful book about his mother, *Artist and Crusader*.

I am, however, glad to say that Richard and his wife Rita, both outstanding students of things Ethiopian, have been good friends of ours—without necessarily agreeing on all aspects of the politics of that region. I was particularly pleased when their son, Sylvia's grandson, became a student of mine at Oxford, working on classical Ethiopic.

*   *   *

My wife and I spent several days, on a number of occasions, at a small place in southern Eritrea, called Senafe, not far from the old Eritrean-Ethiopian frontier. I was greatly attracted to this region, the heartland of Ethiopian civilization. I thought the scenery one of great natural beauty, while my wife felt that the vast rock formations, populated with large numbers of baboons, were a little too stark. Senafe also had a beautiful small British war cemetery commemorating those who died on their way to Magdala, during Napier's Abyssinian expedition of 1867-8, in their quest to free the European captives of Emperor Theodore. In the surroundings of Senafe are several Ethiopian churches of great antiquity, seclusion, and beauty. One of the monasteries is situated on top of the sheer rock face and can only be reached by a rope climb.

Later on, when I served at the Headquarters of the British Military Administration, my desire to be stationed in the Senafe region as a Civil Affairs Officer (=Assistant District Commissioner) became almost obsessive. I raised the matter repeatedly with Colonel Hugh Senior, the Political Secretary, and even with the Military Governor; and when the elderly incumbent of that coveted post was transferred elsewhere, I thought my chance had come. Alas, General Benoy summoned me to his office and explained, in the nicest possible way, that there were two good reasons against my going to Senafe: firstly, he argued, my knowledge of the Ethiopian languages of Eritrea was more usefully employed and required at headquarters; and, secondly, he had no wish to lose his Private Secretary (my wife). The latter was relieved at this reprieve from banishment to the outer recesses, but I felt sure she had not influenced the Governor's decision.

Quite close to Senafe is the tiny locality of Matara with its famous obelisk which bears what is probably the earliest Ethiopic inscription extant, in a still unvocalized script taking us back to a date preceding the fourth century AD. We went there on several occasions and also took some photographs of the obelisk and its inscription. I became increasingly convinced that the explanations and translations hitherto given of the Ethiopic text on this monument were not entirely satisfactory, even though they had been proffered by two of the greatest masters of Ethiopian studies, C. Conti Rossini and E. Littmann. More than forty years later I still marvel at such audacity and impudence of youth. The revised reading and rendering which I published there and then had, I would aver in retrospect, certain advantages in that they were based on the circumstances of the local situation and terrain, but they also produced further problems which in my enthusiasm and inexperience I had failed to recognize.

While my responsibilities in the Ministry of Information were almost exclusively concerned with African publications, the close symbiosis with our colleagues on the *Eritrean Daily News*, the official English and Italian paper, brought me into daily contact with the aforementioned Sgt Fraser and the paper's editor, the late and still lamented Captain Tom Moore, who became a tragic victim of the first Comet aeroplane crash. Fraser and Moore would occasionally ask me to contribute an article to their paper on some subject within my professional competence. These articles seem to have attracted the attention of a curious character, the Marchese Emanuele Del Giudice Barbarossa, who was the editor of a local Italian weekly entitled *Il Lunedì dell'Eritrea*. He approached me with the request to write a series of articles on Ethiopia for his paper. I was not enthusiastic, but Philip Mumford persuaded me that it would be politic to do so.

When the series, under the title 'The Exploration and Study of Abyssinia', was completed, Del Giudice published the collected articles in a booklet which appeared at Asmara in 1945 and was dedicated to Margery and Philip Mumford. It was my first little book.

Del Giudice was a bit of a rogue. He was a journalist on the pre-April 1941 *Corriere Eritreo* and had contributed a series of strongly anti-British articles which were collected in a book, published at Asmara early in 1941, which he called *I negri cominciano a Calais* ('The wogs begin at Calais'). After April 1941 he became an early and enthusiastic convert to a very different view of the world and saw to it that his book was carefully suppressed. His *Lunedì* (Monday) paper (like all others) required to be submitted to military censorship in order to prevent any inadvertent references either to military targets in Eritrea or, by that time more importantly, to the future of Eritrea which might exacerbate the volatile local situation. I remember one Sunday evening when it was my turn to check the paper, very largely a routine inspection, I noticed that Del Giudice had a small piece extending effusive congratulations to a senior member of the Administration who was about to be married 'to the beautiful Mrs . . .', but he had mixed up the name with that of another lady who was extremely plain but answered to a very similar-sounding name. It was not, of course, my duty to censor gaffes of this nature which, while embarrassing to those concerned, had no adverse public-order potential. However, I did draw Del Giudice's attention to the error and was subsequently never forgiven by some of my mischievous friends.

Working at Headquarters

By the end of the war, or in its immediate aftermath, the work of the Ministry of Information seemed to me to lose much of its *raison d'être*. I felt I was getting a wee bit restive by now; our newspapers and journals were running reasonably well, and the challenge had all but disappeared. C. N. Ryan wrote to me from Cairo that there was still 'a lot of spadework' to be done, while Stephen Longrigg, in a letter from London, thought the Ministry of Information was 'a setting sun'. In these circumstances I was glad when the Chief Secretary of the British Military Administration (BMA), Colonel Gerald Kenyon-Slaney (a former Nyasaland District Commissioner), invited me to join BMA Headquarters as Assistant Political Secretary in succession to Dennis Duncanson. Dennis had been a good friend since our early days in Eritrea and was one of a handful of officers (such as Longrigg, G. K. N. (later Sir Kennedy) Trevaskis, B. W. Lee, and some of those already mentioned) who took a genuine interest in Eritrea and had acquired a considerable fund of knowledge on country and people. Duncanson now went as District Commissioner to the Addi Qayyeh division (which included the Senafe district), historically and archaeologically probably the most interesting part of the country with its ancient Axumite remains and significant antiquarian sites. After the war Dennis Duncanson served in the Far East and subsequently taught the politics of that area in the new University of Kent.

To me it was a pleasure, as well as highly instructive, to work closely with and under Colonel Hugh Senior, the Political Secretary and a very experienced colonial civil servant with great knowledge of the colonies in general and of Tanganyika in particular. He turned out to be an excellent, congenial, and utterly unpompous boss—and a valued friend to the present day. At one or two removes above us, we had the interestingly contrasting personalities of Chief Secretary Kenyon-Slaney, with his considerable experience in the colonies, and of General Benoy, the Military Governor, who was inclined to be impatient with the style of administration favoured by professional colonial civil servants and preferred the more transparent command structure of the army.

BMA Headquarters was then situated in the large and sprawling building of the former Hamasien Hotel. While in these premises we may have been short of some of the facilities usually associated with office accommodation, we were at any rate well provided with washrooms and toilets (this was, of course, long before Nancy Mitford taught us not to use these non-U expressions). The Hamasien Hotel was centrally situated on the crest of a little hill and from its upper storeys had fine views over Asmara. After the end of the British Administration it reverted temporarily to its original use, for the new Eritrean Administration sensibly moved into the much larger and infinitely more suitable complex that used to be called, in Italian times and even during the British period, 'Comando Truppe' (army headquarters). While the Italians, preparing for a war of conquest in Ethiopia, plainly required this vast quadrangular edifice, enclosing a fine central court, I am not clear why we did not eject the administration of our small garrison force from there and let the military government of the country take over these spacious premises. By the early 1970s the old Hamasien Hotel had been demolished and a modern luxury hotel had been built, catering for the *then* increasing tourist trade.

When I began my job as Assistant (frequently Acting, when the Chief Secretary or the Governor were away and everyone temporarily moved up a step) Political Secretary, the situation in Eritrea was getting increasingly tense. The genii of democracy and of self-determination which had been so powerfully evoked by our war aims and the concomitant propaganda efforts refused to return to the bottle: Eritreans, especially in the urban areas, became progressively and at times aggressively more concerned with their political future. Ethiopia clamoured for the incorporation of Eritrea, within the Empire, as an historic right; the Muslims in the western lowlands favoured joining the Sudan; others wanted Eritrea to be independent, while a few thought a return of non-Fascist rule by the Italians might be acceptable; finally some felt that partition would be the best solution, with the Christian highlands fulfilling their irredentist aims of going back to their motherland, Ethiopia, and the Muslim parts being annexed by the Sudan. These problems were hotting up with remarkable speed, and unless we managed to restrain some of this new-found fervour we were allowing a situation to arise which we would be unable to control with the limited forces at our disposal. In fact, I was strongly advised by the CID, particularly in periods of tension, not to venture into the indigenous parts of Asmara without a pistol in my pocket.

Among this plethora of rival groups, only two stood out as serious contenders for eventual success and power: the Unionists, that is, those favouring union with Ethiopia, and the so-called Separatists who advocated independence for Eritrea. Within those groups there were various factions and shifting patterns of both views and personalities. Ken Trevaskis, in his book *Eritrea, a colony in transition, 1941–52* (RIIA and OUP, 1960), has analysed these trends and described the politics of intrigue and constant manoeuvring that characterized the years from about 1945 until the United Nations decision in 1950. With only a few reservations I agree with much of his analysis; in any event, this is not the place to rehearse the story or to go into details. Trevaskis had initiated and carried out the creation of the 'Western Province' of Eritrea, amalgamating the two large administrative divisions of Keren and Agordat. After that he joined BMA Headquarters as Political Secretary. In the 1960s he served as Governor of Aden.

Early in 1946, under Senior and myself, we had obtained approval for the creation of a small number of more senior appointments, as Administrative Assistants, for some Eritreans of outstanding ability. Probably the most gifted of these was Tedla Bairu (1914-81). He combined competence, ambition, and charm with a marked penchant for intrigue and dissimulation. He resigned from his prestigious post in the administration in August of the same year, at a strategically crucial moment to which I shall refer presently. He then became Secretary General of the Unionist Party, though his influence and power were more pervasive than the mere title may convey. Upon federation of Eritrea with Ethiopia in 1952, he was elected the first Chief Executive (i.e. the effective ruler) of this new autonomous unit within the Ethiopian Empire. Three years later he resigned on the grounds of Ethiopian interference with Eritrea's internal affairs. But for someone of Tedla's sophistication these reasons appeared naïve, since he had himself striven for complete union for many years. He was subsequently appointed to the Ethiopian Senate and to an ambassadorship, but in 1966 he defected and joined the Eritrean Liberation Front at Damascus. Thereafter he led a life of constant movement and dissatisfaction and eventually died in exile in Sweden. It had been a life of high achievement marred by ambition and an autocratic temperament. I felt sad that a man endowed with such great gifts should never have found peace of mind.

In the Unionist movement Tedla had two principal supporters, both of whom were the representatives of powerful institutions. The first was Abuna Markos, the Ethiopian Orthodox Bishop of Eritrea, who backed the movement of complete union with Ethiopia by committing the influential voice and force of the Church to this cause. In a country like Ethiopia or Eritrea the support of the all-pervasive Church was a crucial element in the attainment of success The second factor was the equally powerful influence of the Ethiopian Government in the shape of Colonel (later General) Negga Haile Sellassie who was appointed the Emperor's personal representative in Eritrea, with the intentionally nondescript title of Liaison Officer. With such well-nigh irresistible backing the Unionist cause was bound to flourish—as indeed it did. In my position I had constant and close dealings with both men. The Prelate was wily, not well-educated but possessed of considerable oratorical powers which made a profound impact on his large congregations. Trying to keep him out of active engagement in politics was a Sisyphean and ultimately futile endeavour. Colonel Negga was an infinitely more agreeable partner in negotiation. He was civilized, humorous, and a congenial companion on many journeys we undertook together in various parts of Eritrea in pursuit of our respective duties.

The Separatists had no such heavy guns at their disposal; their activities had a marked DIY quality about them. Behind them stood the venerable figure of Ras Tessemma Asberom (1870-1964), a man in the great tradition of Ethiopian notables—full of dignity, honour, and years. He was born within two years of Napier's British expedition in 1868, had fought in the famous battle of Adwa in 1896, and had served Ethiopian, Italian, and British Administrations with equal distinction and honesty. But the real impetus behind the movement was the charismatic figure of Dejazmatch Abraha Tessemma (1901-67), the old Ras's eldest son, one of the most versatile men in his country, district chief, engineer, artist, and agricultural expert. He was also a most loyal friend, utterly dependable, and possessed of all those qualities of character which the brilliant figure of Tedla Bairu seemed to lack. During the closing years of the British Administration he was in charge of indigenous affairs. For these services he received the MBE. After the incorporation of Eritrea within the Ethiopian Federation he bore no grudges but served his country nobly when entrusted by the Emperor with the imaginative Zula Dam project.

The third leader of the Separatists was Waldeab Waldemaryam, of whom I spoke in the previous chapter. At this point I ought to say that he was at no time permitted to use the columns of the *EWN* in pursuit of his political aims. Hence a

statement in Trevaskis' book on Eritrea to the effect that the
EWN carried letters in support of the Separatist cause 'under
fictitious signatures' is not correct. Not all those who sent in
letters on either side wished to be identified for fear of being
attacked and were therefore allowed to use abbreviations, but
their true identities and the genuineness of their letters were not
in doubt.

I have said that Tedla Bairu resigned from his post in the
British Military Administration at a strategically crucial moment.
That moment was the day after some tragic and entirely
unforeseeable events that occurred at Asmara on 28 August
1946. It was between 5 and 6 p.m. on that day, when most
members of the Administration had left headquarters and I was
dictating a particularly confidential report to my wife, when we
heard heavy machine-gun fire, loud and prolonged. As soon as
we realized that something pretty serious was happening we
went to the Senior Officers' Mess, less than five minutes' walk
from the Hamasien Hotel, to talk to Colonel Senior. He and I
then went across to the Vice-Regal Lodge to consult the Military
Governor. While we were speaking to him he had a telephone
call from the Brigadier in charge of the garrison troops, largely
Sudan Defence Force contingents. It appeared that some of his
troops had been celebrating the end of the Ramadan fast at the
Asmara market place and had become embroiled in a fracas with
some Christian Eritreans. Their half-drunk comrades rushed
back to their barracks and, with the help of other Sudanese
soldiers, managed to get hold of some Bren-gun carriers on
which they careered through the indigenous part of Asmara,
shooting at any target that moved. We heard later that evening,
after their British officers had finally managed to retrieve the
errant soldiers with their lethal equipment, that about sixty
Abyssinians had been killed and a large number injured.

The already volatile situation at once became extremely tense.
The Unionists, the Church, indeed the entire population were
up in arms, accusing the British Administration of wholesale
slaughter. The garrison commander did not improve relations
with the head of the Administration when he refused to accept
responsibility for these catastrophic events. We at once arranged
for the Military Governor to issue a statement, which was broadcast over the Asmara loudspeaker system situated at strategic

points of assembly in town, expressing his grief and consternation at what had happened and promising that all those guilty of the massacre would be court-martialled.

The political exploitation of what had so plainly been an unpremeditated and wholly unforeseeable occurrence began immediately. Tedla Bairu resigned from the government in protest (although he was perfectly well aware how deeply these happenings were deplored by those in authority) and was now free to become the *de facto* leader of the Unionist Party. He had chosen his moment with consummate skill, and he and his movement were catapulted into a position of unassailable strength and predominance by this tragedy. In this situation fraught with panic and high emotion it was not difficult to persuade the populace that all of them were being attacked by Muslim troops and their British masters.

The funeral of these sixty or so bodies, the victims of British rule (as they were described), was to take place the next afternoon near the Ethiopian Orthodox Cathedral. Hugh Senior and I strongly advised the Military Governor that he, accompanied by ourselves and any other relevant officers of the Administration, should attend the interment. We did not conceal from him that the situation was distinctly dangerous, but we felt that this was the only means of retrieving a fairly desperate state of affairs. The Senior Civil Affairs Officer of Asmara advised the Governor not to attend the obsequies, as there was no way of protecting him in the midst of more than 50,000 highly excited mourners who might be expected to be there. I did not dissent from this analysis but felt that risks had to be taken, because it was right and decent to do so—and because it was politic as well. The Senior Civil Affairs Officer himself declared that he would not go. As these tragic events had occurred within his administrative boundaries, I felt that it was an error of judgement for him to be absent, although I naturally understood his position. But it seemed to Hugh Senior and to me that it was of paramount importance that the Military Governor should be present in full uniform.

He eventually accepted our counsel and also agreed that, even if we had the necessary troops available, their presence would lead to further and potentially greater bloodshed. But there was in any case no adequate contingent of British army personnel at

Asmara, and to take Sudanese troops with us was bound to lead to serious riots—and indeed certain catastrophe. We also decided to go unarmed, for the odd revolver could not have saved us from those vast throngs.

In the end just the three of us went, General Benoy, Colonel Senior, and myself, in the big black Vice-regal Lancia, flag flying. Orders had been given that even Eritrean policemen were to be held back. As we arrived at the burial grounds, we saw a huge multitude of people ranged in an enormous circle around the sixty or so bodies, just wrapped in sheets. To penetrate that crowd from the periphery towards the centre proved to be a dangerous and highly uncomfortable journey. These Eritrean masses who usually bowed to the Governor and treated him with the utmost deference were sullen on that day and very hostile. When finally we reached the centre, the Abuna Markos, standing among the serried rows of white-sheeted corpses, began his funeral oration.

It was an extremely emotional as well as a clever address: We Abyssinians had longed for the British to come and liberate us from the Fascist yoke. We had trusted you to lead us to freedom. But what have you done? You have given us the freedom to die, the only freedom we have received so far. Neither the Italians nor the British, in whom we had believed, will help us. So we must return to our Mother Ethiopia who will receive her Eritrean children with open arms. The only demand we make of you now is: kill sixty Sudanese troops as they have killed our innocent brethren. Will you promise that?

When I had translated to General Benoy what the Bishop had demanded, he asked me to explain that he could not possibly make such promises but that he would undertake to see that all those who were guilty of this heinous crime would be punished. No, this is not enough, was the Bishop's rejoinder, they must be killed, put to death. The situation was tense and perilous, and Senior and I asked the Governor whether it was not certain that at least some of the culprits would suffer the death penalty. He thought that was very likely indeed and asked me to say so to the Abuna. But the latter was still not satisfied: you must promise us that at least sixty will be executed, the same number as our people who died at the hands of these murderers. The Bishop's fierce demeanour was somehow perceived by the vast crowd of mourners, who seemed to become ever more menacing. At this stage I did not think we would ever leave this place alive or unscathed. I tried to convey to the Abuna that nobody knew at this moment how many soldiers had done the actual shooting and killing. If, say, only ten had been engaged in the physical act of firing those weapons, we could not execute another fifty who had not pulled the trigger. I do not think the Bishop was impressed by this argument. But while I was talking to the Primate of Eritrea, the General stepped forward and stood to attention to salute the victim lying nearest to us. He was followed by Colonel Senior and myself and then repeated this gesture by every single body. This exceptional mark of respect by a red-tabbed general and Governor to a humble Abyssinian, indeed to all the anonymous victims, made a deep impression on the Abuna and the large concourse of people. By a hardly perceptible gesture he signalled to those nearest to us to let us go. Our return to the car was much easier, and we breathed a sigh of relief.

Our attendance at the funeral had somewhat defused a very dangerous situation. The Sudanese troops were confined to barracks, and some small British reinforcements were brought to Eritrea. The court martial was convened within two months of that dreadful afternoon of 28 August. I only looked in on one or two of the early sessions of the court, as we were about to depart for Jerusalem. I was not happy about the attitude of the army authorities in charge of the culprits; they seemed to have little compassion for the victims and their relations. I do not know (or cannot now remember) the precise outcome of the court martial, for we had left Eritrea when it was finally concluded. But I think no single death penalty was imposed, for I believe that the judge advocate held that the burden of proof was so exacting that it had to be clearly established that soldier X had killed Eritrean Y. If this interpretation is correct, then it is obvious that it was impossible in the circumstances to make such identifications and prove such links beyond reasonable doubt.

* * *

The politics of the following years were dominated by the Unionist party, while the other parties, the Separatists in particular, were increasingly prone to splits, re-alignments, and further fragmentation. There were periods of considerable agitation and violence. But when the United Nations finally reached a decision on the future of Eritrea in December 1950, their solution (to be implemented in September 1952) in many ways constituted a combination of the aims pursued by the two main aspirants to power: Eritrea was to be self-governing in domestic affairs, but foreign relations and trade as well as defence and communications were to be vested in the Federal Government of Ethiopia. This was a solution which seemed eminently fair and sensible in the circumstances.

From 1952 to 1962 Eritrea had her own Parliament and Administration, presided over by a Chief Executive who was responsible to the Eritrean Assembly. Both Parliament and Administration, drawing inspiration from British models and having been prepared and eased into position by British officials, worked with exemplary efficiency. Many improvements, especially in the area of education, were carried through. It was a poignant experience for me to go back there a decade after the war, less than five years after the internally autonomous Eritrean government had been constituted, and find that the young clerks and interpreters of yesterday, who so recently knew little or no English, had become directors-general of government departments or other senior executives, writing minutes and memoranda with almost equal facility in English, Tigrinya, and Amharic. Their adaptability and competence were encouraging and they were deeply conscious of a sense of adventure and achievement. It was, as I have already indicated, a cardinal error of judgement on the part of the Federal Government to bring this excellent arrangement to an end and to incorporate and absorb Eritrea as just another province of the Empire. The 1962 vote by the Eritrean Parliament to dissolve itself and to dismantle the federal structure must have been taken under pressure. The Emperor's Government stored up for itself endless and wholly unnecessary trouble, while the revolutionary regime since 1974 has transformed an already difficult situation into sheer catastrophe.

It is an interesting reflection on the mutability of human motives and affairs, of political judgements and affiliations, that those who in the 1940s clamoured most vociferously for complete union with Ethiopia were the first to become disillusioned and to agitate even more noisily for separation and liberation. 'The wheel is come full circle.'

An unusual request

It was, I think, towards the end of 1945 that Prince Y of a well-known principality requested a visa to enter Asmara, Eritrea, for medical treatment. There was nothing uncommon in such an application, as the medical skills of Italian doctors in this Italian colony, under British Military Administration since 1941, were much in demand over a wide area of East Africa and the Middle East. The application was granted, and the Prince arrived and settled down in the comfortable CIAAO Hotel. We observed that he seemed in no great hurry to enter hospital or have his ailments seen to.

After quite a few weeks, his secretary made contact with the Chief Information Officer and requested him to call on His Highness. As the matter HH wished to discuss was strictly confidential and no interpreters were, therefore, permitted to be present, it would be necessary for the British Information Officer to be able to speak HH's language. Alas, such linguistic gifts had not been vouchsafed to this official, whereupon he requested me (at that time in charge of the local British Ministry of Information's African Publications) to wait upon His Highness on his behalf.

I promptly repaired to that well-known Asmara hostelry and called upon the Prince. He sent his retainers out, locked the door (somewhat disconcertingly to me), and asked me whether I could keep a great secret. I did not quite know how to answer this question satisfactorily but assured HH that I had signed the Official Secrets Act (I recall that I had great difficulty in rendering this term into his language). He seemed convinced and then came straight to the point. His father, the ruler of his country, was old and was unlikely to live for many more years. He, the Prince, had about nineteen elder brothers (I do not now remember the exact number, but it was sufficiently high to impress me with his father's interest in procreation); they were, of course, the sons of several wives, and the Prince also possessed a remarkably large array of younger brothers and half-brothers. However, the latter were of no direct concern to us today; the elder siblings were the subject of his *démarche*.

He felt quite sure that after his father's demise he would be the most suitable ruler of his country. His brothers had neither the education nor the moral fibre to undertake such a complex and onerous task. Also, he was by inclination strongly pro-British, a disposition unlikely to be shared by his seniors. Was it not, therefore, in Britain's best interests to see him on the throne of his country rather than those wastrels who could not be relied upon to know what the true concerns of their nation demanded? Did I agree so far?—Well, I hesitated and stammered that I had been privileged to be acquainted with him for only a few minutes and did not possess even that advantage in relation to Their Highnesses, his brothers. So, how could I possibly be expected to form a judgement? Moreover, I was so junior an official that I had no means of assessing where the best interests of the British Government lay.

He responded that I had perhaps not quite grasped what he had intended to convey. Was it not true that Britain needed friends in these anxious times? He, when ruler of his country, would be such a steadfast friend. Very little was required of the British Government in return. After all, the English ruled half the world and it could scarcely be a major undertaking for them to arrange for some nineteen or so of his brothers to be 'excluded'. My familiarity with his native tongue was not such as to appreciate its semantic subtleties to the full, and we had to spend a little while on the hermeneutics of the term 'exclusion'. With good reason he found me somewhat slow in my mental processes, and I judged him to be a bit reluctant to use any of the more clear-cut synonyms of that expression which I knew existed in his language in ample measure.

He brought the discussion to a conclusion by asking me to pass his modest request to higher authority and then let him know in due course. I felt able to give him that assurance. He promptly unlocked the door and asked his secretary to escort me to the foyer of the hotel.

I reported this unusual conversation to my chief who seemed less startled, though no less entertained, than I was and at once enciphered a message to the next higher authority. It took about a month for the upward and downward hierarchical processes to be completed. Our instructions from on high were that such a proposal, whatever its precise meaning, could not be countenanced and that it would be advisable to employ as neutral a vocabulary as possible in replying to HH.

These instructions were scrupulously followed when I went to see the Prince. Our interview this time was brief and to the point. He seemed a little sullen but observed the customary courtesies. The secretary was summoned almost immediately to accompany me downstairs.

Whenever my wife and I lunched or dined at the CIAAO Hotel, which—apart from the Officers' Club—was the social hub of Asmara, we saw the Prince and his entourage. He appeared to be well enough and in no need of medical attention. We bowed to each other and smiled stiffly.

A few months later I was transferred back to the Headquarters of the British Military Administration. One day the Military Governor minuted to me, as Acting Political Secretary, that he wished me to be present, for advice and interpreting, when a certain Prince came to see him. I told the Governor what I knew and what I expected the subject of the conversation to be. He at once decided that HH should be ushered into my room instead and that he should be taken into the gubernatorial presence only if his business was of a markedly different nature.

When His Highness crossed the threshold of my door, there was a momentary hesitation, but he regained his composure at once. He betrayed no sign of recognition, either by gesture or by word, and proceeded to explain his proposal. The only hint of our prior acquaintance was conveyed by the fact that his exposition this time was much briefer and did not include a pause for enquiring after my views. He took his leave very quickly.

When the customary channels of communication had been followed, as on the previous occasion, and the not unexpected reply, virtually identical in substance, had been received, I thought I should spare the Prince the embarrassment of having me call on him once more. Instead, I composed a confidential note in his language, the drafting of which took me many hours, and delivered it to his hotel in person. .

A year after these events, some time in 1947, I served in the Secretariat of the British Mandatary Government of Palestine. Although I had some personal acquaintance with the Chief Secretary, in my junior position I did not normally have occasion to see him on business. But one day I was summoned by him; I think it was a purely private matter, but as I was on the point of

leaving his office at the conclusion of the interview, he called me
back and asked whether in the course of my service in Eritrea I
had ever visited a certain country. He had just received a
somewhat cryptic note from a Prince originating from there; His
Highness was in Palestine for medical treatment and wished to
see him. While I had some suspicions, I could scarcely believe
that there was any life left in that hoary tale. But I told the Chief
Secretary what I remembered of that particular experience at
Asmara. Ah, well, he said, he had better be received by you.

The Palestine Secretariat in those days was situated in the
security zone of the King David Hotel at Jerusalem. Compared
with my modest room in Asmara, I now had a sumptuous apartment worthy of receiving a Prince. He appeared on the appointed
day, but even his royal composure seemed a little frayed when
faced by the same man. It would surely be a small matter for the
British Government, he suggested, to comply with his request—
at any rate compared with the trouble they must have taken
moving one man around Africa and the Middle East just in order
to turn down his proposal. 'Perfidious Albion', he may have
thought—or words to that effect. Incidentally, the Secretary of
State did not vary the substance of his reply.

III

Back to Ethiopia

My informant at the Itege Hotel

The Itege Hotel is the oldest hotel in Addis Ababa. The city itself, the capital of Ethiopia since the reign of Emperor Menelik II (1889-1913), is new, just about a century old, though by now a large sprawling town covering a vast area at a height of 7,500-8,000 feet. With the exception of Gondar in North-West Ethiopia (imperial headquarters from the seventeenth to the early nineteenth century), the country had not had a capital city since the days of the Aksum Kingdom. The capital was where the Emperor and his Court decided to reside for the time being. Emperor Menelik, and especially his consort Taitu, chose Addis Ababa ('the new flower') because of the proximity of the hot springs of Filweha or Finfinni.

The first hotel in Addis Ababa was built by Empress Taitu in 1907; initially she thought it might be a suitable residence for herself. It was called Itege, 'queen consort'. Occasionally the Empress stayed there herself, and I was told that she preferred the central room on the first floor, No. 3, which is large, has an *en suite* shower room and toilet, and has a balcony commanding superb views over Addis Ababa and its mountain scenery. In later years I stayed in that room myself, often for many weeks. The political vicissitudes of the present century brought about remarkably frequent changes of names: Itege (Itégué) or Imperial in the early days; Impero or Imperiale under the Italians; since 1941 again Imperial; and, for a long time, once more Itege. But under the present revolutionary military regime it has become Awraris ('rhinoceros'), for reasons which elude me—save perhaps that these animals are untainted by any Imperial connection.

Emperor Menelik's biographer, Gabra Sellassie, tells us (final paragraph of chapter 75) that the Itege Taitu caused 'a large house for strangers' to be built and that 'that house was called "hotel"'. As this house offered 'the choicest European and

Ethiopian dishes, the Emperor used to give banquets there'. People who wished to eat there would 'pay according to the fare they consumed'. These quaint expressions indicate the novelty of such an institution in Ethiopia.

I first stayed at the Itege (then the Imperial) during the war. At that time it was crowded and was devoid of character or atmosphere. By the 1950s and 1960s, when I lodged there for lengthy periods, it had shed wartime crowds and the feeling of military billets. In fact, because several other hotels, some of international renown, had been established for the rapidly growing tourist trade, the Itege had reverted to being a genuinely Ethiopian hostelry with predominantly Ethiopian guests. During the 1950s one would meet quite a number of Ethiopian students there, some on the point of departing for their studies abroad, and others who had recently returned and were waiting for assignment to their first jobs. Both categories were also expecting to be received by Emperor Haile Sellassie, who liked to see students before their departure and on completion of their studies. With the establishment of a university at Addis Ababa and the increasing flow of students both at home and abroad, this attractive custom had to be largely abandoned.

With time the Itege Hotel became somewhat dilapidated in its furnishings and fittings, but its atmosphere as a hub of Ethiopian activities did not suffer. It was the only hotel in Addis Ababa where Amharic was still *de rigueur*, and this alone had attractions for a professional *éthiopisant* which eclipsed even the desire for comfort. When, in 1964, I travelled to Ethiopia in company with my colleague C. F. Beckingham, Professor of Islamic Studies and an authority on the historical geography of Ethiopia, I warned him *en route* of the shortcomings of the Itege. I also explained to him the custom of ordering food from the reasonably extensive menu by number rather than by the name of the dish. A brief lesson on the aircraft of the Amharic numerals from one to twenty was sufficient for my friend's linguistic prowess; I never had to repeat the lesson, and Beckingham never went hungry for want of numeracy in Amharic.

My room, the occasional apartment of Emperor Menelik's Consort, was perfectly adequate and large enough to receive visitors in the sitting-room corner. The only trouble was a small leak in the cistern of the water closet. No amount of remonstration with the management had any effect. The leak remained, and the floor of the shower-room required regular mopping up. Five years later I stayed in the same room together with my wife. Before our arrival I had expressed the hope (I thought jocularly) that the leak would have been repaired in the interval. When the servant assigned to that set of rooms (by then an old acquaintance of mine) took us up to No. 3, I saw at once that nothing had changed—including the leak. On my wife's face there was a look of stark horror—yet no words were spoken. But clearly her facial expression was more eloquent and more effective than my complaints five years earlier (and no doubt those of all the guests in the interval), for on the next day the leak was repaired.

Professor Beckingham's adjoining room, No. 5, had a different problem in 1964: his apartment had a bathtub, not just a shower, but the stove heating the hot-water supply was remarkably temperamental. For its efficient working it required a hard knock by the servant at precisely the right point of its structure. When *we* tried to administer that blow to the stove, it had no effect whatever. So my colleague needed a further instalment of Amharic words in addition to his command of the numerals, i.e. *muq weha*, 'hot water', which at once sent the floor-servant into action for the skilfully aimed knock to the hot-water system. Patience and a sense of humour were the most essential qualities in order to feel happy in the Ethiopia of old.

Whenever I visited Ethiopia for any length of time I was anxious to obtain the services of an Ethiopian who knew no English and who would visit me daily after lunch for an hour's Amharic conversation. In Addis Ababa, in contrast to the countryside, there were by now quite a large number of people whose knowledge of English varied from a slight smattering to an excellent command of the language. They were of no use for my specific purposes; and my Ethiopian colleagues at the university of Addis Ababa spoke English so well that they could not be expected to have much patience with my fumblings in the Amharic colloquial.

I ought to mention that the modern Semitic languages of Ethiopia—as distinct from classical Ethiopic, called Ge'ez—are possessed of a remarkable linguistic complexity, particularly in the field of syntax. To the western student of Amharic, its involved sentence structure is unquestionably the gravest

obstacle: the verb is placed at the end of the sentence, and subordinate clauses are encased and precede the main clause.
Complex periods are often of inordinate length and without
adequate marks of punctuation. The relative clause, in its
various guises, represents the central feature in this network of
subtle and intricately poised enclosures and encasements. The
guiding principle in the order of words demands the determining
or qualifying elements to precede the determined or qualified
ones. I still possess a message which was handed to me at Addis
Ababa thirty years ago. Its 'English' text is a straight reflection of
the writer's native Amharic speech: 'The previously party at
8 o'clock having been fixed at 8:30 taking place saying they
telephoned for you' (anglice: someone telephoned to say that the
party which had previously been arranged for 8 o'clock has been
postponed to 8:30).

When, in 1975, I translated Emperor Haile Sellassie's autobiography into English (still, I believe, the most substantial piece
of Amharic rendered into English), I endeavoured to do justice to
the original, not of course by trying to imitate the shape of
Amharic syntax but by using a similar level of speech. The
resultant ungainliness of the English style was intended to mark
it unequivocally as a translation in its archaizing tendencies, in
its involved sentences, and in its faithfulness to the 'feel' of the
Amharic original. Anyone who has ever tried his hand at translating the highly convoluted sentence structure of a language like
Amharic into a European tongue will be conscious of the
extreme complexity of such an undertaking which at times
approaches the boundaries of translatability. While it is plainly
impossible to emulate the organization of Amharic syntax, it is
feasible, and indeed desirable, to stay as close as practicable to
the sinews and tendons which hold together the framework of an
Amharic sentence.

Thus, while as a university teacher I had ample opportunities
of practising my Amharic reading and writing and everything
connected with the academic study of the language, the occasions
for speaking it were fairly limited. Hence I grabbed with both
hands the chances of living contact in Ethiopia and did what
would be anathema in Europe: talked at length to any waiter, to
any taxidriver, night-watchman, messenger, to the girls at the
reception or the bar, the boys at filling stations, policemen,

priests (of whom there were very many), salesmen, and anyone with whom I came into contact, however tenuously. Whenever I had an audience of the Emperor, he would ask me how long I proposed to stay in the country. And when I replied that I was already close to the end of my visit, since I had wished to brush up my Amharic before being ushered into his presence, he seemed puzzled and uncomprehending. With accustomed royal charm (which he possessed in ample measure) and a high degree of hyperbole he preferred to think that my Amharic speech was always *gerum* ('wonderful'). Alas, I knew better; and so, I imagine, did His Majesty.

What I needed, therefore, was that regular daily contact (to which I have already referred) with an 'innocent' native speaker of Amharic with whom I could spend an hour or so on subjects of my choice. On three or four such visits to Addis Ababa (and, of course, one required time to visit other parts of the country as well) I was fortunate to engage the services of Getahun, a simple and in many ways very characteristic and typical youngish Ethiopian gentleman. He came to my room at the Itege Hotel every afternoon for a long chat. I remember well my dis-comfiture on an early occasion when my interviewing techniques led me sadly astray. I could not recall having seen any butcher's or baker's shops in town and assumed that all (?) Ethiopian women baked their own bread (*injera*—a flat circular pancake-like unleavened bread made of millet (teff) or barley), but what about meat? Would your wife, I asked him, get a whole animal, say a sheep, or are there shops where she could buy meat by weight—say a kilo or two? He told me that there were some shops—not many—where she could purchase meat by weight rather than the whole animal.—So would she buy one kilo?—Yes.—Or two?—No.—I was puzzled: if she could obtain one kilo, why not two? Could she buy three kilos? (perhaps only uneven measures were available?)—Yes, she could buy three kilos. It took a very long time for me to establish that he was referring to actual occur-rences, and not to theoretical possibilities: thus it had simply not happened that she had purchased two kilos, but she had got one, three, four, or five.

The next day I lunched with an Ethiopian friend of mine who had, together with three other young noblemen, been an under-graduate at Oxford in the late 1940s when I held an appointment at the Oxford University Institute of Colonial Studies under Dame Margery Perham. Ten years later he was Ethiopian Ambassador to Britain and subsequently served as a Minister in the Ethiopian Government. When he was his country's representative at the United Nations in New York, he was a candidate, widely supported, for the post of Secretary-General of the UN. In 1974 he was briefly Prime Minister of Ethiopia until he was dismissed and murdered by the present rulers of that country. His name was Endalkatchew Makonnen. He was a man of many gifts; he served his country well; he was a proud man and no doubt had his faults, but neither he nor his many colleagues deserved the cruel fate that awaited him and them in the terrible events of 1974 and the following years. Fortunately his three Oxford companions are still alive, and I have something to say about them elsewhere in this book.

But back in 1964, at that lively lunch party in Addis Ababa, in Endalkatchew's home, I told him of my experience with Getahun the previous day and expressed particular interest in the fact that he seemed totally unaccustomed to even so small a measure of abstraction as to envisage contingencies that had not actually arisen, such as the notion of buying two kilos or seven or any other number used for exemplification rather than as a reflection of a real event. My friend did not dissent from these observations, but he rebuked me, with every justification, for having asked Getahun about his wife's purchases of meat: Don't you know, as a student of things Ethiopian, that in our country meat is traditionally always bought by men and never by women? —No, to my shame, I had not known that—and, to my greater shame, I had asked a leading question, instead of a neutral one, by assuming that his wife would be buying the meat. When, later that day, I spoke to Getahun, he explained, with the dignity and respectfulness for which all true Ethiopians are renowned, that he could not possibly have contradicted me: *ayeggäbbam*; *tägäbi aydälläm*, 'It would have been improper, unseemly'. I hope I learned from that experience never to ask questions of my informants which embodied part of the answer.

On another occasion, when Getahun visited me at the Itege Hotel one afternoon, I noticed that he was somewhat restless and a little less concentrated than was usually the case. But in response to my question he politely denied that there was anything amiss. Finally I prised it out of him that it was *Timqat* ('baptism') today, the feast of Epiphany, one of the greatest and most spectacular celebrations in the Ethiopian Church. It was January 19th, when *Timqat* would be observed and officiated at Jan(-Hoy) Meda, the vast racecourse in Addis Ababa, in the presence of the Emperor, the Patriarch, large numbers of clergy, and many thousands of Ethiopians. It was always a wonderfully colourful spectacle, strongly reminiscent of King David and all the House of Israel playing before the Lord on harps and lyres, drums and sistra, dancing with all their might and bringing up the ark with shouting and the sound of the trumpet (2 Samuel 6:5, 14–16). In Ethiopia the Old Testament was still fully alive, and the scene described in 2 Samuel was not so much re-enacted as it was part of a continuing and active mode of life, observed in all the details described in the Bible. I do not know how, since 1974, the Marxist-Leninist military regime of the country manages to cope with such deeply rooted traditions—at any rate in the remoter regions.

However, there was no problem on 19 January 1964, when I readily agreed to accompany Getahun to Jan-Meda for the *Timqat* celebrations. The proceedings had begun: the Emperor was seated in a large tent at one end of the vast concourse, with the Ethiopian dignitaries on one side of him and the diplomatic corps on the other. The priests and the people were mustered in an immense semicircle in front of the royal tent. Shortly after Getahun and I had joined the multitude of the people on the periphery of the semicircle, my trusty informant whispered to me that His Majesty wished me to join him in his tent. I, too, had observed that Haile Sellassie had motioned (almost imperceptibly, as was his wont) to Tafarra Worq, the Minister of the Palace, and the latter, by similarly discreet gestures to equerries down the hierarchical line, had me fetched into the tent. It was a somewhat embarrassing walk, in the middle of the great ceremonies (and I was decidedly not dressed for the occasion), and probably seemed much longer than it really was. I was glad that I was placed among the Ethiopian notables, not far from the ever friendly Crown Prince Asfa Wossen, rather than amidst the diplomatic corps. My friends on the other side of the Emperor, Ed and Pat Korry, the American Ambassador and his wife, had smilingly watched my awkward and no doubt blushing countenance as I progressed towards the royal presence.

When Getahun and I met the next day for our usual hour of Amharic colloquy, he seemed even more polite and respectful and told me that he now knew that I was *tilliq säw* ('an important man'), for he could easily recognize how pleased His Majesty had been to see me. I tried to disabuse him of this notion and asked him what had changed since yesterday, for he had long known that I would occasionally be received by the Emperor— and he, Getahun, had himself brought a newspaper along a few days earlier, with a picture showing Professor Beckingham and myself at the *Gibbi* ('royal palace'). Ah, that was quite different, he replied, for on this occasion he had been a witness; after all, he added, you have told me yourself not to believe every word one reads in the newspapers!

Alas, disillusionment was to come to Getahun a few years later. When he came to one of our customary meetings in the afternoon, with my wife sitting out on the balcony of our room, I thought it would be a good topic of conversation if we talked about our normal mode of living at home. I began to question him first about his household. I already knew that he was a senior messenger somewhere, with a steady job, but not well paid. I also knew that he was married. He said he had three children, a boy and two girls, and two servants. At this latter piece of information I expressed polite surprise, for I was aware of the level of his modest wages. It was impossible to be without servants, he explained, for even one of his servants had a servant at his own home in the country. How many servants did I have? —My nil return proved to be a severe shock to his system.— Perhaps a cook?—No, and I pointed to my wife on the balcony who did our cooking at home. His disenchantment became even more severe.—And what about a gardener?—No, my wife liked gardening. But then I had a bright idea and told him, in the hope of redemption, that I had a secretary at the university. After carefully interrogating me on this point he decided the secretary did not count because she was paid by the university and not by me. He made one final attempt: what about a chauffeur?—No, not even that, I actually liked driving. This was too much for him, and he exclaimed: 'But I thought all these years that you were *tilliq säw*, an important man!' In the end he approached my wife on the balcony for confirmation, in case I had just been teasing him.

I had some unworthy doubts whether Getahun would turn up the next day. Of course he did. He was as polite as ever, but it was obvious that he was more than a little disillusioned on account of my patently lowly station in life. I had always introduced my informant to my Ethiopian friends as *astämarinna tämari* ('teacher as well as pupil') which I thought was an apposite description, for, while I acquired from him a good deal of practice in Amharic conversation, I taught him a little Amharic grammar and literature. Hitherto Getahun had modestly demurred at my description of him as both teacher and pupil; henceforth he accepted this expression and occasionally used it himself.

I retain an affectionate recollection of Getahun, our conversations, and his wonderful Ethiopian manners. I often wonder what may have become of him in revolutionary Ethiopia. Would he still have his two servants and could he still go to *Timqat* celebrations—perhaps somewhere in the depth of the country?

Ethiopian miscellany

Each of my return visits to Ethiopia is associated with some particular piece of research I wished to undertake or with some special event, some lectures or a conference, and quite often with travel in various parts of the country, visits to friends, etc. There was a long hiatus between our departure from Eritrea late in 1946 and my first journey back to Ethiopia early in 1958. In the meantime I had had to build my academic career which had started at Oxford and was, in the 1950s, being continued at St Andrews University in Scotland. My main lecturing commitments were concerned with Arabic, Hebrew, and other Semitic languages, among which the Ethiopian tongues occupied at that time a relatively modest place in terms of my teaching duties. My published work, books as well as articles, was, however, principally devoted to Ethiopian studies.

At St Andrews I nevertheless had opportunities, on a few occasions, to teach classical Ethiopic or Amharic to advanced or research students. David Hubbard, an American Biblical scholar, wrote an exceptionally important PhD thesis on the remarkably far-flung as well as strangely syncretistic literary sources of the Ethiopian national saga, the medieval *Kebra Nagast* ('Glory of the Kings'). Unhappily, this fine work, which, even in its unpublished form, has been widely quoted with approval, has never been technically published, largely because its author was appointed President of a Theological College, on his return to the USA, and thus seems never to have found the time or inclination to prepare his pioneering study for the printers. About the same time the Government sent me a mature student for training in Amharic who made exceptionally good progress in this complex language.

Later, when I was at Manchester and London Universities, these arrangements continued, and there was a steady trickle of Foreign Office candidates preparing for service in Ethiopia. The most remarkable of these was Ewen Fergusson who devoted himself to the mastery of Amharic with singleminded dedication and astonishing success. When he served in Ethiopia in the early 1960s, his attainments in the language were widely noticed and admired by Ethiopians; I do not think that any other member of the British Embassy in Addis Ababa, at any rate since the war, has made a comparable impact. In later years Fergusson rose to some of the most senior posts in the Foreign Service; at the time of writing he is British Ambassador to France. Perhaps I might mention here, parenthetically and as a minor curiosity, largely the result of my long connection with Ethiopia and of advancing age, that I must be the only person alive who has known, with varying degrees of closeness, all fifteen British Ambassadors to Ethiopia since Sir Sidney Barton (Minister at Addis Ababa before and during the Italo-Abyssinian war) to the present day, though not invariably *in situ*.

My first return journey to Ethiopia during the early months of 1958 was financed jointly by St Andrews University and the Carnegie Trust for the Universities of Scotland and had as its prime object the hope of refreshing my living acquaintance with Amharic and of collecting material and, above all, new impressions for a general book on the country and people. When I got back to St Andrews there were just two months left of the long university vacation; and I knew that, if I did not write that book immediately, during term my heavy teaching load would prevent me making any real progress and, additionally, my vivid recent impressions of the country would become somewhat blurred. So I settled down at once and wrote *The Ethiopians* (published by the Oxford University Press) in fifty-four days, almost in one sitting, and deliberately without recourse to works of reference. This genesis accounts for many of its blemishes but also, perhaps, for some of its merits. In the thirty years since it was composed, the book has gone through several editions and has also been published in paperback. Were I now to rewrite it completely, temper some of the more general assertions, qualify a few of the hasty judgements, and document as well as argue many of the statements in the light of recent research, a wholly different book would emerge, better no doubt in some respects but no longer the impressionistic picture of the Ethiopians which I had had in mind and which had not basically altered since I first saw the country, now more than forty-six years ago, at any rate until the revolution of 1974.

That 1958 journey was poignant in many respects, for in the intervening years great progress had been made in almost all areas. In the urban centres in particular the changes were very marked. Perhaps the most pleasing aspect was the emergence of Ethiopian women. Ten or twelve years earlier they were hardly ever seen at official functions; now they acted as helpmeets to their husbands, as charming and competent hostesses. I do not think that in 1945 there was any woman in Ethiopia or Eritrea who could drive a car. Now there were many who could be seen at the wheels of large American and small Italian cars (alas, very few British ones). While Asmara had not changed very greatly, the transformations in Addis Ababa were considerable and continued at a similar pace over the following years. Whether one liked these changes or approved of African townscapes resembling their European and American models so closely, is quite another question.

I had travelled to Ethiopia via Rome and had visited Enrico Cerulli (born 1898), the greatest living master of Ethiopian studies, scholar, diplomat, and proconsul. In that last capacity he had been Vice-Governor General of Ethiopia during two years of the short-lived Fascist occupation. While his acceptance of such an appointment was, of course, controversial, Cerulli's own conduct remained untainted by any act that fell below his own high standards. Emperor Haile Sellassie had had indirect contacts with him even during the 1935-6 conflict and retained the greatest respect for him throughout his life. He had first known him during the 1920s when, as Ras Tafari, he was Regent and Crown Prince at a time when Cerulli was serving in the Italian Legation in Addis Ababa. He was then (and, for that matter, has remained ever since) one of the very few foreigners to possess a fluent command of Amharic. When I was received by the Emperor during my 1958 visit, one of his first questions was about Cerulli. In fact, this was the occasion of a royal repartee which I remember very clearly. His Majesty had asked me about my library of Ethiopian books; I told him that it was quite good but could not compare with Cerulli's splendid collection. Ah, he replied, but you have *bought* your books! (*irso gin matsahifton baganzab gaztawal*—in the rather more telling Amharic original). This was a jocular reference to the rumour, entirely unfounded, that Cerulli had had privileged opportunities of acquiring Ethiopian books by virtue of his exalted position.

Another great change and innovation in 1958 had been the recent establishment of a university college, at that time a fairly modest affair and still in its initial stages; it was run by Canadian Jesuits. After the brief revolt in December 1960 the Emperor gave his palace to the college which now became the Haile Sellassie University and gradually expanded considerably. Of particular note was the Kennedy Memorial Library, originally established with American funds, which developed into an excellent collection, very largely thanks to the care and efficiency of its librarian, Mrs Rita Pankhurst, daughter-in-law of the suffragette leader Sylvia Pankhurst of whom I spoke in an earlier chapter.

At the university and in government offices one could now see a goodly number of Ethiopian typewriters. This statement is not as hackneyed as it may appear at first sight, for the Amharic (Ethiopic) syllabary consists of more than 250 characters and is thus very difficult to fit on to a machine of conventional size. Shortly after the war a well-known firm of typewriter manufacturers got in touch with me to discuss devising a method by which the Ethiopic writing system could be adapted to the parameters of a normally sized apparatus. We experimented with a number of systems, especially as I was personally interested to make that typewriter suitable for writing all Ethiopian languages, including Tigrinya. The result was perfectly serviceable, although it always remained a little unsightly and was never able to reproduce the authentic ductus of the Ethiopic characters. In Ethiopia itself, and indeed for scholarly purposes elsewhere, a good indigenous calligraphy remained preferable; and the xerox machine has replaced the typewriter in many university-based contexts. I am not sure that the initial investment in this project was ever amortized.

On my return trip from Addis Ababa I stopped off in Asmara, the first time I had seen the town since I had lived there for close on five years during the war. The palace and its beautiful grounds (which we had used first as an officers' club and later, perhaps more appropriately, as the English Institute and the headquarters of Kynaston-Snell's Department of Education) had reverted to its original purpose and was now occupied by the Emperor's Representative (*Endarase* up to 1962—after the full incorporation of Eritrea the title became 'Governor General'). In 1958 that Representative was Ras Andargatchew who was married to the Emperor's eldest daughter, the Princess Tenagne Worq. The dinner party they gave for me was a glittering affair, and they had thoughtfully invited as many of my erstwhile Eritrean friends, chief among them Dejatch Abraha Tessemma, as they could discover. Sadly, the Princess has been incarcerated, together with other princes and princesses, ever since 1974—for reasons wholly unfathomable. I understand, however, that, despite her age, her spirit is unbroken and she is a great source of strength to other captive members of her family.

In Asmara it was a great joy to walk through familiar streets and places; yet everything seemed much smaller than I had remembered it: the Italian cathedral appeared less imposing, and the *Comando Truppe*, now Government HQ, stood on a much lower elevation than I had imagined. Only the Ethiopian cathedral and the mosque measured up to the picture that had remained in my mind. I looked at our last house, but the present Greek occupants seemed somewhat bothered when I stared at it from the outside. The CIAAO Hotel, still quite good, was totally unchanged. There were the same Eritrean waiters and front-desk clerks. It was a joyful reunion. To my surprise I could still remember their names, and to my greater astonishment found that my Tigrinya was less rusty than I had thought. But most amazing of all was that 'my' waiter on the first night remembered my favourite dish and brought it along unasked: *ravioli in brodo* followed by tournedos, medium to rare.

Politically there was a certain restiveness at the unnecessarily heavy hand of Amhara officialdom which was inclined to interpret the functions of the federal authorities a little too generously. In the mundane context of the CIAAO Hotel that resentment could take amusing forms. Quite often the Ethiopian Air Force Chief of Staff, who was then staying at the hotel, would join me at breakfast. He would place his order in Amharic, the only Ethiopian language he knew, whereupon the Tigrinya-speaking waiters, who a dozen years earlier had been only too anxious to show off their knowledge of Amharic, pretended not to understand him. They would turn to me and ask me in Tigrinya to translate to them what he had said in Amharic. They hugely enjoyed this charade, performed with completely serious faces and no little acting skill.

Some of my Eritrean friends of old, now motorized as ministers or directors-general, also took me on excursions into the country, to all the familiar haunts. The only snag was that they had little interest in time and punctuality and would often turn up much later than had been arranged. I must, however, admit that in this respect they could not hold a candle to my old friend Zewde Gabra-Sellassie of whom I speak elsewhere in my story. When he was *kantiba* (mayor) of Addis Ababa, he invited me to accompany him on a trip to Ambo (Hagara Heywat), a lovely valley with thermal springs, some eighty miles due west of Addis Ababa. He promised to collect me early one Sunday morning; and when I expressed some doubt that he would fulfil his promise to come early, he said 'You will be surprised!' Indeed, I was, for he came hours late; and when I remonstrated with him, he said disarmingly, and perhaps not without some justice: 'I thought you were an expert on Ethiopia!'

* * *

In 1959 Enrico Cerulli convened the First International Conference of Ethiopian Studies. It took place in Rome at the Italian Academy (Lincei) of which Cerulli was a prominent member, but at that time not yet its President. Participation was by invitation only, and in those days we were still a small band of some forty or fifty scholars from all over the world. We were lavishly treated, fed, and accommodated in the magnificent premises of the Corsini and Farnesina Palaces belonging to the Academy. The second such conference was held in 1963 at Manchester, where Charles Beckingham and I were then serving, in conditions of markedly lesser splendour. But the University was able to confer honorary doctorates on three of the greatest *éthiopisants*, Cerulli, Polotsky, and Marcel Cohen of Paris. At Manchester we received an invitation from the Emperor, brought to us by Richard Pankhurst, to hold our next meeting at Addis Ababa in 1966. This turned out to be the largest congress so far, partly because of the participation of many indigenous scholars and partly because admission was no longer restricted to those formally invited. The congress was opened by the Emperor himself, and the venue was, of course, in most ways ideal for specialists in Ethiopian studies. It was also an occasion for seeing new parts of the country that we had not visited before.

Our friends, the American Ambassador and his wife, Ed and Pat Korry, invited my wife to stay at their embassy. We gratefully accepted this generous invitation, and I cabled my wife to join me as soon as possible. Alas, she arrived with a broken foot which she had sustained at Heathrow Airport. It was only thanks to the Korrys' wonderful hospitality and the superb facilities of their embassy that the visit proved to be as enjoyable and as memorable as it did. Another visitor to Addis Ababa at that time was Arnold Toynbee who gave a lecture at the American Embassy. I asked him about our North Talpioth neighbour who, it may be recalled, had written to him to point out some error, real or alleged, in Toynbee's *Study of History*. I was not surprised that he had no recollection of that event.

I had met the Korrys two years earlier in the course of a visit to Ethiopia. We were all guests of the then British Ambassador and Lady Russell. I subsequently encountered the Korrys at the Timqat celebrations (described in the previous chapter) and later spent many happy hours in their company. I also gave Pat Korry a few hours of instruction in Amharic. She was a very able and spirited pupil, and if she did not at that time make appreciable progress, it was scarcely her fault. Ed Korry, the Ambassador, had in a very short time acquired an enviable knowledge of the Ethiopian governmental machine and of the Byzantine ways of

Ethiopian politics. The Korrys made an excellent ambassadorial team, with Pat Korry working hard and strenuously on many social and communal enterprises, including the artistic production of Ethiopian-cum-Western calendars of great beauty and interest. But above all it was her remarkable personality that impinged so prominently and agreeably on the Ethiopian social milieu.

I think it was during the same journey to Ethiopia that Professor Beckingham and I parked our car outside the Addis Ababa Post Office where we wanted to buy some stamps. I might mention here, parenthetically, that such visits to the Post Office were apt to be prolonged, for the counter clerks quite often engaged one in conversation: either they criticized some Amharic word on the envelope or postcard or they liked to discuss some particular Amharic expression—even on occasion the details of the Ethiopian spelling and writing systems. Such conversations could also involve a request for full biographical information and how and why one had learnt Amharic, even how many students one had and what progress they were making. If I wanted to despatch some of my Ethiopian book purchases to my home address, the parcel had to be left open for customs inspection. This almost always led to long questions about Amharic literature, what other books one had or had not read, and occasionally to some on-the-spot test of one's prowess in Amharic reading. I did not normally have any reason to shun such entertainment, since everything of that kind was designed to improve my fluency in Amharic and to bring me into agreeable contact with the ordinary Ethiopian public.

As Beckingham and I emerged from the Post Office on that occasion, we found our car surrounded by quite a few urchins and a busily scribbling policeman. He was about to issue a parking ticket, for since my last visit to Addis Ababa that latest urban refinement, the parking meter, had been introduced to the capital; being unprepared for this innovation at an otherwise familiar spot, I had not noticed that instrument of torture. My argument that we were strangers here failed to carry weight or conviction, for, the policeman argued, 'strangers do not speak Amharic'. But before I could offer a rejoinder to that, a newspaper vendor interrupted us and held one of his papers up to the constable, pointing to a front-page photograph depicting the Emperor receiving Professors Beckingham and Ullendorff. Indeed, we had had an audience of His Majesty on the previous day, but we had not realized that our appearance at the palace would rate such prominent coverage. It was very clever of the boy to recognize us from the photograph, and his intervention brought him the sale of several papers and a handsome baksheesh into the bargain; for the policeman, on being convinced of our exalted identity, tore up the parking ticket and offered us his apologies. I signed the photograph in one of the papers and presented it to him. I hope he has long disposed of that memento, as I cannot think it will advance his career in present political circumstances.

Our visit to Addis Ababa coincided with a tour of inspection by Lord Bridges, that exceptionally distinguished former civil servant who had been Secretary to the Cabinet and Permanent Secretary of the Treasury. He was now Chairman of the British Council and had come to look at the activities of the Council in Ethiopia. His fame had gone before him, and we counted ourselves fortunate to meet him at several of the official entertainments laid on at that time. I was greatly taken with his wide knowledge and experience, his charm, and his recollections of his father, the Poet Laureate. We were both invited as guests of honour to a dinner given by the Ethiopian Society of Oxford graduates, presided over with much aplomb by Lij Endalkatchew Makonnen (Oriel College and a future Prime Minister) and also attended by my wartime colleague Sirak Heruy (Brasenose College and translator into Amharic of Dr Johnson's *Rasselas*). Lord Bridges and I both had to make speeches, but I was very glad that mine preceded his, for to follow his captivating and consummate performance would have been a sad anticlimax.

* * *

In 1898 Queen Victoria sent a recording of her voice to Emperor Menelik of Ethiopia and his Queen, the Itege Taitu. The phonograph message was accompanied by some essential technical equipment. Queen Victoria's recording was made at Osborne and consisted of only two or three short sentences of conventional greetings, whose text has been preserved, though the actual recording was destroyed on the Queen's instructions. She was said to have disliked the squeaky character of her voice and the poor quality of recordings at that time. Emperor Menelik and his Queen were reported by the British Agent in Ethiopia, Colonel J. L. Harrington, to have been greatly impressed by this manifestation of technology. Harrington and the Emperor's Swiss adviser, M. Ilg, had to confirm, on the basis of credentials sent with the message, that it was a true record of the Queen's voice. The Ethiopian royal couple listened to the message amidst much ceremony and an artillery salute. Queen Taitu was delighted to recognize her own name, and the Emperor had the recording repeated several times.

Menelik and Taitu subsequently recorded a message of their own addressed to Queen Victoria and performed on the equipment sent by the Queen. Unfortunately, neither the Amharic text nor an English translation of their words were known to be extant, but the original cylinder on which the Ethiopian royal message was grooved has been preserved in the Royal Library, Windsor Castle, and was kindly brought to my attention in 1967 by Sir Robin Mackworth-Young, then HM's Librarian. The cylinder could only be played on instruments available at the Science Museum in London, but the quality of the recording was by that time such that it required to be repeated very many times before my colleague, Professor Abraham Demoz, then of Addis Ababa University, was able to transcribe it. His acumen and perseverance were deserving of much credit and commendation. Fortunately, we had taken tape-recordings of the earliest of our re-playings before the cylinder became even balder. Abraham Demoz published the Amharic texts of Menelik's and Taitu's messages together with English translations. The Emperor's speech was of a markedly more political nature than Queen Victoria's purely formal words had been.

With the gracious permission of Her Majesty Queen Elizabeth II, I took two tapes of the Menelik and Taitu recordings with me to Ethiopia in 1969 and presented one to Emperor Haile Sellassie and the other to his son and heir Crown Prince Asfa Wossen. The next day the Addis Ababa newspapers carried headlines 'Menelik's voice heard again'. I also brought them Abraham Demoz's transcripts of the Amharic texts, for without these it would have been very difficult to make out what was being said; but accompanied by the text the original voices of Menelik and Taitu were reasonably audible and comprehensible. It was an enjoyable as well as an unusual piece of research.

A few years later I came across an amusing exchange of Foreign Office minutes, dated 1898, between the Permanent Under-Secretary at the Foreign Office and the Marquess of Salisbury, Prime Minister and Foreign Secretary at that time. The Foreign Office was pondering the text of a suitable message for Queen Victoria to record for the benefit of the Ethiopian royal couple. They submitted to the Prime Minister what they termed 'a draft of banalities' but wondered whether some more political matters, such as the railway to Jibuti or frontier problems, should also be broached. To this Lord Salisbury responded with the following terse minute:

I think your proposed formula will do admirably. If HM desires to add sentiment or admonition, she will do it better than we can.

S.

I have referred here to Crown Prince Asfa Wossen who is, of course, since the death of his father, Emperor Haile Sellassie, in 1975, King of his country. With characteristic modesty and self-effacement he has, however, refused to assume the title until such time as the Ethiopian people are free to make a decision. On my visits to Ethiopia it was always a great pleasure to be received by His Royal Highness. His eldest daughter, Princess Mary, had been at school in England, and his son and heir, Prince Zara Yacob, was an undergraduate at Oxford and a frequent and welcome guest of ours. Apart from their home in Addis Ababa, the Crown Prince and Princess had a villa at Debre Zeit on Lake Bishoftu in superbly beautiful surroundings. Once or twice my wife and I were invited to lunch there, and we greatly enjoyed the loveliness of the place and the warmth of the hospitality.

In 1973, a little over a year before the initially peaceful but increasingly sanguinary revolution, the Crown Prince had a stroke which left him somewhat handicapped but saved his life from the horrors of the military junta, for he had been flown out for treatment in this country immediately the illness struck. Since then he and Crown Princess Madfariash Worq, together with their children, have lived in this country in conditions of much physical and mental deprivation and anguish. The Crown Prince's serene disposition in the face of much adversity is wonderful to observe, and the Crown Princess's devoted care and solicitude for her husband set an admirable example.

* * *

In 1963 Emperor Haile Sellassie established, by charter and trust deed, a Prize Trust with the object of 'encouraging the activities and proficiencies of Ethiopians and others, particularly in the advancement of health, prosperity, and the exercise of the Fine and Applied Arts, and also to strengthen spiritually and culturally the bonds between the peoples of the African continent and of the whole world; recalling also the splendid example of the Nobel Foundation in its work for the education and enlightenment of all mankind'.

The Haile Sellassie Prize Trust was financed during the ten years of its existence from the income of properties and estates donated by the Emperor. Its charter and procedures were deliberately modelled on those of the Nobel Foundation. It had a number of high-powered trustees who appointed an executive council which, in its turn, annually despatched proposal forms to relevant persons all over the world who were asked (*à la* Nobel Prize) to return them with their reasoned suggestions and nominations for the various awards. These awards were given in two separate categories, national awards (for achievements in Ethiopian agriculture, industry, humanitarian activities, fine arts, education, and Amharic literature) and international awards (for African Research and Ethiopian Studies). Both types were accompanied by a gold medal, a diploma, and a cheque in Ethiopian dollars. Between 1964 and 1973 thirty-two national and nineteen international prizes were awarded; of these, ten were for Ethiopian studies and six for Amharic literature.

There is no reason to suppose that the Ethiopian Trust was any more infallible in its selection of prizewinners than the various Nobel committees have been. One need only think of some very odd choices in the Nobel Literature or Peace awards; and almost inevitably judges are influenced quite often by considerations of a fair distribution among nationalities rather than by absolutely strict criteria of sheer merit. In the awards for Ethiopian Studies there were two glaring omissions: Enrico Cerulli and H. J. Polotsky. In neither instance can the failure of inclusion have been due to lack of proposals; rather there must have been extraneous considerations at work: in Cerulli's case these were undoubtedly connected with his political career, despite the Emperor's well-known benevolent attitude towards this great Italian scholar. It is more difficult to fathom the reasons for Polotsky's omission—unless it be the result of his extreme reticence, his failure to visit Ethiopia, and the fact that his extraordinarily wide range of scholarly expertise allotted to Ethiopian studies an important but not a predominant place.

When my turn came, there were good personal reasons to accept the honour, despite some misgivings: these were connected partly with the omission of the two great masters to whom I have just referred, and partly with the awkwardness of accepting a monetary award in addition to the splendid gold medal and diploma. But in the latter respect there existed means of applying the money to purposes concerned with Ethiopia. I would be lacking in honesty if I were to pretend that the thought had never occurred to me that one day I might be chosen for the Ethiopian Studies award, but when the telegrams arrived it was nonetheless a total surprise—not least because there was only one week left before our expected appearance in Addis Ababa.

The easiest part of our feverish preparations was the Ethiopian visas issued to my wife and myself and the complimentary tickets given to us by Ethiopian Airlines. Inoculations and cancellation of all other commitments were a little more difficult. Messages of greeting were produced in record time from the British Academy (thanks to the efficiency of Sir Mortimer Wheeler) and from the Vice-Chancellor of London University (at that time fortunately the Director of the School of Oriental and African Studies, Sir Cyril Philips). Such messages were considered *de rigueur* in Ethiopia. But the hardest of all was to comply in such a short time with all the dress regulations carefully laid down for both my wife and myself. I did not at that time own an evening suit with tails, and hiring such an outfit in Oxford was becoming difficult. And then, of course, there was the drafting of the Amharic address of acceptance and thanks.

When eventually we took off, it proved to be 'a week out of time' (as my wife put it in a brief account of the trip), a wholly unreal interlude of a kind not usually bestowed on ordinary people like ourselves. Gone were the days when the comfortable Ethiopian planes were half empty, with plenty of room for passengers to spread themselves and their belongings over several seats. Tourism had by then arrived in Ethiopia and planes were usually filled to capacity. We had the embarrassing experience of sitting next to a lady who told us that she was to be off-loaded at either Rome or Athens (I forget which) because 'two priority passengers had had to be squeezed in, as they were to receive some prize from the Emperor'. We sympathized with her very genuinely, but were too cowardly to confess our guilt. When we arrived at Addis Ababa at dawn the following morning, we were met at the airport at that ungodly hour by the Director of the Prize Trust and by the British Chargé d'Affaires (the new Ambassador, the late and much lamented Sir Willie Morris, was to arrive the next day and had to present his credentials to the Emperor just before the Prize Trust ceremony in the afternoon).

The rest was one whirl of official and social functions. The youngest son of the late Ras Kassa (the Emperor's cousin and war lord during the Italo-Abyssinian war), Ras Asserate Kassa, had been good enough to put one of his cars at our disposal, a large Mercedes, in whose unaccustomed luxury we managed to drive from one appointment to another—and also on one or two quick spins outside the capital to revisit at least some of the lovely surroundings. On the morning of the official ceremony a dress rehearsal was held at Africa Hall, in the great circular assembly hall which had been built for the inauguration at Addis Ababa of the Organization of African Unity. All the participants in that afternoon's proceedings, the prizewinners as well as their presenters, were assembled and put through their paces. As a reflection of the hierarchical structure of Ethiopian society (unchanged, I understand, in these days under Marxist leadership), it was interesting to observe the carefully judged intervals of time at which the Ethiopian dignitaries arrived in strict order of seniority, as if guided by some innate timepiece; it certainly operated like clockwork.

The actual ceremony was modelled on the Nobel Prize proceedings, and, apart from the speeches, also resembled the Olympic Medal awards, including the playing of the prizewinner's national anthem. The Emperor, though clearly ageing, was as gracious as ever, both during the ceremony itself and afterwards at the picture-taking session and subsequent reception. At that reception he had my wife called over to him and was as gallant as

he always was to her and to ladies in general. One met so many of
one's Ethiopian and other friends on that occasion, among them
the doyenne of the British community in Ethiopia, Mrs Christine
Sandford, who, with her husband, the late Brigadier Sandford,
had lived in Ethiopia since 1920 and had become a legendary
figure. I also cherish a photograph with Willie Morris, an
excellent one of him, taken at that reception.

When I now look at the official photograph, taken after the
ceremony against the beautiful stained glass window of Africa
Hall, with the Emperor at the centre of our group, I can only
be filled with sad and melancholy thoughts: of the eleven persons
in the picture, the prizewinners and their presenters, the Emperor,
the Crown Prince, and President and Mrs Tolbert of Liberia
(then on a state visit to Addis Ababa), at least six (including the
Liberian leader) have since been murdered, a dreadful reflection
on the world in which we live and on the transience of human
affairs.

*   *   *

When I moved in 1964 from the Chair of Semitic Languages at
Manchester to the newly established Chair of Ethiopian Studies
at the School of Oriental and African Studies, London University,
I became involved in the affairs of the Anglo-Ethiopian Society.
In the days of Sylvia Pankhurst, during and after the Italo-
Abyssinian war, the Society had been very active, but later on it
became increasingly dormant. When I was elected chairman in
1965, it was with the express intention of re-activating the
Society. The then President had not taken any real part in its
deliberations for a very long time, and we were now seeking
someone who was both eminent in British public life and had
also had some involvement with Ethiopia.

It seemed to me that there could be no one who fitted that
description better than Anthony Eden, the Earl of Avon. When I
wrote to him, he suggested that we should discuss the matter and
he and Lady Avon invited my wife and myself to visit them at
their splendid home at Alvediston near Salisbury. It was a most
interesting experience to meet someone who had played such an
outstanding part in world affairs since the 1930s and who had
also prominently impinged on Ethiopia at three crucial stages:
he became Foreign Secretary in December 1935 when the ill-

fated Hoare-Laval plan about the partitioning of Ethiopia compelled the resignation of Sir Samuel Hoare; and Eden himself resigned in 1938 largely (though not exclusively) because Chamberlain insisted on extending *de jure* recognition to Mussolini's conquest of Ethiopia; finally, after the liberation of Ethiopia in 1941 the Emperor asked Eden to intervene (which he did most effectively) to stay the hands of some over-zealous senior colonial officials. The Emperor had always had a high regard for Anthony Eden, and after the war one of the main thoroughfares in Addis Ababa was named 'Anthony Eden Avenue'.

Lord and Lady Avon attended the Anglo-Ethiopian annual dinners, invited the Ethiopian Ambassador and, later, Prince Zara Yacob, the Emperor's grandson, to their home, and did much to revive the Society and to encourage its members. At our first annual dinner in 1965 Prince William of Gloucester (who had travelled extensively in Ethiopia and whose tragic death in 1972 caused much distress) was our principal guest, while at our last (as it turned out) annual dinner in 1974, under Lord Avon's presidency, Princess Anne graced our proceedings (she had recently returned from a visit to Ethiopia). She made an excellent speech, admirable in its knowledge and practical approach, and without a single note in front of her. It was an inspiring finale to a dying era.

*   *   *

Sir Mortimer Wheeler, who, apart from being an eminent archaeologist and highly distinguished Secretary of the British Academy, was also a Director of Swans Hellenic Cruises, had on several occasions requested me to go as a guest lecturer on one of Swans' recently inaugurated Ethiopian tours. While I was attracted by the idea of travelling in Ethiopia, I had a distinct phobia of group travel or organized jollifications (which I had imagined, quite wrongly, were a concomitant of such tours) and had more than once chickened out of such an undertaking—even in timorous defiance of Sir Mortimer's somewhat imperious manner. But it was not possible to resist his blandishments for ever, and, when he bribed me by suggesting that I take my wife in lieu of a fee, I became an easy prey to his cajolery and charm. In the event, we never regretted having gone on this superb tour (the last one, as it turned out) despite some unforeseeable problems and mishaps.

Our tour took place during the second half of March and early
April 1974, a month or two after the beginning of the initially
slow and then still bloodless revolution. Hopes of bringing about
peaceful change under the new government of all talents were
high, although some senior ministers feared that the situation
might have to be viewed less optimistically than it appeared. Less
than an hour after our arrival at Addis Ababa, early in the
morning, I was summoned to the Palace to see the Emperor. The
taxi driver who took me there was distinctly nervous and hesitant
as we entered the precinct of the Old *Gibbi* (palace) and I had to
coax him to carry on. In the Palace itself the Emperor was surrounded by some of the new men, but a few of the old guard
recently dismissed were still lurking in the background. Haile
Sellassie seemed rather more frail than when I had seen him a
few months earlier on a visit to his ailing son and heir in London.
Quite frequently during audiences in the past he would stand,
but now he was seated and bade me sit down on a chair close to
his. He talked only very briefly on the situation in Addis Ababa
and expressed the hope that calm had now returned to the
capital. He mainly wanted to know about his grandson Zara
Yacob, the sick Crown Prince's son, then studying at Exeter
College, Oxford. I was glad to tell him about the young Prince's
progress and above all about his maturity and delightful
character. Two or three weeks later I read in the papers that,
before a large assemblage of people at the Palace, Haile Sellassie
had nominated his grandson as his successor, in case of the
Crown Prince's incapacity. Strictly speaking, this was an act of
supererogation, as the Ethiopian Constitution made such pro-
visions in any event.

Our Swans tour numbered some twenty-five to thirty people,
predominantly Americans and Britons, the agreeable numerical
limitation being imposed by the capacity of the DC-3 planes used
on internal flights and by the tiny grass airstrips at some of the
localities visited. It was a congenial group, which included a distinguished and witty Oxford lady don, an historian, an American
lady doctor, and a professorial cousin of mine and his family.
The afternoon of the first day was spent sightseeing in Addis
Ababa after an introductory lecture on the history of the city and
its outstanding features. We were staying at the Ghion Hotel,
close to the Jubilee Palace, and in the early evening a much re-

juvenated Haile Sellassie came to visit his stables and horses.
I was surprised how much more sprightly he seemed compared
with earlier in the day. He had always been happiest in the
company of children and animals.

The next day we flew to Dire Dawa in the east of the country,
the halfway point on the Addis Ababa-Jibuti railway line. Each
movement was at that time connected with a measure of uncer-
tainty; the incipient revolution imposed certain restrictions on
flights and affected the modalities of ordinary life, at any rate to
some inevitably unpredictable extent. The bus ride to the
medieval city of Harar, past Lake Haramaya with its great
variety of water birds and the adjacent colourful market, was full
of interest. And, of course, the walled city of Harar, set high on
the southern ridge of the great rift valley escarpment, had been a
focus of attention to many, including Sir Richard Burton and
Rimbaud. It was also the traditional family fief of the Emperor,
his father's governorate and later his own.

After our return to Addis Ababa, full of rumours of impending
events, we flew north-west to Bahar Dar on the southern shore of
the great Lake Tana. We visited the spectacular Tississat Falls
where the waters of the Blue Nile plunge 200 feet into a chasm
at the start of their 1,000-mile journey to meet the White Nile.
Next day's cruise on Lake Tana, landing at several of the islands
to see their ancient churches, was one of the highlights of our
tour. It was also the first (and last) time I had been *on* Lake Tana
rather than just by its shores.

We now flew the short distance north to Gondar, situated in an
area of exceptional natural beauty. It is a former capital of
Ethiopia and the site of a remarkable array of Portuguese-
inspired castles. At each of these places one had to lecture and
explain their significance in the history of the country. Then
onward in a south-easterly direction to the miraculous sights of
Lalibela, centre of the monolithic churches cut from the living
rock, one of the great wonders of the world and testimony to the
power that religion can exert.

At Lalibela, the most inaccessible of places, we had to abandon
the tour temporarily, as for some days now I had been suffering
from an abscess on a tooth which failed to respond to antibiotics
given to us by our American doctor friend. She warned my wife,
as my temperature rose higher than I had ever experienced

before, that I needed to have immediate treatment if my life was not to be endangered. My wife, with a great deal of string-pulling, had us flown out of Lalibela to Asmara where, we knew, an American dentist was located. Alas, he was away, and the only salvation lay with an Italian lady dentist. She called in a physician and, after some penicillin injections to be repeated twice a day, cut the abscess without an anaesthetic (which, I understand, could not be administered because of the high temperature). After a repeat performance the next day I was almost back to normal and could resume the tour which by now had reached Asmara via Axum.

My wife and I found it a moving experience to show our Swans group the sights of Asmara, the place we had known so intimately during the first years of our married life. The atmosphere now was at once tense and eerie: the soldiers and their officers did not know exactly what was happening at Addis Ababa and what posture they were to adopt. They were cautious and wary, but also jumpy and trigger-happy. Yet when one spoke to them in their own language, Amharic or Tigrinya, they would still smile and let one go through, even into the Palace grounds. The boys on the gharries, as ubiquitous now as they had been in the early 1940s (then the principal local conveyance), were still beating their emaciated horses, and I would again urge them in my best Tigrinya to remember that these horses were God's creatures just as they were. This always seemed to convulse them with laughter, but at least they would stop their cruel use of the whip—temporarily. It all seemed so unchanged in many ways, but we knew that the intervening thirty-odd years had trans-formed the world and Ethiopia with it. And the greatest change of all in that country was just beginning to happen—right in front of our eyes. We were witnesses to the early phases of a revolution in Ethiopia and Africa, the end of which is not yet in sight.

I did not know it then, but when our plane finally took off it was the last time I would see Ethiopia, the country whose mountains, lakes, and valleys I had loved, whose people I had admired, and whose languages and civilization had been the mainstay of my career.

IV

Emperor Haile Sellassie

Late in 1973 I wrote a paper on the then recently published auto-biography of Emperor Haile Sellassie. That paper was delivered as a lecture to the Accademia dei Lincei at Rome (at the invitation of its illustrious president, Enrico Cerulli, the Nestor of Ethiopian scholars) and subsequently also served as an introduction to my annotated translation and English edition of the Emperor's autobiography (Oxford University Press, 1976). Its opening paragraph read:

Whatever the future of Africa in general and Ethiopia in particular may hold, the place of Emperor Haile Sellassie in the twilight period of emerging Africa is assured. I do not mean to imply that there will be no argument about the nature of this place, that the verdict of history (whatever this may mean) will be unequivocal, or that even now there are not some among the young urban intelligentsia in Ethiopia who would not echo Cromwell's imperious words to the Long Parliament (used so effectively, in 1940, by Leopold Amery in relation to Chamberlain): 'You have sat too long here for any good you have been doing. Depart, I say, and let us have done with you. In the name of God, go!' But such cries of impatience are not likely to be confirmed by the calm view of a longer perspective . . .

These lines were penned exactly two months before the beginning of the initially slow (subsequently savage and brutal) revolution in February 1974. I can claim no gifts of prescience, for the portents of impending change had for some time been writ large over the twilight horizon of Haile Sellassie's long reign, which effectively extended from 1916 to 1974. But few people had expected that change to be as cataclysmic as it turned out to be and as contaminated with ideologies that flourished far from the native soil of Ethiopia.

Droves of western journalists, excusably innocent of the Ethiopian milieu, attended the obsequies of the dying régime in 1974 and filed despatches which were often as wayward in their political orientation, assiduously and skilfully fed by a fervent politico-military propaganda machine, as they were ignorant of the historical and cultural background. They employed a jargon in which 'feudal' stood for 'traditional', 'autocratic' for 'moderate', and 'progressive' for 'communist'. That background, at once mythopoeic as well as opaque, played similar tricks with journalists, aid organizers, and others during the droughts of the 1980s or the exodus of the Falashas from north-west Ethiopia to Israel.

We live in an age when Winston Churchill can be accused of assassination and Haile Sellassie of 'salting away' $4,000 million (*sic*). The calumny receives all the glare of publicity but never the refutation of such defamation. There are few who have heard that the mythical millions do not exist, yet the original libel continues to reverberate.

In the mid-1970s my wife and I spent some time in Zurich and other parts of Switzerland at the behest of Haile Sellassie's son and heir, Crown Prince Asfa Wossen, in search of those billions. But despite the helpfulness of the Swiss (and indeed British) banking authorities nothing was found. Even the Marxist régime in Ethiopia accepted this fact, but the western media periodically resuscitate that hoary myth. His alleged fortune is still mentioned, bracketed with those of the late Shah and President Marcos of the Philippines. At one stage there was a persistent rumour that pilots of Ethiopian Airlines had been charged by Haile Sellassie to deliver parcels filled with gold to the manager of a Swiss hotel at which the Emperor had occasionally stayed. On investigation it turned out that the rumour was substantially accurate and that parcels had indeed been sent to that gentleman, but they did not contain gold—only bags of Ethiopian coffee for which the manager had developed a penchant. Thus a gesture of royal thoughtfulness was interpreted as an act of imperial plunder.

Those who truly knew Emperor Haile Sellassie of Ethiopia and felt the remarkable impact of his unique personality will long find it hard to come to terms with a world from which he has been removed. Four generations of his family are still mourning the disappearance of the beacon that illuminated and guided all their actions, and his many friends—all those who have remained steadfast in adversity—are bewildered at the loss of the figure which had such qualities of calm endurance and profound dignity. The very full obituaries in the world press in August 1975 were in themselves a tribute to the first African leader to receive such exceptional coverage. Haile Sellassie and the Earl of Avon (Anthony Eden) had been the last survivors among the major statesmen on the world stage in the years between the two world wars.

Haile Sellassie, as the young Tafari, had already made a deep impression on the ageing Emperor Menelik in the early years of this century. There is a photograph in existence, taken in 1905 when Tafari was aged 13, showing Emperor Menelik with this young boy who was the son of the Emperor's cousin, Ras Makonnen. There was at that time little reason to think that this young nobleman would ever ascend the ancient throne of Ethiopia, yet anyone who studies the photograph, even with no knowledge of subsequent events, will assume that the boy with the delicate features, slender build, beautiful hands, and those extra-ordinarily penetrating—indeed imperious—eyes is the Emperor, accompanied in this picture by an elderly retainer. It is that overpowering personality, contained in so small a physical frame and prominently manifest from early childhood to great old age, that has been the key to Haile Sellassie's success and international stature. As Regent of his country since 1916 and Emperor from 1930 onwards he was the major force in Ethiopia throughout the twentieth century; and there is little doubt that—whatever the revolutionaries may decree—the remainder of the century will stay under the shadow of this remarkable man.

During the first phase of his rule, from 1916 until the Fascist invasion in 1935-6, Haile Sellassie was far in advance of even the most enlightened elements in his country; and what resistance there was to his stewardship came from people who considered that his programme of reform was too fast and too radical. In the second phase, from the restoration in 1941 until the middle or late 1950s, there was a high degree of equilibrium between the ruler and his subjects, while the third period ushered in an era of increasing, if at times concealed, turbulence among the young urban intelligentsia. But Haile Sellassie could fairly claim that he was Emperor of 25 million Ethiopians scattered over his vast and beautiful domain, not just of some 1,500 or 2,000 young men who wished to go faster than he, in his later years, considered safe.

But the time has not yet come for a final assessment of his achievements and failings in statecraft, partly because the necessary documentary material is far from being available and fully assembled and partly because the prevailing atmosphere is not conducive to reaching calm and dispassionate judgements.

The time is, however, appropriate to consider the overpowering and truly charismatic personality of this Emperor. Such an assessment has to be undertaken at this stage before eyewitnesses disappear and the insidious propaganda now being disseminated against him begins to attain its intended object. It is a fact that Haile Sellassie not only made a profound impression on over-awed Ethiopians or on foreigners unaccustomed to finding themselves in the presence of royalty, but he had the same effect on his fellow-monarchs among the reigning houses of Europe, on American Presidents, on Communist leaders from Stalin to Mao, and, above all, on other heads of African states who were reared in a very different tradition. And it is noteworthy that some of the most radical among these pleaded most eloquently on his behalf with the newly established military dictatorship in Ethiopia.

It is, of course, impossible to describe such a singular personality to those who have not come under its spell. And in any event, any judgement of this kind is of necessity highly impressionistic. Yet foreign envoys who visited Ethiopia when Tafari was in his early teens and fairly far removed from the throne reported his regal bearing and spoke of the strong impact the young prince had made on them. His retainers were fiercely devoted to him from his early youth to old age. His children may have been in awe of their father but they always had a close and intensely human relationship with him. And this applies equally and especially to Crown Prince Asfa Wossen (despite many baseless reports to the contrary) who has not only been a loyal and devoted son but is a remarkable, though very different, personality in his own right. If he had not been abroad in 1973 and 1974, stricken by a cruel illness, developments in Ethiopia might well have been different. And the present regime deprived themselves of a fine constitutional monarch when they revoked their earlier invitation to him to return as King.

Emperor Haile Sellassie's relationship to children and animals was always exceptionally close and empathic. He felt at ease with them, free from the constraints of kingship, while they discerned that combination of inner strength and genuine kindness which are the marks of greatness. His adult granddaughters in particular were fierce in his defence in public, yet they were among the few who would on occasion voice criticism and doubt to the Emperor himself, who received such unaccustomed candour with grandfatherly indulgence.

His lifestyle, as indeed that of every Ethiopian, was strictly regulated by the hierarchical arrangements of Ethiopian society and by the carefully adjusted checks and balances of a traditional framework. This was a society in which every member knew his precise position, his rights as well as his vulnerability. Access to the person of the monarch was, in practice as well as in theory, open to everybody, though naturally the quality of that contact could vary a great deal. Throughout his life he was immensely hard-working and unsparing of his personal convenience and comfort.

This work-load is vividly described in his autobiography. The book is couched in the Emperor's stately Amharic prose. Amharic, Ethiopia's official and national language, was used by him with consummate skill. He was the only Ethiopian I have ever met who was intuitively conscious of the prodigious complexities of Amharic syntax and would produce sentences of a shape and structure with which a western student of Amharic could cope. His French was very serviceable, but his English remained halting, though he comprehended more than his active command would suggest. For all official purposes he relied exclusively on Amharic.

Of all his qualities I would single out supreme dignity and composure in adversity. He would be clement when the situation warranted it, but he could be stern and demanding. A foreign envoy once told me that he had been instructed to address some words of censure to the Ethiopian Government. But when the appointed day came, he faced His Imperial Majesty with some polite generalities and sent the rebuke in written form instead. In private, though never in public, the Emperor could be humorous. To ladies he displayed an old-world gallantry to which they almost invariably responded with profound devotion to his person.

When he died, unattended by doctors who 'could not be found', the new rulers had to bury him secretly at an undisclosed place for fear of popular demonstrations in his favour. His daughter, grandchildren, and all members of his family then present in Ethiopia have been imprisoned in humiliating circumstances ever since 1974.

In attempting to give a brief outline of Haile Sellassie's life and career (it is much too early to write a full-scale life, and any of the present endeavours are mere journalistic exercises and doomed to failure in serious historical terms), I must begin by offering a superficial glimpse of some of the material at our disposal.

In the first place, there are a number of western accounts which deal directly with the life of the Emperor. Among these I might mention the late Mrs Christine Sandford's brief and uncritical outline entitled *The Lion of Judah hath prevailed* (London, J. M. Dent, 1955). As the oldest British resident in Ethiopia she had exceptional opportunities of observing the development of the Ethiopian polity under Haile Sellassie. Mr Leonard Mosley's story takes us up to 1964; and while the external events are adequately chronicled, the author was not deeply steeped in the Ethiopian ambience (*Haile Selassie* (London, Weidenfeld & Nicolson, 1964)).

Of a different calibre altogether are some of the books which deal not with Haile Sellassie's life but with the political aspects of his reign. Here I would select three works of a fairly disparate nature which, cumulatively, convey a tolerably full picture of the official and public *persona*. They are the second edition of Dame Margery Perham's *Government of Ethiopia* (London, Faber & Faber, 1969); Christopher Clapham's *Haile Selassie's Government* (London, Longmans, 1969); and particularly John Markakis's *Ethiopia: Anatomy of a traditional polity* (Oxford, Clarendon Press, 1974); cf. my review in the *TLS*, 20 Sept. 1974. The authors—students of history and politics—make a critical assessment of the Imperial influence, but inevitably their studies represent the outsider's view of the Emperor's impact. Their empathy for the authentic Ethiopian milieu is at times uncannily close (this applies especially to Markakis), but it takes an Ethiopian to describe what it felt like to have lived in Haile Sellassie's realm. Such a literary event has not yet occurred. The appearance of an indigenous product of this nature does not, however, guarantee either dispassionate analysis or gifts of descriptive imagination coupled with truth and candour and free from ideological claptrap.

Of course, there exist many other books on various aspects of Haile Sellassie's reign, but, unlike those I have referred to, the great majority suffer from one of two grave defects (or at times from a combination of both): they betray a distinct political commitment and measure events and institutions against alien criteria; or they show a marked lack of familiarity with Ethiopia, her languages, civilization, and history. Here one might well ponder the sage words of Kenneth Clark (*Civilization*, xvii): 'I have the feeling that one should not try to assess a culture without knowing its language; so much of its character is connected with its actual use of words.' (While the present book was going through the publication process I noticed an announcement by the University of California Press about the impending appearance of a biography of Emperor Haile Sellassie by H. G. Marcus).

Apart from these works, bearing directly or indirectly on the Emperor's discharge of his royal functions, there are, of course, the foreign archives; and here I am thinking primarily of British, Italian, French, German, and American sources. While the material in these archives is now accessible, for the earlier period at any rate, no comprehensive use has so far been made of it. Indeed, it may be wise to defer such treatment until the full range of archival sources is open to inspection and to dispassionate historical scrutiny.

As far as Ethiopian archives are concerned, their precise nature and condition were not generally known during the Imperial régime, and this is *a fortiori* the case at the present time. Whether the Emperor's private documents were seized, destroyed, or doctored by Ethiopia's military dictatorship is purely within the realm of speculation. In any event, access is impossible now.

A source readily available is the collection of royal speeches, assembled in a number of volumes under the title *fere känafer*, 'fruit of the lips' (of Emperor Haile Sellassie). The volume in front of me as I write was published at Addis Ababa in 1951 and contains 225 speeches, chronologically ordered, from 1924 to 1950.

The most immediate source is, of course, the Emperor's autobiography. This was published in Amharic under the title 'My Life and Ethiopia's Progress'. The first volume, taking us from his birth in 1892 to the famous Geneva speech to the League of Nations in 1936, was issued early in 1973; a second volume,

covering the Imperial exile and the Ethiopian campaigns of
1940-1, appeared in mid-1974. The third and final volume may
have been dictated in part, but its fate is not known. I have
already alluded to the annotated English translation of the first
volume which was carried out by me, originally at the request of
the Emperor. The problems associated with this autobiography
have been discussed in the introduction to that work. Historians
of the life and reign of Haile Sellassie will have to be as adept at
reading between the lines of the Amharic work as they have to be
in scrutinizing the actual text.

It is interesting to observe that the autobiography is exclusively concerned with the life and activities of its author. There
are few reflections of a general kind and certainly no comment
whatever on the events and personages of his era. Thus Ras
Tafari, on the first visit abroad by any Ethiopian ruler, arrived in
France in May 1924 in the middle of a major government, and
indeed constitutional, crisis. Yet the book has not a single word
about the severe problems which were convulsing France as the
Ethiopian Regent stepped on French soil. His serene aloofness
from events and exclusive preoccupation with the minutiae of
etiquette are like an unbroken thread running through the whole
course of this work. There are no thoughts on the nature of
western society or technological progress, nor are there any
comparisons with the conditions in which Ethiopia then found
herself. The writing is not philosophical but essentially annalistic,
enumerative, catalogue-like.

Similarly, while we are given a full list of the princes,
noblemen, and officials who accompanied the Regent on his
European tour, no further mention is made of any of them in the
course of the narrative. We are not told what they thought of
their great experience and whether Jerusalem or Alexandria,
Paris or Stockholm, Cambridge or Athens held their attention.
We only know from other sources that, while Ras Hailu went on
a tour of the sights and indulged in a vast shopping spree, the
Prince Regent visited schools, universities, and hospitals. There
are no references to Ras Hailu's antics as the *enfant terrible* of the
party. Thus it is said that King George V asked Ras Hailu
whether he knew any English, French, or Arabic. When he had
to answer all these questions in the negative, he, in his turn,
asked the British monarch whether he could speak Amharic,

Tigrinya, or Galla. The reply was a predictable 'No', whereupon Ras Hailu said to the King, allegedly to the latter's huge enjoyment, 'Then, Your Majesty, it would appear that we are both equally ignorant.' None of this will be found in Haile Sellassie's autobiography; there are no anecdotes, there is no *bon mot*, no wit; its purpose is austerely and severely serious, moralistic, and didactic.

Apart from this major material of first relevance, there are a good many secondary and indirect sources. I am here thinking of references to Emperor Haile Sellassie in Amharic literature, prose and poetry; of fiction in which his person is mentioned; and of all the paraphernalia of royal exposure to publicity and the media of press, radio, and television. Recordings of his voice on tape and of his appearance on film must cover a great deal of footage and must indeed run to a formidable total. In 1977 I published (in the *Journal of Semitic Studies*) transcripts and translations of tapes of the Emperor's last two pronouncements: of 14 April 1974 when he spoke of unrest in the country and nominated the son of the gravely ill Crown Prince as his successor; and of 12 September 1974 when army officers arrived at the Palace to depose him. Both are pronouncements of great dignity. But very little of this considerable material will be informative or instructive in any real sense, for the imperial reserve and reticence have only been pierced by the most astute and linguistically prepared observers—and even then, 'touched' rather than 'pierced'.

While I can think of many instances of humour and acts of personal kindness and considerateness on the part of the late Emperor, his public persona was self-contained and aloof. This self-absorption was undoubtedly a source of strength, but in critical moments during the last years of his reign it led to isolation as well as to insulation from the inexorable fragmentation of Ethiopian urban society.

In addition to the historical sources and records to which I have referred, there exists, of course, the vast amount of material relating to the Italo-Ethiopian war of 1935-6, its antecedents as well as its aftermath, when Haile Sellassie first ascended the world stage on which he remained for so long by sheer dint of a remarkable personality. And now we are witnessing the unfolding of a propaganda literature of imperial debunking and defamation, when the vultures descend to feed on the carrion of a once great reputation, when snide dismissal replaces the spectacle of sycophantic toadyism.

A few lines of general background:

Haile Sellassie, a great-grandson of King Sahlä Sellassie of Shoa with whom Queen Victoria had concluded a treaty of friendship and amity in 1841, was born (as Lij Tafari) on 23 July 1892 at Ejärsa Goro, not far from the famous medieval city of Harar. He was a son of Ras Makonnen, Emperor Menelik II's cousin and principal adviser (who in 1902 had attended the coronation of King Edward VII), and of Wayzaro Yäshimabet. His mother died before he was 2 years old, and his attachment to his father was exceptionally close.

The education he received was that usually given to young Ethiopian noblemen. He explains in his autobiography that 'there was no undue softness about that education as used to be the case with princes of that period'. He soon took lessons in French, first with a physician from Guadeloupe and later with a French-mission-educated Ethiopian, Abba Samuel, who remained his friend and companion for many years until his untimely death in a boating accident on Lake Harämaya, in which the future Emperor was one of only two survivors.

Ras Makonnen died when his son Tafari was aged only 13. The young prince and his retainers had expected that the Governorship of Harar province would be given to him, but Menelik, under the influence of Empress Taitu, appointed Tafari's elder half-brother Yelma and sent Tafari himself to govern the district of Sällale. Even when Yelma unexpectedly died, in October 1907, Tafari did not yet inherit the prestigious family fief of Harar but had to content himself with the Governorship of the large and fertile province of Sidamo. His patience, perseverance, and hard work were, however, rewarded when, in March 1910, before he was 18 years old, a proclamation was issued appointing him Governor of his father's province of Harar.

It was here that for the next six-and-a-half years he studied and applied the craft of rulership, reformed land and tax administration, and introduced, carefully and deliberately, many new ideas which were progressive in their effect, yet not so novel as to be disruptive of the traditional fabric of Ethiopian society. In this way Dejazmatch Tafari prepared himself for higher tasks yet to come, for, though he was born without direct and immediate prospects of ascending the throne, he was from an early age profoundly conscious of the destiny which was eventually to be his.

That moment came when, in 1916, Menelik's grandson and designated (though uncrowned) successor Lij Yasu had made himself thoroughly unacceptable to the Christian majority of his people, partly by his unreliability and dissolute way of life and partly by his flirtation with Islam. Tafari became the rallying point, though neither the instigator nor the leader, of the forces of resistance which finally brought about (under the auspices of the Abuna, the head of the Church) the deposition of Lij Yasu and the crowning of Zawditu, Menelik's daughter, as Empress, with Ras (as he now became) Tafari as Regent and Heir to the Throne.

The dyarchy of the Empress Zawditu and the young Regent was a delicate arrangement, but it brought peace and a large measure of stability to Ethiopia. Tafari Makonnen was now firmly set on the road (which he always trod with superb skill, admirable patience, and complete trust in the outcome) to his eventual succession to the Crown.

Zawditu was conservative in outlook and the focus of all those elements most deeply opposed to change, while Ras Tafari was progressive and the embodiment of the aspirations of the younger generation. Yet as Regent and later as Emperor he showed a remarkable feeling for the pace of progress and reform at which the country as a whole could move without undue disturbance or upheaval. He always insisted that Ethiopia must evolve its own concepts and forms suitable to conditions prevailing in that ancient realm. And when, after nearly sixty years in power, he did finally succumb, it was to an alien ideology and to trends, aims, and forces for which his traditional outlook and upbringing had not prepared him and which neither he nor most of his people could comprehend.

When he first assumed effective control in 1916, he appointed ministers and began to build up the rudiments of a civil service and all the other paraphernalia of a complex polity. But within the Ethiopian hierarchical system he remained the source of every major initiative, of every important decision (at times of very trivial ones as well), of every success as well as of every failure.

One observer (John Markakis, *Ethiopia: Anatomy of a Traditional Polity* (Oxford, Clarendon Press, 1974)) has offered a characterization that is formidably to the point:

Profound ambition pursued with judicious caution; limitless patience coupled with the ability to act decisively; benevolent disposition and gentle manner matched with great ruthlessness in matters political . . . the capacity to attract and manipulate mutually antagonistic forces simultaneously . . . and a sense of supreme self-confidence in his ability to rule the destiny of the Ethiopian people.

These words could scarcely be bettered in their striking appositeness.

No less apt is the same writer's description of the obverse, the relationship of the people to their ruler:

There is a strong element of dread mixed in the profound reverence accorded to their emperor by the Ethiopians. Despite the constant exposure of his person to his subjects, Haile Selassie has preserved an aura of awe-inspiring mystery which, instead of dissolving, thickens with the passage of years, and has turned the aging monarch into a legend during his own lifetime. Perpetually frozen into a posture of . . . regal isolation, the sombre figure of the ruler stands across a psychological divide which even his most trusted retainers cannot cross. Seen in the midst of his tense, scurrying courtiers, the . . . Emperor gives the impression of remote aloofness and icy calmness that easily dominate any scene of which he is part. Men of great importance in their own right are reduced to insignificance in the Emperor's presence . . .

In contrast to so much current meretricious writing on Ethiopia, the author of that characterization does not pretend to be privy to the Emperor's thoughts, motives, and plans. Even those capable of breaching the formidable barrier of the Amharic thought-categories would have been foolhardy to engage in such speculations. The picture here drawn is as accurate for 1904 as it is for 1974; of the boy Tafari as of the venerable King at the close of his life; of the young nobleman of 12 who so impressed a delegation of seasoned German diplomats (see my *Haile Sellassie's Autobiography*, OUP, 1976, pp. xxiv-xxv) as of the deposed monarch who struck such terror in the hearts of the revolutionaries attempting to interrogate him.

But we must revert to the chronological sequence. In 1923, the Regent had a conspicuous success in the admission of Ethiopia to the League of Nations. In the following year, as we have already seen, he visited Paris, London, Rome, and other European cities and thus became the first Ethiopian ruler ever to go abroad. In 1928 he assumed the title of *negus*, 'King', and two years later, when Empress Zawditu died, he was crowned Emperor (*negusä nägäst*, 'King of Kings') in St George's Cathedral, Addis Ababa, and took the regnal name of Haile Sellassie, 'Might of the Trinity'. It was in another St George's, the Chapel at Windsor Castle, far from his own realm, that a memorial service in his honour was held forty-five years later, in 1975. The only person, I believe, who was present at both services, in both St George's churches, was his son and heir, Crown Prince Asfa Wossen. Prince Henry, Duke of Gloucester, represented King George V at the 1930 coronation at St George's Cathedral, Addis Ababa, while his widow, Princess Alice, Duchess of Gloucester, attended the memorial service for Haile Sellassie at St George's Chapel, Windsor Castle, in 1975.

One of the first things the new Emperor did after his coronation was to offer his people a written constitution. This act has often been derided in later times, but every political event has to be judged against its proper background and within the time range in which it occurs. True, measured against the expectations of the last quarter of the present century, it was a pretty modest affair, but in the Ethiopia of 1930-1 it was an act of progressive statesmanship and mass education. When a revised constitution was promulgated a quarter of a century later, it was a much more advanced and sophisticated instrument under which several general elections were held. It also produced a parliament which, though not organized on party lines, was vigorous in its debates and, when united, could on occasion throw out some major government measures.

It must always be borne in mind that, when the process of decolonization in Africa gathered momentum in the 1950s and 1960s, power had to be surrendered to vocal urban minorities by the various colonial powers. Haile Sellassie's regime was an indigenous one and was under no such immediate compulsion; he judged it right to wait until a majority of his people—rather than a foreign-indoctrinated and at times violent minority—was ready for a responsible and genuinely representative transfer of power. That in the end this turned out to be a miscalculation (perhaps only by a narrow margin) need not necessarily be held against him.

Next to the promulgation of a constitution came education and administrative reforms. When this work was about to reach serious dimensions, the Fascist invasion of 1935–6 compelled the Emperor to turn his attention from domestic amelioration to the more urgent matter of preserving the country. Amidst the holocaust of bombing and poison-gas raids as well as the debates of a virtually impotent League of Nations, there stood out the lonely, slight, and noble figure of the Emperor who in 1936 went to Geneva to plead the cause of his people.

Some of the most poignant passages in the imperial auto-biography are concerned with the hopeless fight against an invader provided with an arsenal of modern weapons, and with calls to a League that was embarrassed by this clamorous voice appealing to the international conscience for justice and peace.

To his own people he said: 'We shall strive for peace till the end. But even if our exertions and our manifestations of good will achieve no result, at least our conscience will not reproach us' (my ed. of the Autobiography, 221).

The fighting itself is described by the Emperor with a wealth of detail which makes us relive those terrible days of the mid-1930s. This account must now be set beside the justly famous narrative by the late George Steer in his classic *Caesar in Abyssinia* (London, Hodder & Stoughton, 1936).

The climax of the volume (and perhaps of the Emperor's entire life) came on 30 June 1936 with the monarch's address to the League of Nations. He was silent, unmoved, and dignified when Fascist journalists shouted abuse and M. Titulescu, the Rumanian Foreign Minister, turned on them with his long-remembered 'A la porte les sauvages!' His address was the more impressive because it was delivered with that quiet dignity which was so peculiarly his own:

Mr. President, Envoys of the Nations!
I should have liked to speak to you in French. But it is in the Amharic language alone that I am able to speak my mind from my heart and with all the force of my spirit. . . . I, Haile Sellassie, Emperor of Ethiopia, am present here today to ask for the justice due to my people and for the help which 52 nations had undertaken to extend when they affirmed that a war of aggression, in violation of international law, was being

waged against Ethiopia. This is the first time that a king appears before this assembly, but it is truly only today that violence of this kind is being committed against a people now falling victim to the aggressor.

Those were his opening words. Then followed a detailed rehearsal of the origin and development of the conflict, punctuated by such prophetic passages as: 'If Europe reckons that this matter is an accomplished fact, then it is right to consider the fate which awaits it and which is bound to come upon it.' And it did come upon it, within three years. And again: 'The Ethiopian Government does not expect other countries to shed their soldiers' blood in the defence of the League's covenant. What the warriors of Ethiopia did expect was merely the means they required for their defence, the funds for the purchase of arms. We were denied this assistance.' Was this not an anticipation of Churchill's famous words to President Roosevelt in 1941: 'Give us the tools, and we will finish the job'?

He concluded with these words: 'Representatives of the world assembled here! I have come to you to Geneva to carry out the saddest duty that has befallen a King. What answer am I to take back to my people?'

If this was, perhaps, Haile Sellassie's finest hour, it would be wrong to lose sight of many important achievements yet to come.

After four years of exile in Britain, Haile Sellassie went to Khartoum in 1940, shortly after Italy's entry into World War II, and helped to organize the Ethiopian campaign which culminated in the Emperor's re-entry into his capital in May 1941. The transformation of the country from chaos, destruction, and political fragmentation into a viable structure was his abiding achievement.

The post-war years in Ethiopia may roughly be divided into two decisive periods. First, the years of consolidation and reconstruction, free from virtually all serious internal conflict (and including the federation with Eritrea), lasting from 1941 to 1955 and associated with the powerful figure of the Minister of the Pen, Waldä Giyorgis Waldä Yohannes. When he was removed from power, Ethiopia enjoyed another five years of tranquillity and relative prosperity, while all around her Africa was awakening from its long slumber and scores of new, independent nations were rising up. Then, in December 1960, an unexpected and short-lived revolt occurred while Haile Sellassie was visiting

Brazil. The physical disturbance may have been relatively slight, but the psychological effects were deep-going. The next fourteen years are associated with the steady ascendancy of Prime Minister Aklilu, Ethiopia's identification with the Organization for African Unity, and the Emperor's gradual withdrawal from internal affairs into the arena of foreign relations. While he may at first have been slow to realize the value to Ethiopia, and indeed to himself, of a movement of pan-African solidarity, once he had grasped the potential of this organization he embraced it eagerly and became the father-figure of an incipient African supra-national body.

The corollary of higher education, African nationhood, and freer international exchanges was the rise of an ideologically based and at times violent student movement which plagued the declining years of Haile Sellassie's reign. It fed upon the obscene contrasts of abject poverty and ostentatious riches within the urban (thought not rural) scene, on comparisons with other newly independent African countries which had passed through the colonial phase with considerable economic and administrative benefits, and on indoctrination from abroad. The students, in their turn, worked hard on the politicization of the junior ranks of the army, while senior military officers culpably failed to realize what was happening.

For seven months, from February to September 1974, Ethiopia had a government of which Haile Sallassie was merely the constitutional head and which was carried by four men of probity and experience: Lij Mikael Imru, Dejazmatch Zewde Gäbrä Sellassie, Lij Endalkatchew Makonnen, and General Abiy Ababa. Trade unions flourished, western-style democracy was fully operative, newspapers were free and interesting, and parliament attained real influence. But it was too late, as Kerensky had experienced fifty-seven years earlier, for orderly and progressive reforms. The national socialists and dedicated ideologists had arrived, who spoke of the will of the people but wrought murder and ruthless suppression. Thus a short-lived, frail, yet eminently worthwhile experiment came to an abrupt and violent end. If men such as Mikael Imru and Zewde Gäbrä Sellassie had been allowed a little more time, Ethiopia might have set a new pattern of genuine democracy and civilized conduct in Africa.

Emperor Haile Sellassie was deposed on 12 September 1974 and placed under detention. He died on 27 August 1975, suffocated by Ethiopia's new rulers who had come to fear his continuing popularity among the people (*The Times*, 21 June 1976). He was mourned by all those in all parts of the world who saw in him the very embodiment of Ethiopia. He had outlived his time. Emperor Menelik's polity, into which Lidj Tafari was born in 1892, was farther removed from the so-called socialist republic of Colonel Mangestu, in which Haile Sellassie died in 1975, than it was from Ezana's Aksumite Empire, 1,600 years earlier.

Haile Sellassie was a de Gaulle figure rather than the amalgam of Stalin's cruel ruthlessness and Nixon's wicked manipulation of power which much uninformed writing now attaches to him.

Thus a life ended of which (like Moses in Deuteronomy 34) 'no man knoweth of his sepulchre unto this day'. And until his last days 'his eye was not dim nor his natural force abated'. Those of us who really knew the man and the king will long mourn the passing of Haile Sellassie, for there will not arise in Ethiopia anyone quite in his image.

Epilogue

Jerusalem: the experience of the 1930s, the early days of the Hebrew University, the *Yishuv* in its pioneering stage, the renaissance of Hebrew, the sounds of Arabic, and of other Semitic languages still spoken in this unique conglomerate of tongues and melting-pot of struggling nationalities and nationalisms, the beauty of the past and the harsh realities of the present; and Ethiopia: the story of its Semitized inhabitants and the sounds of its vigorously surviving and indeed still burgeoning Semitic languages, its peoples in the historic heartlands heavy with ancient traditions plucked from the world of the Old Testament, men and women of impeccable manners and stout hearts, all those true to their heritage and free from alien ideologies—these are the twin loyalties of my life, the two principal pillars on which my university career was built.

Of course, fresh experiences and loyalties were laid upon these substrata. Oxford and the splendours of its colleges, the seemingly unchanging scene of its academic life, but also the less welcome intrusion of the world as it is now. St Andrews and Scotland, the former with its ancient university, its calm and seclusion so conducive to scholarship, and its smallness in an age when ever larger and more powerful structures are formed, and the latter with its mountains and lochs and islands, its sparsely populated land, outside the big conurbations, places of solitude, isolation, tranquillity, and great natural beauty. Manchester, with its fine university, its great local traditions and vigorous cultural life, its lovely surroundings, and its attractive parochialisms—a city and a university which even after many years of absence compel a nostalgic loyalty. And the School of Oriental and African Studies, a small island in the busy metropolis and a still minor cog in a vast federal university structure—yet for thirty years after the Second World War the most comprehensive and, perhaps, the foremost place for the study of the rich plethora of Oriental and African languages.

All these and their associated impressions have crowded into a life which has never moved very far from its twin foundations of

The Two Zions in its academic concerns. At times this life has been busy and full and in the centre of those activities and pursuits, but now it is increasingly contemplative, though still attached to, and admiring of, the excellences of scholarship (much of it represented in the British Academy), though worried about, and aloof from, so many contemporary trends that seem to be closer to the sphere of advertising and public relations than to that of the groves of Academe. And amidst it all are the wonderful consolations of books and reading and writing, of good friends, and of a contented private life.

Index

abaya, 42
Abdullah ibn Hussein, Amir (later King),
  50, 58, 114
Aberdeen, 164
Aberdeen University, 74
Abiy Ababa, General, 234
Abraha Tessemma, Dejazmatch, 182, 204
Abraham Demoz, 209
Abu Tor, 12, 24
Abuna, 229
Abyssinia(n), 127, 135, 141-3, 145,
  148-50, 165, 183, 185-6
Abyssinian Expedition (1867-8), 176, 182
Abyssinian Street, 9, 11, 15, 31, 130
Accademia dei Lincei, 205-6, 219
Adamson, Jr. Comm., ATS, 153-5, 157-8
Addi Qayyeh, 179
Addis Ababa, 93, 112, 135, 141-2, 159,
  170, 172-5, 192-8, 201-10, 212-18,
  225, 231
Addis Ababa University, 193-4, 209
Aden, 93, 173, 181
Adwa, 170, 182
Aešcoly, A. Z., 9
Africa, 99, 115, 131-2, 150, 153, 155, 161,
  167, 175, 191, 202, 211, 218-19, 222,
  231, 233-4
Africa Hall (Addis Ababa), 213, 214
Agaw, 149
Agnon, Esther, 34
Agnon, S. Y., 32-6, 77, 79, 80, 98
Agordat, 133, 158, 181
Ahad Ha'am, 62, 80
Akkadian (Babylonian-Assyrian), 51
Aklilu Habta-Wold, 234
Aksum/Axum, Axumite, 130, 141-2, 150,
  179, 192, 218, 235
Albright, W. F., 86
Alexander, Samuel, 62
Alexandria, 226
All Souls College, Oxford, 53
Allenby, Gen. Sir Edmund (later F-M
  Viscount), 96
Allenby Barracks, 12, 13, 24
Allon, Gedalya, 28
Al-Usbu', 172

Alvediston (near Salisbury), 214
amba, 144
Ambo (Hagara Heywat), 205
America(n), 37, 40, 46, 50, 55-6, 63, 78,
  86, 89, 102, 105-6, 108, 138, 140, 159,
  198, 200, 202-3, 216-18, 222, 225
American Colony, Jerusalem, 10
American Embassy, Addis Ababa, 206
Amery, Leopold, 219
Amharic, 10, 11, 14, 128, 130, 148, 163,
  166, 169-71, 173-5, 187, 193-6, 199-
  201, 203, 205-9, 211, 212, 218, 223,
  225-7, 230, 232
Amharic Language Academy, 171
Andargatchew Massai, Ras, 204
Anglo-American Committee on Palestine,
  58, 119
Anglo-Ethiopian Society, 112, 214, 215
Anglo-Ethiopian Treaty, 93
Anglo-Saxon, 63
Anne, HRH The Princess Royal, 215
Anseba, river, 163
'Anthony Eden Avenue', Addis Ababa,
  215
'aqāl, 42
Arab(s), 5, 6, 9, 11, 13, 15, 16, 22-4, 35-7,
  40-3, 47, 50-1, 55, 57-9, 69, 71, 103-4,
  114-18, 120-2, 128, 139
Arab-Jewish accord, 22, 50, 55, 57, 58,
  61, 69, 75, 92
Arabia(n), 15, 130, 137, 150, 173
Arabic, 4, 5, 13-16, 19, 20, 23-4, 34, 40-4,
  51-4, 71-2, 83-4, 88, 90, 91, 94-8, 117,
  121, 137-9, 141, 166, 170-2, 200, 226,
  237
Aramaic, 14, 15, 51, 54, 75
Arberry, A. J., 172
Aristotle, 64
Ark of the Covenant, 130, 141
armon, 13
Arnona, 29
Asfa Wossen (Haile Sellassie), Crown
  Prince of Ethiopia, 198, 209-10, 214,
  220, 222, 227, 231
Ashkenazi, 95
Ash-Shahr, 172

Index

English (language) (*cont.*)
62-3, 66, 71, 74, 93-4, 96, 98-9, 105,
  109, 140, 160, 164, 170, 174, 177, 187,
  194-5, 209, 219, 223, 226
English Institute, Asmara, 204
Epstein, J. N., 51
Eritrea, vii, 4, 20, 28, 41, 45, 59, 60, 67,
  85, 90, 93, 101, 103-4, 110-12; passim
  in Part II
Eritrean Daily News, 164, 177
Eritrean Liberation Front, 181
Eritrean Weekly News (EWN), 166-71,
  182-3
Ethiopia(n), vii, 4, 9, 10, 13-16, 20, 21,
  28, 45, 59, 67, 85, 90, 92-3, 101, 103,
  110, 112, 237; passim *in* Part II
Ethiopian Airlines, 212, 220
Ethiopian Church, 141, 147, 181, 183,
  198
Ethiopian Church, Jerusalem, 9, 11, 15,
  130
Ethiopian languages, 9, 10, 14, 20, 52,
  81, 85, 101, 177, 211-12, 214, 218
Ethiopian Orthodox Patriarchate,
  Jerusalem, 15
Ethiopian Studies Conferences, 205-6
Ethiopians, The, 202
Ethiopic (Classical), 28, 41, 51, 83, 127,
  141, 149, 163, 176-7, 194, 200, 203-4
Europe(an), 5, 11, 16, 35, 40, 43, 46, 49,
  56, 64, 69, 77, 84, 96-8, 103, 105-6,
  109, 116, 144-7, 161, 176, 192, 195,
  202, 222, 226, 231, 233
Exeter College, Oxford, 61, 216
Ezana, 235

Faitlovitch, Jacques, 9, 151-2
Falashas, 9, 10, 93, 149-52, 220
Faranjiyya, 42
Farnesina, Palazzo, 206
Fascism, 134-5, 137, 151-2, 160, 185,
  202, 221, 232
Feigenbaum, A., 31
Feiwel, B., 55
fere känafer, 225
Fergusson, Sir Ewen, 201
Ferro Luzzi, Giovanni, 154-5
fetfet, 145
Filweha, 192
Finfinni, 192
Fitch, Marc, 138, 140
Florence, 70
Foreign Office, London, 104, 201, 210

France/French, 23, 40, 62, 96, 98, 201,
  223, 225-6, 228, 232
Frankfurt, 70, 77
Frankfurt University, 69, 70, 71
Franks, 42
Fraser, George S., 164-5, 177
Freier, Recha, 25
Freund, Edgar, 25, 26
Freund, Elly, 26
Friends of the Hebrew University, 93,
  105, 113
Frumkin, *see* Segal, H. L.

Gabra Sellassie, 192
Gabriel, Gavino, 129
Gafat, 149
Galilee, 22
Galla (language), 227
Gash, river, 132
de Gaulle, C., 235
gazoz, 39
Gedaref, 132
Ge'ez, *see* Ethiopic (Classical)
Gehenna, 12, 17
Genesis, 10, 99
Geneva, 175, 225, 232-3
Genizah, 15
George V, King, 226-7, 231
German/Germany, 34-5, 37, 40, 42-3,
  52, 56, 69-73, 77, 79, 80, 83, 93, 96-8,
  116, 131, 225, 230
German Colony, Jerusalem, 10, 42
gesho, 145-6
Getahun, 196-200
ghafir, 7
Ghion Hotel, Addis Ababa, 216
Gibbi, 199, 216
Givat Ram campus, 50, 58
Glasgow, 164
Gloucester, Princess Alice, Duchess of,
  231
Gloucester, Prince Henry, Duke of, 231
Gloucester, Prince William of, 215
Glubb, Sir John, 122
Goldziher, I., 14
Gondar, 192, 217
Gordon Memorial College, Khartum,
  132
Gorgora, 162
Gort, F-M Viscount, 118
Göttingen, 82
Government House, Jerusalem, 12-14,
  16, 112